Praise for COHEALING:

"COHEALING is an INVALUABLE RESOURCE FOR RECOVERY AND HEALING. Addictions and other dysfunctional behaviors are causing agony in millions of households. Both the sufferers and the professionals who work to help them heal themselves need this rare combination of personal story and new method of healing!" — David Loye, Ph.D., *author of* The Healing of a Nation

"Hope Sinclair's book is *caring and compassionate*. It will help patients, parents, and those who work with persons with eating disorders. The reader will find the story fascinating and true to the distortions eating disorders produce. The focus is on . . . aiding recovery and rehabilitation. I am IMPRESSED BY THE HIGH QUALITY AND EXTENT OF HER CONTRIBUTIONS to the advancement of the field." — Walter E. Barton, M.D., *Professor of Psychiatry, Dartmouth Medical School; Past Medical Director, American Psychiatric Association*

"Hope Sinclair's wonderful, insightful book, COHEALING is brimming with her namesake quality, hope, for which the world is hungry! Those struggling with eating disorders and other addictions are given solid advice on how to triumph over their dependencies by using the innovative principles of *cohealing* and *co-independence*. These concepts foster co-equal relationships and effective control of one's life. The author's message is WARM, PERSONAL, AND VERY IMPORTANT FOR ALL OF US!" — Sue Patton Thoele, *psychotherapist, seminar leader, and author of* The Woman's Book of Courage

"DESTINED TO BE A CLASSIC in the arena of interpersonal relations, COHEALING *should be in every library* so that it is available for all to read. Hope Sinclair, in addition to telling an intense personal story, has carefully researched the field. Compassionately and interestingly written, this book leads us through near tragedy to a sense of robust well-being, showing us along the way how other families can overcome an abusive past." — Emily Cohen, *Senior Librarian, New York Public Library system*

"In COHEALING, Hope Sinclair tells the *moving story of the partnership* between her and her daughters that SUCCEEDED WHERE ALL OTHER APPROACHES FAILED to facilitate her daughters' recovery from severe eating disorders. I highly recommend it." — Riane Eisler, *author of* The Chalice and The Blade

"COHEALING by Hope Sinclair encourages mothers to act on their potential. It offers illuminating insights on how to provide a role model for daughters to follow. Although this warm and heart-rending story is about a mother and her two daughters who overcome an abusive family system to build fulfilling lives, its uplifting message is universal for all families. COHEALING is destined to be one of the PIVOTAL BOOKS OF THIS DECADE. Deeply perceptive, its suspenseful tale of courage and compassion should inspire us all." — Rhoda Scherer, M.A., O.T.R., *therapist with the New York Board of Education*

"COHEALING is empowering for anyone, and particularly so for those struggling with eating disorders or other addictive behaviors. THE ULTIMATE IN SELF-HELP, it bypasses professional hype and involves the entire family in the healing journey. It is an impressive contribution and a good thing for parents to read!" — Margot Edwards, R.N., M.A., *therapist with Health Associates: A Mind Body Approach and author of* Reclaiming Birth with Reclaiming Death

"Most eating disorder clinics have only minimal results — this book on COHEALING REPRESENTS A METHOD THAT HAS WORKED, AND CAN WORK FOR MANY OTHERS!" — John Frykman, Ph.D., *Director of Addiction Services, Ross Hospital, Kentfield, CA; Former Director of Drug Treatment Services, Haight Ashbury Medical Clinic, San Francisco; author of* A New Connection: A Problem-Solving Approach to Chemical Dependency

"A BRILLIANT, MARVELOUS, BEAUTIFUL book! The *cohealing process* has significantly improved the relationship between my teenage daughter and me. Though I am disabled and confined to a wheel chair, I gained a wonderful sense of personal power and freedom from the book's emphasis on individual rights and on establishing emotionally *co-independent relationships*. No matter what circumstances and limitations we face, COHEALING is a powerful, enlightening gift of hope and expanded possibilities!" — Judith Dadak, *Quadriplegic Artist*

BEFORE YOU BEGIN

Some people who've been given this book have reported wondering at first, "Why am I being told I should read this? It seems to be about weight, dieting, and abusive relationships — these aren't my problems!" However, once into the book, they report that the practical new concepts and insights presented, brought them new awareness on many levels. They began to recognize that interwoven within the story were valuable clues they could use to greatly improve their own situation including their relationships. They see daily events in a new light, particularly those they now perceive as being destructively competitive or controlling, limiting or stifling.

COHEALING has been passed from hand to hand and person to person since it first appeared. It's been gathering followers, with individuals joining together with others to put the innovative concepts described in this book to use in their own lives.

Compulsive-addictive problems, unsatisfactory relationship patterns, and dysfunctional behavior in general, *have common threads*. This book deals with these and takes you through the cohealing process, moving from the pain and frustration of addiction, authoritarian relationships, and codependence to — co-*independence* with new, satisfying ways of being and of relating.

So, as you read, look for what this book may hold for you. Remember that though it's written about a particular set of addictive behaviors and relationship problems, these are a means of demonstrating the *attitudes* and *approaches* that encourage healing and a sense of abundant well-being — the consistent use of problem solving, self-awareness, personal responsibility combined with mutual support, and distress-as-motivation for creative, life-enriching change.

Adapt and use what speaks to you and then, if it suits you, simply consider the rest as a memorable story of growth beyond despair and a restrictive, abusive past to a joyous sense of personal freedom, self-awareness, and the ability to thrive!

Cohealing

Cohealing
The Shared Quest
for Optimal Well-Being

Hope Sinclair

Introduction by Claire Burch &
Foreward by Lester A. Gelb, M.D.

MILLENNIA BOOKS

Publisher's Cataloging-in-Publication Data
Sinclair, Hope.
    Cohealing: the shared quest for optimal well-being / Hope Sinclair.
    p. cm.
    Includes bibliographical references and index.
    Preassigned LCCN: 95-80872.
    ISBN: 0-9649014-4-7

    1. Eating disorders–Treatment. 2. Compulsive behavior–Treatment.
3. Healing.   I. Title.
RC533.S56 1996   616.85'227
                      QB195-20649

WORKSHOPS AND LECTURES
We welcome your feedback on *Cohealing: The Shared Quest for Optimal Well-Being*. Write: Center for Cohealing, 4546 El Camino Real, B10 – Suite 150, Los Altos, CA 94022. If you would like to schedule a speaking engagement or workshop by the author, on Cohealing, (or a "Cohealing for Couples" weekend retreat), please contact the Center. *Cohealing* books and other information on this subject, are also available.

Contents

PART I

A PARENT'S RESPONSE TO SELF-STARVATION

PART II

A COHEALING RESPONSE TO BULIMIC BINGE-PURGING

PART III

RECOVERY — GROWTH AND TRANSFORMATION

NOTES

COHEALING AND CO-INDEPENDENCE HIGHLIGHTS

Acknowledgments

I would like to thank the following people:

My daughter Jacqueline (who in the opening chapters is referred to by her given name, Barbara), for her contributions to this manuscript. This includes all the audio tapes she recorded and transcribed about her personal experiences with eating disorders, hours spent typing her recollections, and helping collect research materials. I have profound admiration for the persistent courage she showed during the years she struggled to recover.

My daughter Brenda, for patiently reading segments of the manuscript and giving me perceptive reactions, based on her own recovery from bulimia. My daughter Lisa, for spending countless hours helping type and edit the manuscript during its early development. Her ideas, suggestions, and enthusiasm were consistently helpful and much appreciated. My son Roger, for his male point of view and his urging to complete the project so it could get into the hands of those who could benefit by it. Without having shared the process of cohealing with my children, and without the valuable input they gave me while this book was in progress, it could never have been written.

Riane Eisler and Dr. David Loye, for taking time from work on their own books to offer their invaluable suggestions on organizing the mass of notes from which this book was written, their helpful guidance on the manuscript from the early stages of its development to its completion, and their steadfast belief in the importance of its message.

Dr. Jean Rubel and Dr. Marlene Boskind-White, authorities on eating disorders and addiction, for providing helpful materials that have been incorporated into the book.

Dr. John Frykman, addiction specialist, for his belief in my work and its potential for helping others. Margot Edwards and Debora Capers, eating-disorder specialists, for their enthusiastic willingness to contribute to this project and become involved in this work. My mentor and friend, Ken Jones, for forever changing my life with his powerful insights on how to live a satisfying, effective life.

Sonya Kaufman, head of reference services at the University of California Education-Psychology Library, for her continuing interest in the project, as well as for conducting the extensive computer searches that helped locate the research material upon which it is based.

Claire Burch, social commentator and critic, for taking time from her own writing and film-making projects to read through this book line by line. Her enthusiasm for my work is much appreciated. Cynthia Shireling and Agatha Walker for editorial suggestions on portions of the manuscript, and Sue Thoele, for her support and interest in my subject matter.

My friends, for their belief in me and the book. Their continuing supportive caring and encouragement to complete this project, as well as their comments on the manuscript, have added significantly to its final form.

Introduction

COHEALING offers profoundly helpful approaches to making satisfying choices that improve our lives and support others in doing the same. The concepts of *cohealing* and *co-independence,* introduced in these pages, have unlimited ways in which they can and need to be used. Both are "grounded in coequal power, trust, affirmation, and respect, along with the actualization of individual potential."

Cohealing and *co-independence* are logical, direct, and broadly applicable to all types of recovery and to building relationships based on egalitarian values. Both concepts provide us with a new ways to visualize and work toward "the cooperative, shared search for optimal well-being" that the author discusses.

Hope Sinclair presents cohealing in the context of three generations of her own family. Drawing on a near-tragic experience in which one of her daughters almost died, the author speaks with compassion and authority on overcoming a legacy of abuse and addictive behavior. After more than ten years of research in the field, she's produced a definitive work on the subject of shared healing that conveys reassurance, guidance, and *hope.*

What makes this book all the more useful is that the family system presented in it is so *typical,* so relevant to those whose own lives echo similar problems — of stifling gender stereotypes, entrapment in hierarchal family systems, oppressive dominant-submissive roles, physical and verbal abuse, dependencies and addiction, incest and family secrets, and beyond this, of divorce, rape, sexual harassment, and much more.

We're painfully aware that these issues are so commonplace that they've become the norm. They reflect our shared legacy of combativeness and conquest, of intolerance and domination. Can anyone question the need for us to *re-image our possibilities for healing ourselves, our families, and our social systems so that cooperation and partnership can become the overriding values of the day?*

In this story, we see the process of *cohealing* unfold, at first subtly, then gaining momentum as cohealers in the family begin experiencing the benefits of open communication, persistent questioning of the family system, and mutual support. We watch as they become allies in the process of change; of relinquishing ineffective habits, beliefs, reactions, and repressive relationships, and in time, reclaim their lives.

Cohealing and co-independence are based on egalitarian values. Both lay the groundwork for moving away from the current exploitation and domination that have proven so destructive to human relationships and our environment. This book is a pioneering, indispensable resource for everyone, but particularly so for those in dysfunctional families and those with any type of compulsive-addictive behavior, whether related to drugs, alcohol, destructive emotional involvements, eating disorders, or other dependencies.

Self-help programs have proliferated in recent years but unfortunately the basis of most of them has been on holding separate groups for individuals with different kinds of personal problems, such as for specific addictions or particular personal traumas, as well as individual groups for the parents, children, and spouses of these people. Yet we do not live life in compartments; our problems tend to be multiple and interrelated, and very much tied to the environment in which they occur.

The cohealing dynamic is, instead, based on approaches that are, as the author notes, "holistic rather than divisive and based on transformation rather than on dysfunction." It fosters involvement in, and commitment to, working together to improve our personal lives. This reverses the trend of splintering people's problems into defined categories (such as the literally hundreds of distinct types of support groups), and encourages professionals and non-professionals alike to move away from compartmentalized thinking to a sense of integration and wholeness regarding the healing process. This makes fundamental sense since making *whole* is, after all, the essence of healing.

Cohealing is in a very real sense, an ecumenical stance but without the required religious components that are an essential part of most self-help programs. Further, cohealing fosters a sense of personal power (as opposed to individuals declaring they're powerless to help themselves). It points the way to developing physical, mental, emotional, and spiritual well-being, and clearly shows us how to "thrive, not just survive." This work uses low self-esteem, learned helplessness, submissiveness, and addictive problems, plus reactions to other abuses, to demonstrate cohealing and co-independence. But beyond these examples, there are undoubtedly innumerable other applications of these principles that are as yet to be explored.

COHEALING makes a major contribution by emphasizing the need for creation of an environment that supports individual well-being, and by demonstrating how this can be achieved. It uses the recent upsurge in destructive eating-patterns and body-dissatisfaction among females as a tool for understanding that these are merely symptoms and that it is the social pressures and mores of our times, most particularly the current dominator paradigm, that creates this tragic situation. And it gives us *tools for transformation and resolution.*

No previous work has so documented how, by joining forces and moving forward together, family members can support each other in their growth beyond dominator conditioning. This book encourages open communication regarding problems with self-image, self-esteem, and self-identity issues as well as mutual support in becoming more aware of the countless double binds and often subtle gender discriminations they continually encounter. The author shows how mothers and daughters can lend encouragement, compare insights, and be an inspiration to each other, in the process forming a bond that releases past restrictions, reclaims their personal rights, and allows co-independence for both.

For the most part, in the past, mothers communicated acceptance of female-role restrictions to their daughters but this has changed in recent years, since former guidelines no longer have the stamp of general validation and there is a new openness to women's right to equitable, non-sexist treatment.

Given these circumstances, Sinclair demonstrates how both mothers and daughters are challenged to determine for themselves what would make their lives most satisfying, what work would be most meaningful, what relationships most nurturing and expansive, what attitudes and approaches most helpful in dealing with the cross-fire of divergent social pressures and attitudes that they face due to hidden and not so hidden conflicts between entrenched gender-based inequities and the ongoing struggle for full equality.

Over the last quarter century, life-distorting eating disorders and related compulsive-addictive behaviors have become progressively more common among females in westernized countries. A large share of our young daughters (often as young as seven and eight) and women of all ages are plagued with body-image obsessions and chronic dieting, with many also bingeing, purging, and fasting.

Because these problems tend to be chronic and continue even after extensive professional treatment, there's been a pressing need for new, more effective approaches to recovery. This book addresses this need, giving penetrating insights into how to promote recovery, including a modus operandi for families to move forward together through the healing process.

Food-based compulsivity has become so common we've largely come to accept it as a "sign of our times," a signature of today's generations of females. In fact, one would have to say that a definition of what's considered "normal" for westernized women, includes perpetual anxiety about their body shape (believing it is misproportioned and too big), their weight (believing they are too heavy), and what they eat (believing it is too much). The impact of this epidemic was brought home to me recently when one of my daughters mentioned that at least 12 of her friends are bulimic!

Food-related obsessions have become a major public health threat as women struggle to cope with the confusing and conflicting pressures involved in trying to form a new, contemporary female identity. After more than 5,000 years of patriarchy, the frustrations females are experiencing in attempting to redefine their role and its possibilities, are causing huge numbers of them to turn inward on themselves, hating their bodies, attempting to dissipate their frustrations and rage by obsessively trying to control their appetites.

For the millions whose lives are being affected by this epidemic, this book skillfully shows how to progress from illness to recovery. In addition to guiding the reader through an engrossing story, it emphasizes personal responsibility along with demonstrating how to make healing a shared experience in which all benefit, plus showing how this creates a basis for positive self-exploration that leads to greater personal awareness and fulfillment. Further, it keys in on the difference between what the author defines as "hyper help" that's detrimental to recovery and "real help" that is supportive of recovery and well-being.

Sinclair describes easily applied, innovative solutions for overcoming dysfunctional patterns. Subjects are organized to make it easy for support groups and professionals to use the book as a basis for discussion.

Therapists will find it beneficial to assign specific chapters as "homework" for both clients and family members to quickly convey helpful information and supportive attitudes that augment counseling. Of particular interest are illustrations of the benefits to be derived when family members become personally involved in the healing process.

In the years ahead this work will undoubtedly be joined by a number of books on cohealing, written by others who will have adapted its concepts to their needs. Cohealing Support Groups for individuals, families, and others, some attended by therapists, will also undoubtedly develop many additional useful applications for cohealing that will have a beneficial impact not only on the lives of those personally involved, but also well beyond.

Therapists who become participants in self-help Cohealing Support Group activities should have much to offer and much to gain personally from involvement in this holistic approach. Cohealing Therapy Groups are a logical extension of principles described in this work.

The principles of *cohealing* and *co-independence* are summarized in Chapter 19, but throughout this book we see applications of both concepts. The attitudes, approaches, and results derived from them are illustrated so that we, as readers, *live through* the story and sense the magnitude of the transformation that can result from cohealing and the adoption of a co-independent stance in our own relationships. The author brings these concepts alive, helping us visualize how we ourselves might apply them to making our own lives more satisfying.

Sinclair speaks with the authority and conviction of years of personal experience and, by example, shows us how these innovative approaches to integration, cooperation, and equal status are within our reach.

No one who hasn't overcome a restrictive, abusive past plus devastating family problems, and who hasn't talked with physicians, guidance counselors, educators, and others who have first-hand experience with the traumas of abuse, addiction, and dysfunctional behavior in general, could have had the overview and personal insights necessary to develop the ground-breaking concepts of cohealing and co-independence that we see unfold in these pages. The author's unique perspectives give us a reliable, sensible framework for overcoming past and present problems and for regaining control of our lives.

No one who hasn't lived through years of anguish, discouragement, apprehension, and fear created by a legacy of shame and abuse, and of a family system reflecting coercive dominant-submissive scripting and who hasn't reclaimed her own life could have envisioned the powerful principles presented in these pages, or have given us this shared path to reclaiming our own lives.

The practical and profoundly useful approaches explained in these pages have proven highly successful and life-enhancing. Both lay-people and professionals will find them illuminating as well as provocative, and readily adaptable to a wide variety of situations.

This work offers us a splendid foundation for developing a broad-based *cohealing movement* to repair the social and psychological damage created by millennia of oppressive hierarchical social and family systems, and facilitate acceptance of new approaches based on mutuality and partnership.

Claire Burch, *Director of Art & Education Media, producer of numerous television documentaries on addiction, poverty, and mental health for PBS; an editor of Network News, Northern California Psychiatric Review; author of Careers in Psychiatry for the National Commission on Mental Health Manpower, Stranger in the Family, and other books, plus features in many national magazines (Saturday Review, The New Republic, Life, McCall's, Good Housekeeping, Women's Life, Mademoiselle, and others).*

Foreword

Hope Sinclair is the mother of two daughters who were afflicted with such compulsive-eating disorders as are becoming epidemic among day's young women. She shares her poignant struggle to confront herself and her loved ones with what she has learned about their addictive behaviors.

She demonstrates that healing and recovery from dependencies and other dysfunctional behaviors need to involve the entire family. She also beautifully illustrates a self-healing method that produces positive change. She communicates her insights and experience in a lucid and straighforward way that can be of help to everyone who reads COHEALING.

It is to the shame of the many professionals who have a wealth of experience with anorexia and bulimia as well as other eating disorders that few can write about them without the use of a maze of arcane and sometimes inane psychoanalytic jargon.

Furthermore, the author of COHEALING is convinced that these addictive problems are promoted by perverted social values that secondarily infect the family. Parents reflect the values of their social environment, but environment also independently affects our young people. Daughters in particular are pressured by parents and by society to be "the best," to "succeed," and to "win," by being physically attractive. The various media bombard young women with advertisements to buy cosmetics, skin creams, and products to "reshape the body" to comply with today's "fashion." Along with these pressures, there is often insufficient opportunity for daughters to develop adequate self-esteem, which is another issue this author addresses.

Children lose their "sense of self" when they feel compelled to please and impress parents and peers so as not to lose love, support, and social opportunities. When what is defined as success by a culture is elusive (such as the imperative that females be thin), many give up; in the case of women, many overeat so as at least to enjoy the pleasures of food. Some, like the daughters in this book, become anorexic or bulimic in a desperate attempt not to lose out. What a tragedy! *Not enough people have learned one of the main messages of this book — the importance and joy of self-motivated striving to achieve necessary or desirable goals without having to compete with others.*

With eating disorders as well as with other compulsive-addictive behaviors, times of crisis, failure, and defeat are almost inevitable. For this reason, competent professional support is needed. Yet, because social environment is of critical importance, such counseling needs to be combined with creative approaches to family awareness and shared healing such as those presented in this book. Thus, therapeutic help needs to involve a combination of professionals and family members who *share the cohealing process* in a "recovery network," as so movingly discussed by this author.

I have long advocated a collaborative, socially integrated approach such as the one Hope Sinclair demonstrates, and this book reinforces my conviction. Therapists who want to improve their skills, or readers who suspect they may have an eating disorder or problem with low self-esteem (which makes them vulnerable), are well advised to read and learn from it!

Lester A. Gelb, M.D., *Consultant Emeritus and former Clinical Director, Department of Psychiatry, Maimonides Medical Center, Brooklyn, N.Y.; former Director of Mental Health Services, International Center for the Disabled, New York; Fellow, The American Academy of Psychoanalysis, author of* Masculinity-Femininity, A Study in Imposed Inequality.

The Cohealing Response

This book was begun when one of my three daughters was still bulimic. It was written over time, through the stages of her recovery. The writing has been a labor of love: it started out of concern for her, though eventually we all benefited from the effort and years of research involved, and it ended with compassion for all who are suffering from dysfunctional patterns and a legacy of dominator-submissive relationships, including addictive disorders, as well as those who love and care about them.

We are living in an age of compulsive-addictive eating problems. Most of us have close friends or relatives caught in these destructive patterns or are caught in them ourselves. Currently, countless young girls, and women of all ages, are suffering from eating and self-image disorders that are damaging their mental, emotional, and physical well-being. They are among the millions privately obsessed not only with controlling their weight and food intake, but also with what they perceive to be the unacceptability and shortcomings of their bodies.

They perennially feel guilty for what they've eaten and try one diet program after another, never feeling comfortable with how they look or who they are. They keep hoping for an improved self, with a body they feel will be acceptable and appealing. Frequently they lose touch with reality, in terms of their body-image.

From personal experience, I know that seemingly innocent dieting behavior (such as two of my daughters developed in college) can develop into life-threatening food addiction.

In the course of researching and writing this book, I gradually developed the concepts of *cohealing* and *co-independence*. Cohealing establishes a mind-set that makes co-independence not only seem possible, but also desirable as the foundation for our relationships. Cohealing thus provides a basis for us to pull ourselves away from our shared hierarchal-patriarchal past, and release ourselves from "dominator"[1] thinking so that we can be receptive to cooperative partnership approaches to solving personal, local, and even global problems. Partnership attitudes are based on mutuality as a healthy, satisfying, and constructive approach to life.

Cohealing gives us a mental construct, an easy way to envision responding compassionately to ourselves, to those we care about, and to the world in general. In an age of addictions and compulsivity, brutality and prejudice, the process I call *cohealing* offers us with a way to *conceptualize shared healing and the benefits to be gained from making satisfying, comfortable choices that improve our own lives and that support others in doing the same.* It is a response that is basic to *recovery from any type of addiction, whether from alcohol, drugs, destructive personal relationships, eating disorders, or other dependencies.*

Cohealing not only profoundly changed and improved my daughters' lives, but my own as well. Though this book is devoted primarily to a shared personal healing experience between my daughters and me, fathers, husbands, brothers, and other male members of a household who become part of a family cohealing system can, of course, add immeasurably to the overall process and in so doing gain valuable insights, direction, and closeness to other family members. Sharing in the cohealing experience fosters an openness and exchange that is enormously supportive as well as expansive, and this opens new avenues for relating to one another on a healthier basis.

Males are in a position to model healthy aspects of what we think of as the "male archetype." These include offering a sense of protection and security that makes home a safe place to be, along with practicality and worldliness, self-sufficiency and independence. Further, males and females alike can, as they heal themselves, become examples of individuals with a strong, positive personal identity while at the same time offering love, nurturing, and acceptance that help others in the cohealing network to more easily love and accept themselves. Both genders contribute to the healing process by modeling such traits as persistence, courage, forgiveness, integrity, creativity, and inquisitiveness. In this way, they help others with whom they are cohealing to do the same.

Beyond this, males and females can both show that it is okay to make "mistakes" and learn from them, to be spontaneous and enjoy life, to be courageous yet vulnerable and share one's vulnerability. They can, by showing appreciation and closeness, provide others with a feeling of self-acceptance, the sense that "I am okay. I can take care of myself. I am worthy. I am lovable." All of these are priceless gifts that can be offered by either gender in the cohealing process. They are supportive of health and life satisfaction, of a sense of well-being, wonder, and personal fulfillment.

Households in which eating disorders and other compulsive-addictive problems develop, tend to be restrictive and authoritarian and to accentuate gender stereotypes rather than self-definition. Often they are more rigid than fluid, more restrictive than allowing, more critical than affirming, more hierarchal than partnership oriented. For this reason, sharing the cohealing process can be particularly helpful since it can help release family members from role-bound, self-limiting interpretations of what it means to be human.

Despite the growing epidemic of eating disorders, there has been far too little supportive material available to help those whose lives are affected, though such information is vital. This book gives guidelines on how to develop a *cohealing network* when someone we care about, or we ourselves, are suffering from compulsive-addictive problems, dependencies, or other dysfunctional behaviors; examples given, related to eating, include bingeing, harmful dieting, self-starvation, and purging, as well as cross-over addictive problems. Because the vast majority of those with eating disorders are women, I have written from their perspective.

Those with eating disorders and related addictions usually wait several years before seeking therapeutic help, during which time the individual and her family often not only feel helpless to deal with illness-related problems, but are also in a quandary as to what they could be doing to promote recovery. Since the cost of professional treatment can be devastating to a family's financial situation, often outstripping its resources, relying solely on such help is often untenable, and even unaffordable. Because the individual suffering the disordered patterns needs a supportive, nurturing personal environment in which to recover, cohealing and self-help approaches become imperative.

I have dealt, in this book, not only with addictions and eating disorders, but also the gamut of family trauma and dysfunction, showing how the cohealing process proved invaluable in recovery from such painful events as *incest, rape, spousal threats and intimidation, and shaming and physical abuse by parents*. Ultimately, these and other negative influences yielded to the powerful influence of cohealing.

My writing is dedicated to helping parents and children, husbands and wives, sisters and brothers, friends, colleagues, counselors, and others to overcome personal legacies that are restrictive and damaging, limiting of personal growth, freedom, and potential, so that they can reclaim their right to freely choose what is in their own highest good as long as this does not infringe on someone else's similar rights. "Reclaim" is synonymous with *recover*, and reclaiming our rights to a heathy, fulfilling life is basic to the cohealing process.

COHEALING shows how to make the healing process a mutually beneficial, shared experience to reclaim our innate personal rights, and to build the good life we deserve. It shows how to break free of destructive relationships, replace negative mental dialogues with positive self-talk, find freedom from perfectionism, work through unexpressed anger, overcome the habits of guilt and self-blame, replace depression with emotional buoyancy, move from inertia and procrastination to constructive action, and initiate caring intimate relationships. It shows how to cope with and overcome gender stereotypes and double binds that promote and sustain low self-esteem and dependencies, including eating and weight problems.

Most important is being imaginative in exploring the cohealing process and its unlimited applications, for it is an approach that is applicable to each of our lives since all of us experience traumas that call for *healing*. The personal story presented here is related to traumas we experienced and dysfunctions in our own family system, because that is the setting in which our cohealing developed. *But take this just as an example of how this process can work, and from it adapt and apply it to your own situation to make it most useful to you.*

Cohealing provides a mind-set that supports us not only in overcoming the legacy of a dysfunctional personal past, but also in working together to overcome the legacy of the damaging hierarchical social past to which we have all been subjected. Co-independence is essentially a "partnership" approach, and it takes cohealing (shared interactive recovery) to heal the wounds of our previous authoritarian socialization in which relations have been based on domination/subordination, through force, fear, and other means of control. Cohealing increases our awareness of how we have been affected by our detrimental personal and social past, and helps us establish attitudes and approaches that heal these wounds.

It is the *bridge* that can help us move from the precepts of, and the pain caused by, dominator thinking and from unquestioning acceptance of the injustices, imbalances, and destruction it produces — to accepting and even requiring the freedoms, personal responsibility, and equality that are implicit in co-independence. It is the *bridge* that can help us visualize the benefits to each of us, and to all humankind, that will come about from establishing a new partnership ethos in which co-independent relationships are the norm, not the exception.

The principles of cohealing support us in acquiring the attitudes and behaviors that foster our desire and our ability to create healthy, mutually beneficial relationships based on justice and mutual respect. They help us clearly understand and acknowledge that we ourselves benefit when each of us is empowered and given the opportunity to actualize our unique potential.

Cohealing principles can foster cooperation within families, communities, and other groups; principles for working together to break the status quo that passes painful, dysfunctional patterns from generation to generation, unwittingly perpetuating them. It can be seen as a primary way to facilitate personal and social healing, and to transform personal and social interactions so that they become more satisfying and respectful, cooperative and just, rewarding and humane.

Looked at another way, cohealing provides us with principles for questioning the basic assumptions that have limited us in the past so that we are able, at last, to freely choose from more appropriate alternatives. It offers the key for replacing acceptance of our destructive "dominator" socialization with attitudes that allow us to visualize and accept co-equal, co-independent relationships as beneficial to all concerned.

I have written with the thought in mind that many who are deeply involved in addictive, abusive, or other destructive situations, might want to quickly jump to the chapters that sound most applicable to their problems. I've therefore arranged the material so that it can be accessed in any order, though of course a sequential reading is preferable for following the story.

Also, particularly in Part I, chapters present events from different perspectives, with each focusing on particular types of problems though many of them were being addressed at the same time. For nine years, the daughter about whom this book is written, worked to release herself from her addictive behaviors. During that time and also subsequent to it, as part of the recovery process, our family system went through significant changes.

Through cohealing, we as a family, gradually moved from "codependence" to "co-independence," a condition that *resolves the dichotomy between autonomy and intimacy, aloneness and relating.* Co-independence affords a solid basis for establishing intimate, caring relationships while at the same time maintaining one's own identity. *Cohealing* combined with *co-independence* brings a sense of freedom and closeness, providing tools for abundant living. I hope that our story will make the way easier for you.

What would I tell you if I knew you were experiencing problems and distress that diminish your ability to enjoy the miracle of being alive?

I'd tell you that you're a very special person. I would let you know that I care about you and have faith that you can find ways to make your life meaningful and rewarding. That you can overcome whatever problems you face and find a deeper sense of satisfaction than you ever dreamed possible. That you have a right to make healthy decisions for yourself and look out for your own highest good. And that I believe you can become the powerful, dynamic individual you were meant to be!

Note: As you read and perhaps reread COHEALING, record your reactions, insights, and ideas in the "Personal Cohealing Journal" section at the end of the book. Date your entries so that you can follow your progress and get a feeling of momentum and direction. Good luck on your journey!

PART I

A Parent's Response to Self-Starvation

CHAPTER 1

Midnight Phone Call

For us, the cohealing process evolved gradually. Back when my daughter Barbara was slipping deeper into anorexia, she didn't phone me, refused to have lunch with me as we'd done in the past, or see me on any terms, and was terse in phone conversations I initiated. She talked with her sister Brenda, about going some place where none of us could ever find her.

I was worried about her, though I had no idea how ill she had become. For months she had been much too thin, and I heard reports from her sisters that she engaged in marathon eating sessions which she followed with self-induced vomiting. As she became more ill, she withdrew from my life, rarely phoning home. When she did, she refused to discuss her eating problems or her low weight.

Anytime I mentioned the subject, she stopped me. According to her accounts of how her life was going, everything was "just fine" and I had absolutely nothing to worry about.

I was asleep when the phone rang, and as I made my way through the darkness to the living room, I had the feeling something was wrong. I lifted the receiver, and all I heard was sobbing. Looking back on those heart-stopping moments, I recall my mind racing, trying to figure out who was on the other end of the line. Could it be that someone had died and this person was too distraught to let me know?

"Who is this calling? Please tell me who you are. What's happened; has someone died?" But I only heard unrecognizable sobs.

Finally, I realized that it was Barbara: "It's me, Mom, I'm dying. I'm slowly starving myself, and I don't know why. I haven't been able to keep any food down for days, and I'm so weak it's difficult to walk. I'm so depressed I don't know what to do."

At last she was calling. Why had she waited so long?

It had been disturbing, on the brief occasions when we had been together, to see that Barbara was continuing to lose weight and yet refused to hear comments about it. Since she was an adult, I couldn't force her to get medical or psychological help. Months had passed before this midnight phone call.

Despair

"Mom, I'm so afraid. All evening I've been thinking about killing myself. Nothing seems worthwhile. You wouldn't believe how much I eat, yet I can't keep any food down. Last night I ate and vomited five double-layer cakes. I don't know what's wrong with me. I just can't help myself."

Her words came in rapid succession as she continued weeping softly: "Today the landlord came over and handed me an eviction notice which says that if I don't pay my back rent by noon tomorrow, I'll be out on the sidewalk. I've spent everything I had for food."

Barbara said she had borrowed money from the university to pay her past-due bills but had spent these emergency loans on food. Now the loans were due, and she would be expelled for nonpayment. The utility company was going to shut off power, and her phone was about to be cut off.

She explained that, after running out of money, she'd continued writing checks to buy food. "I wrote them hurriedly, hoping the bank wouldn't notice them."

The shambles her finances were in and the state of her mental disorganization showed further when she explained that dozens of overdraft notices had arrived from the bank and that she'd hidden some of them in the phone book and others behind her bureau and couch, while throwing others away.

She talked rapidly, in staccato fashion: "I keep thinking of suicide and how easy it would be. I've planned it many times. I'm such a failure and life seems so sad and unhappy. There's really nothing to live for. I'm terribly afraid of the future."

Each time she paused to catch her breath and blow her nose, I filled the silence by telling her I loved her more than she could possibly know, assuring her that she had much to live for.

Then she said, "While I'm telling you all this, you may as well know that I'm not the only one who is vomiting. Brenda comes over here all the time and porks out and vomits too, so it's not just me."

I hadn't known about Brenda's involvement. Not just one daughter was caught in this bizarre behavior. How could this be happening?

She talked for 45 minutes, often repeating herself, telling about how she hated her classes and was too weak and tired to regularly attend them. She was failing her three remaining courses and had not been showing up for her campus work-study job. She was sure she'd be fired. Emptiness and desperation echoed through her voice: "Mom, I feel so terribly lost and confused; I don't even know myself anymore."

I suggested that I pick her up and bring her home.

"Yes, yes, that would be wonderful." She said she'd wait until morning, but I questioned her to make sure she could make it through the night.

Before hanging up, I told her again how much she meant to me, saying I'd see that her bills were paid in the morning and reassuring her that she wasn't alone, that I would help her.

Hanging up, I sat there trying to sort out what I had just heard. Barbara had reached out, and in so doing, the cohealing process had begun, though we didn't realize it at the time nor did we have a name for it.

Coming Home

The next morning, as I pulled into the driveway of Barbara's apartment, she opened the door a crack, motioning for me to come in. Not having seen her recently, I was shocked at the change. She was listless, gaunt, pale, and skeletal, moving slowly as in a despondent dream. The drapes were drawn, and in the dim light, evidence that her life had caved in around her was apparent in the piles of debris haphazardly strewn about the apartment.

Since she seemed incapable of gathering her own possessions, I began packing them. In the kitchen, clouds of fruit flies hovered over moldy dishes, and garbage spilled out of soggy bags onto the floor. Tattered window shades filtered light across her bureau drawers where soiled clothes lay among bowls of hardened cake frosting. Under her bed an earthenware bowl lay hidden, a spoon glued to its side with cake batter. The stench from the bathroom permeated the air.

As I packed her things, Barbara moved lethargically from chair to bed to be near me. She was too ill to care or be embarrassed by the condition of the apartment. I sensed that she had come to accept the mess without question and was unable to picture how it might look to me or anyone else.

Her possessions were few — some rumpled clothing, dirty dishes, two drinking glasses, a saucepan, some baking trays and pans, bedding, and forgotten, half-done homework assignments. On the way home we stopped at her landlord's house so that Barbara could hand him my check for her back rent and explain that she was moving out. By mid-morning she was back home in her once-familiar bed, covers tightly pulled around her shivering body while I went off to pay her bills, past-due loans, and bank overdrafts.

Barbara remembers that day also, saying, "There was a feeling of relief when I walked through the front door, recognizing the familiar rooms and furnishings that were home. As Mother put my belongings in my old room, I thought, 'Everything's going to be all right now.' At first I slept most of the time. I was exhausted and depressed. Sleep was an escape. I felt like a wounded soul seeking refuge until I could gain my strength again. I didn't trust anyone and was terrified that someone would try to change me."

In the following days Barbara clung to the hope that somehow I could help her, yet at the same time she resisted my attempts to do so. Looking back, even after years of research into anorexia and bulimia, it still hurts to remember the extent of the disintegration of Barbara's life. I tried to fathom this illness so devastating to mind and body. How could such a bright, good-looking young woman have let her life fall so completely apart?

Catalyst for Cohealing

Compulsivity and addiction are associated with family systems that are often referred to as being dysfunctional, shame-based, codependent, or addictive.

Bulimia, anorexia, or other forms of disordered eating can be looked on as a catalyst for making beneficial changes. The daughter or other loved one can then be recognized not as "the problem" but as "having problems" related to multiple factors, among them family interactions.

Although social factors are often minimized, and far too much blame has been leveled at the family, when a loved one develops disordered eating or other addictive problems, we need to recognize that certain types of interactions between family members are related to the occurrence of compulsive disorders. For this reason, one of the most helpful things we as parents, husbands, and other relatives can do to support an individual's recovery is make changes that improve our own lives. This is particularly true if we are part of her home environment.

Everyone is stressed when a family member is seriously ill. When someone we care about is hurting, we are affected and have our own anxieties — anger, helplessness, defensiveness, resentment, guilt, denial; you name it. These too need healing. At times when the pain is greatest, the discouragement overwhelming, we are, however, far more likely to make substantial changes in our own lives. Distress can be a great motivator. It can force us to get in touch with our feelings, propelling us toward more effective, life-enhancing decisions and actions.

During Barbara's years of eating problems, I considered the many ways in which we had patterned our home life in relation to society. It seemed that we had replicated our society in miniature. Both our household and culture were hierarchical, based on dominance and submission rather than on equality and partnership. Both were role-bound, with innumerable limitations and expectations based on gender. Both were based on controlling, not on negotiating. Having assumed the position of authority in the family (mirroring our patriarchal society), the children's stepfather had set the rules, judged compliance, criticized, and punished, according to what he felt was appropriate.

Thus cohealing had its beginning in Barbara's turning to me for help when she was starving, an event that opened the door of communication between us. This developed gradually, imperceptibly, with most of the initial efforts in the direction of helping her gain a foothold on recovery. But this very process of discussion, of trial and error, of setbacks and progress, shook loose long years of habit. Cohealing unfolded gradually as we worked together to develop greater awareness of family and social influences so that we could make healthier life choices.

While Barbara was anorexic, her dire health situation was paramount; we needed to move her toward recovery as quickly as possible to stabilize her health. Much of what transpired between her and other family members had to do with her feelings, perceptions, needs. In time, her fears, dissatisfactions, and anxieties would trigger other family members to examine their own, and these too became fertile ground for joint discussions in a discovery process that developed into cohealing. The impetus was anorexia and our need to understand, to find answers, to change things so that recovery could take place.

When ill with anorexia, she seemed too emotionally fragile to give back to anyone else. Her body and her will to live were so tenuous, there was nothing to do but for me to become involved in working with her to get her life back together. It was a process of listening to her, affirming her, reassuring her, giving her reality checks.

Family members supported Barbara in regaining control of her life with infusions of love, hope, and approval, non-judgmentally accepting her as okay — "I love you as you are" came across abundantly. To a great extent, then, it was a one-way street in the beginning, with each of us trying to understand how to avoid making matters any worse and, hopefully, gradually make them better.

Barbara's anorexia was a time of reassessment for all of us and a growing awareness that our family system was related to her illness. If she was to recover we would have to somehow understand the problematic aspects of our family life and change — but how? During the cohealing process, we would find answers.

However, it would not be until after Barbara regained a more normal weight and had reestablished a firmer grip on life that cohealing would develop into a powerful force affecting all of our lives. We had all been aware that there were problems within the family, but for the most part, we had avoided or worked around them. The need to overcome anorexia heightened this awareness; however, more importantly, it triggered our doing something about our problems. In time, we eventually realized that our family system was one that would be described as being "codependent" and that as a family, we were moving from codependence — to co-independence.

Anorexia pushed us toward making positive changes in our lives. It caused us to set a pattern of exploring and going beyond previous limitations, propelling us toward greater understanding and resolution. Cohealing would eventually involve major life changes to reduce the anxiety created by rigidity and the obsessive need to control, allowing family members to develop as individuals and make each of our lives much easier and more relaxed.

Cohealing

We all need nurturing relationships in our lives, particularly when we are recovering from illness, pain, sadness, anxiety, or any type of compulsive/addictive problem. There is nothing more healing than caring, loving, interpersonal involvement.

Healing — recovery from anxiety and disease — restores us to sound health, a state of optimum functioning emotionally, mentally, and physically; even spiritually. "Co," of course, relates to something that is shared with others. I think of the cohealing process *as the cooperative, shared search for optimal well-being.* I chose this descriptor because it *focuses attention* on interactions and attitudes that are beneficial and highlights the mutual support needed for recovery. It gives a sense of direction, an appreciation of how we can become involved in the healing process and why this is beneficial to all concerned.

The cohealing mind-set helps each of us accept the need to grieve, learn, and grow with the help of supportive people. The recovery process does not occur in isolation. Cohealing offers us a way to conceptualize moving through the healing process together, forming a basis for healthy, mutually gratifying, co-independent relationships.

Co-Independence

Co-independence provides a useful mental construct that combines mutuality and partnership with individuation and autonomy, in a balance that is healthy for the individual as well as society in general. Cohealing is an attitude and approach. Co-independence is a state or condition. Both are healthy ways of relating to one another. Cohealing works with addictions of all types as well as in other distressing situations, for even at the best of times, there are rough moments that need emotional balm. Co-independence is essential for a good life regardless of social context. Both cohealing and co-independence are grounded in coequal power, trust, affirmation, and respect, along with the actualization of individual potential.

Cohealing is essential to family members resolving problems in a way that encourages everyone's fulfillment and well-being. Becoming part of this recovery process helps us move beyond our own emotional turmoil aroused by the illness and/or addiction of a loved one and provides us with an opportunity to expand and enhance our own life possibilities.

Although cohealing would have seemed almost impossible at the time Barbara came home so ill, it did evolve.

So don't give up hope. Keep reaching out to the loved one who is having addictive problems. Stay with it — there is no way to predict the time-frame for recovery. Even when everything seems most hopeless, it is important to remember that things can turn around. Although those with addictive problems struggle to make it appear that they have their lives totally together, they may feel that nothing they do is good enough. Often they suffer from feelings of worthlessness. We can let them know generously and regularly that we care and that we accept them for who they are.

CHAPTER 2

Dieting Becomes Addiction

With Barbara at home it became possible to piece together her version of how she had become ill. During her first year and a half in college, her weight had slowly inched upward, so she had experimented with fad diets. But in spite of attempts to regain control of her eating, she had added 30 pounds. Life had been a struggle, and eating had provided temporary solace and escape.

Vomiting had been a way of sidestepping the normal cause-and-effect relationship between overeating and weight gain. She had begun to eat more and yet lose weight. Gradually her eating had escalated to full days devoted to stuffing herself, punctuated by trips to the bathroom to disgorge.

At some point, vomiting was no longer a choice — it was something she felt compelled to do after eating, the final act that completed food intake. The thought of not carrying through on this ritual filled her with panic. Barbara came to experience time as a "frightening empty space" that could best be filled by eating, yet she thought of food as a pleasurable but poisonous substance that must not be allowed to remain in her body.

Three years later, Barbara would record the following thoughts on how she had unknowingly and progressively moved from the deprivation of weight-loss dieting to addiction. She hoped my including her comments might forewarn others of obsessive dieting and help them to avoid the devastating effects of eating disorders.

Problems and Disappointments

"I want to tell you what it was like. Maybe you'll recognize yourself here — or your daughter, or someone else you know and want to assist.

"As a high school senior I'd never worried about calories or dieting. I'd had a strong body and an athletic build. Thinness had been of no concern to me. But two years later, in college, the need for it was an obsession every waking hour of the day.

"Worry over my size dominated my life, and I heard voices demanding that I starve, or vomit if I ate. Whatever had happened had been gradual but unrelenting. Before graduation from high school, I'd earned enough money baby-sitting and working in local farmers' fields to cover two years of college expenses if I lived at home. My parents had offered this, but at the time I thought I needed to be on my own.

"It was difficult to trade that security and help for the shaky prospect of getting financial aid through the college as an independent student. I would have to live away from home and could receive only the smallest stipend from any relative in order to meet the requirements for this student-aid program, but I hoped my savings, plus a campus job, would carry me through."

Snacking Becomes a Habit

"During summer session, I moved into a virtually deserted old rooming house shared with three other students. The two-dollars-a-day rent bought me a small L-shaped room with a broken three-legged desk, a mattress on the floor, and a small walk-in closet with a single 40-watt bulb. Because I was too poor to buy more expensive foods, I stretched my budget with a monotonous routine of canned beans, spinach, and carrots. Protein was supplied by eating hot dogs and peanut butter.

"The combination of being a poorly-paid secretary, attending university night-classes, and living in a dark, empty rooming house was oppressive. I wanted out but lacked money to buy options and confidence to seek new directions. I felt frustrated and insignificant, lost among thousands of students. It scared me.

"Lunch breaks with my sister Brenda were spent recuperating from the monotony of the morning's work and joking about the tedium to come during the next four hours. I'd describe to Brenda how I was filing 16,000 coded pieces of paper or running errands between five offices. I was the lowest-paid employee, with no benefits and little respect, always ready to hop to a job with a glued-on smile. Why didn't I leave? I was afraid I couldn't find a better way to support myself.

"Alone in my room with school books and papers before me, I rewarded myself after a long day's work by scooping spoonfuls of peanut butter from the jar and spreading them thickly on graham crackers. One, two, three, four, until the jar was half empty. I'd screw the lid back on, then hiding the jar, look for something else to do that seemed pleasurable, but I found little that could distract me from my problems except food.

"It wasn't easy to pull my spirits up after trudging home from eight hours of secretarial work at minimum wage. I'd make a thick peanut butter sandwich for dinner and head off to evening class. I felt that if I had more money, a job I liked, and a man I cared for, I wouldn't rely on food for relief and consolation. Eating relieved my distress but added to my weight, which made me feel more distressed. As 120 pounds became 130 and 135, I focused more and more attention on food and worried about the need to limit my calorie intake.

"There didn't seem to be much to look forward to, and I found myself sleeping late on weekends. That justified combining morning and noon meals. Even if I ate all low-calorie food, it was more fun having a large single meal instead of two meager ones.

"Food was solace and pleasure. I interspersed splurges with days of restriction, but whether I was dieting, abstaining, or exercising to lose weight, food and calorie-counting became more and more important.

"When fall term arrived, Brenda and I moved into a large campus living group, and I thought my attitude would lighten with the new environment. What I didn't know was that I'd committed myself to live in a setting in which the majority of students were either in upper division or graduate school. It was a stiflingly quiet academic atmosphere I hadn't anticipated.

"At registration — another blow. My financial aid had been denied so I had to take out a substantial loan to stay in school. More debts and more scrimping. The law had been changed during the summer so I no longer qualified. Heartache.

"Brenda had more money since she had been awarded scholarships. I was envious too of her go-getter approach to everything, and it didn't help one bit that I compared myself unfavorably to her. She'd been active in social clubs in high school and in community activities as well. She was an honor student who'd received various awards. Who was I? Just Brenda's younger sister, quiet, unsure, wanting acceptance but never quite feeling acceptable.

"In high school I'd been active in sports, but the pace of college and work promoted a sedentary life, and for the first time I developed a heaviness on my hips, thighs, and stomach that made me feel pear-shaped. To offset this weight gain, I tried lots of weight-loss schemes. All of them failed.

"I blamed my sparse dating life on my increasing weight, convinced that if I were thin, my life would be filled with male escorts. I was sure men would not find me attractive unless I were slender. I felt self-conscious about the fullness between my waist and knees. I began masking my increasing insecurity with an aloof air of superiority.

"I wanted to fit the media image of what is sensuous and attractive in makeup, hairdos, clothes, and body shape. I looked beyond my mother for a female role model that would give me an aura of glamour, and decided the entertainment world would be my guide. It seemed clear that actresses and models offered examples of a more stimulating and adventurous life than the role of housewife/mother.

"Yet at the same time I desperately wanted marriage and a man who was self-reliant and confident, who could protect and provide for me. I hoped that in college I'd meet such a man.

"Over the following months my evening nibbling and occasional splurges increased to all-out binges. Having a light frame and being five-feet-nine inches tall, at 137 pounds I knew I needed to change my eating habits but felt unable to resist buying a half-gallon of ice cream, a dozen cookies, and a bag of doughnuts, and consuming them in a single sitting.

"Some nights I'd be nauseous from the amount of food I'd eaten. Looking in the mirror at my reflection, I thought anything would be better than living in this body. My social life was nonexistent, my shape unsightly, and my job boring. I had no close friends other than my sister. I seemed to spend all my time working and studying, and just trying to keep up with a grueling schedule.

"Feeling in a bind between wanting to indulge and also to be thin, I hit upon the idea of taking laxatives to push the food through my system fast, with minimum absorption. I'd swallow several tablets at a time and wait out the discomfort. This didn't prevent weight gain, but it seemed to slow it.

"The pounds continued to creep onto my hips and thighs, so I bought myself a girdle as an immediate solution. After much tugging, the elastic stretched from my knees to my waist. The girdle cut deep welts into my flesh, and my thighs itched unmercifully. On warm days

I felt as though I was walking in wet diapers. Every moment I was squeezed into it, I felt miserable. But there was a definite improvement in my appearance. The girdle smoothed the bulges, shifting the flesh around so I appeared trim and compact. I gladly traded comfort for looks.

"Over the previous year my weight had gone up from 120 to 148 pounds. I knew this upward climb would continue unless I discovered an effective way to control my eating. Though I was anxious to lose the added pounds, I didn't want to diet all the time, so I decided to limit myself during the week. On Saturdays, I'd allow myself to eat anything I wanted.

"Soon the deprivation from weekdays of limited food intake led to my expanding the freedom to eat what I wanted to entire weekends. Brenda and her girl friend, Sue, also adopted this abstain-splurge resolution, and together we treated ourselves to sweets on weekends. Within a couple of months these binges gradually grew. We consumed more and more rich food at a single sitting. Even our five days of dieting couldn't offset these feasts. I began measuring food in terms of calories rather than nutrition. Eating had become a problem instead of a natural process.

"Perhaps if some reassuring events had happened in my life at this point, I might have been able to again put food in its proper perspective and back off from worrying about my weight and from eating to satisfy unmet needs.

"Instead, I was assaulted and violently raped by a stranger while working alone one evening at my campus job. The emotional devastation of this attack, the bottomless fear it engendered, the sense of helplessness that somehow it might just as unexpectedly happen again, compounded my insecurities. More than ever I felt I needed drastic measures to gain greater control of my body and make it more acceptable."

The Start of Purging

"One evening I sat with Brenda and Sue at a local ice cream parlor. Sue was a tall six feet without shoes, and I remember wondering whether her problems with dieting might be related to her height and her wish to be smaller and less conspicuous.

"This particular Saturday we were commiserating about approaching finals and our non-existent social life. We dwelt on our dissatisfactions as we spooned down ice cream. I ordered a double sundae and, having enjoyed it thoroughly, ordered a second one and then a third.

"With the evening still young, we walked to the pizza parlor, where we leisurely put away a deep dish pizza while listening to the jukebox and drinking diet cola in a feeble attempt to assuage our guilt over the calories we were ingesting. We hardly spoke as we headed home, each of us caught in her own silent thoughts. What was on our minds became obvious when we all headed for the bathroom to weigh ourselves. We took turns, and in disgust and disbelief, I saw that I'd gained another four pounds. I hated my hips and thighs. I hated my stomach as it stretched my waistband, and my ravenous appetite.

"Later, as we sat watching television, I told them about this self-disgust. They laughingly dared me to puke and quit complaining. I took off for the bathroom, lifted the toilet lid, and stuck my finger down my throat. I gagged and retched as the food made its way back up.

"After several minutes I stepped on the scale for a weight check. Elated to find that I'd lost two pounds, I turned back to the toilet with deeper conviction, forcing myself to heave and gag until my stomach felt raw. After washing my hands and face, I stepped on the scale again, and to my relief all four pounds had been expelled! I couldn't believe I'd lost the weight so quickly.

"I had never experienced such an immediate reward of weight loss before. I walked into the living room with a triumphant grin and shared my success! I had discovered my 'salvation' and announced that I planned to vomit all future splurges.

"Their first response was disbelief. Brenda gave me a short lecture about how vomiting was repulsive and abnormal, saying that she'd move out if I continued such warped behavior. How could I communicate that the instant weight loss made me feel a relief I hadn't experienced in months?

"While I loved Brenda as a friend, roommate, and sister, nothing was going to stop me from losing weight. I would have to be secretive. I learned early-on that when she was home the sound of vomiting in the bathroom was too obvious, so I sought other means of disposal."

Deception

"Eventually, I worked out more successful methods of deception. I vomited while pretending to take a shower, using the noise of the water to muffle any sound I might make. I purged into double-layered plastic bags and deposited them in the large apartment dumpster. Or I rode my bike to a nearby laundromat and used their rest room, or found bathrooms on campus that were rarely used. I had three or four staked out for emergencies.

"However, even with my deceptions, Brenda had her suspicions. 'I know you're vomiting your food! You can't be losing weight that quickly without upchucking!' she would say.

"But she had no evidence to prove her accusations, and I was not about to admit my guilt. In exasperation she'd complain, 'I can't go on living with you if you're constantly lying to me. Vomiting is so repulsive! Besides, it's got to be bad for you!'

"I wanted Brenda as my roommate, but I also wanted to be thin. Some people learn to accept smoking cigarettes. Others accept tranquilizers or stimulants, while still others turn to alcohol as a means of coping. I learned to accept vomiting because it helped me get what I wanted — thinness. Snacking and splurging provided emotional escape and relief, and purging let me discard those calories."

Food and Guilt

"The day I realized I didn't have to take responsibility for the food I ate because I could easily bring it back up, was the day I lost my perspective on food. I began making decisions on when to vomit and what to digest based on calorie content. I decided that all foods containing large amounts of calories and all meals over 400 calories would be vomited. Slowly this decision was influenced by wanting to lose weight even faster, and I graduated to digesting almost nothing, some days only an egg, peach, or glass of milk. If I only digested 100 calories a day and vomited everything else, I'd be thin in a very short time!

"Temporarily I wouldn't worry about health or balanced meals. I wanted to be thin before spring term. Later I would go back to eating healthily, once I had my weight under control. I began regurgitating breakfasts, lunches, and dinners. I vomited all daytime snacks and my caloric junk food binges late at night.

"I soon equated food with calories and calories with fat. Some days I purged everything I ate; other days I wondered if maybe I needed some small source of nourishment. There were conflicts in my mind as to how much I could allow myself to digest. Since I was now regularly vomiting eggs, meat, vegetables, bread, and fruit, I associated all of these foods with weight gain. How could I find a balance between achieving thinness rapidly and eating to stay alive?

"My way of thinking became a mass of mental juggling, confusion, and indecisiveness. I might eat an egg, but feel guilty, heave, and flush it down the toilet. If I digested the egg, I felt my requirement for health had been satisfied. I never knew which way I'd decide, and so eating became a game of chance, with my never knowing the outcome beforehand.

"Though my ideas about food and calories had become distorted, Brenda was there to continually remind me that food was necessary for health and a long life. Later, I would regard food as having no beneficial effect at all and would fear it. I remember thinking that purging was more of a relief than the sickly feeling of being bloated with food.

"When my stomach was filled to capacity, sticking my finger down my throat was like a hand guiding out the pain. I figured the food hadn't been wasted, since I would have eaten it and it would have been gone anyway. Again and again I reasoned, 'I've discovered the magic diet. I can't give it up until I'm thin.'

"Each time I lost a pound I heard the words in my mind, 'You did it! You did it! You're one pound nearer your "goal!"'

Thinness and Future Security

"I needed to give myself reassurance I'd soon be thin. It was wonderful being able to cross my legs with ease, to walk down the street without the inside of my thighs rubbing together, and to run upstairs again, easily. In the beginning, I had every intention of giving up vomiting when I reached 126 pounds. But after awhile, vomiting came to seem both natural and necessary. It was a way to eat all I wanted without feeling guilty.

"I so focused on being thin that I thought about it most hours of the day. A good figure would be my answer to peer acceptance and self-esteem. I believed that thinness was the way to be special and attract the type of man I dreamed of marrying someday.

"My stepfather prided himself on having married a beautiful woman. Yet, whenever I confided my wish to look beautiful myself, he warned that I was misplacing my values, insisting that personality and intelligence were far more important than good looks and that I should think less about my appearance. Over the years I took his message to mean, 'It's okay for your mother to be beautiful, but not for you.' In retaliation I'd told myself, 'I refuse to be ordinary, just you wait!'

"In looking for approval, I longed for others to take away my feelings of inferiority. It was funny because when I received compliments, I discounted them by thinking that the person didn't know me very well, or wasn't good enough for the compliment to mean anything, or that something was wanted from me and flattery was being used to get it."

Bingeing Buddies

"It was pathetic watching Brenda struggling to lose weight, trying to restrict herself to meager portions of salad, lean meat, vegetables, skim milk, low-cal cottage cheese, and unbuttered bread. She was determined to trim down, and she agonized over the scale, which fluctuated between 145 and 150 pounds.

"People had begun referring to me as the 'thin' sister. That made Brenda even more frustrated. I felt it was so unnecessary for her to painstakingly measure what she ate, and groan whenever she regained a pound. I was again digesting small meals, but loved being able to indulge in foods I liked (since I had a ready means of reversing the process).

"Some time in March, when the days were cloudy and depressing, Brenda was losing her battle against weight gain and fell into the same desperation I had months before. Snacking during late-night studying for exams repeatedly defeated her best intentions.

"Eventually I admitted my vomiting, which she'd suspected all along. Feeling sorry for her, I asked, 'Why don't you try it? It's not disgusting like you think. You can eat all you want and still lose weight faster than you ever have before.' I must have been persuasive because later she followed my advice.

"She learned quickly, and after the 'event' was over, she weighed herself. She'd lost two pounds. I gave her a hug and assured her, 'If you keep this up, I guarantee you'll be slim in no time!'

"I continued to push, 'This is your saving grace. You'll never have to worry about being overweight again.' I remember saying, 'Think of the Romans! They ate week-long feasts, stuffing themselves and then vomiting repeatedly. If the Romans did it, why shouldn't we?'

"Brenda laughed and said, 'Let's celebrate!' She started for a head of lettuce, and I cracked a sly smile: 'If you want salad that's your choice, but I'm going to indulge in some doughnuts. You know, Brenda, now that you have the secret, you can eat anything you want.'

"'Let's go for it!' she laughed. That evening we whipped up a chocolate cake and a batch of cookies. We began having joint binges, or as we referred to them, porkouts, feasts, splurges. We devoured entire cakes at a sitting, along with dozens of cookies, doughnuts, and various pastries. With her new acceptance of vomiting, our relationship opened.

"For the next six months we spent almost every night bingeing, laughing, and sharing. This ended the hostility that had come between us because of my secretive vomiting. We became slender, and our social lives improved.

"In time, three girl friends joined in our 'bingeing-barfing' get-togethers. As a group, we got together for regular binges and visiting. We joked about toilet counseling for overweight women, and our mottos became, 'Have Toilet; Will Cure! Bow to the Porcelain Altar! Eat All You Want: Calories Don't Matter!'

"Brenda began dating regularly, and I had a steady boyfriend. The men in our lives knew nothing of our 'feasts,' and we were determined to keep it that way. There was a brief time when I thought all would be well again. After several painful male rejections, I met a man who I came to love, who seemed to feel similarly about me.

"Unlike men of the past, Carl showed his affection for me in many ways other than pushing sex. I could see he cared by the way he went out of his way to spend time with me. Because he was ten years older, I felt protected in his company and looked to him for assurance. Though I didn't admit it to myself at the time, I believed everything Carl said, including his talk of marriage.

"To keep up with his athletic pace, I regained some weight and started eating more normally. Though in many ways we were different, I focused on our shared interests — hiking, camping, fishing, and sports. I toned down my makeup, dressed casually as he did, and for the most part, molded my opinions to his.

"He wanted a healthy, intelligent girl friend, so I stabilized my weight at 118 pounds, a compromise. At that weight I was strong enough for excursions into the mountains with him but was still slender. I studied harder and took lots of notes in class, pulling straight A's so Carl would be proud of me. Though I occasionally binged and vomited with Brenda and the others, I began allowing myself to digest a full diet of fresh vegetables, meat, milk, and fruit.

Carl had no idea that I occasionally vomited excess calories. I was not about to tell him. He liked my figure, and there was no reason for him to know."

The Dominos Fall

"After a reasonably happy nine months, things began falling apart. As though dominos were tumbling one against another, the first one fell when my father found out I'd spent a weekend at the coast with Carl. He was outraged, sure that the family would be humiliated if anyone found out. Shouting that I was despicable, that I was no daughter of his, that I was shameful and unworthy of his love, he announced that he never wanted to see me again. I tried to explain, but he slammed down the phone. The second domino fell when I learned that Carl had been dating another woman for almost six months, announcing that now he wanted to spend his time with her. I was devastated. This was the man I'd hoped to marry.

"Then the third domino tumbled as I watched Brenda enter a new, more serious relationship. All she could talk about was her new-found happiness with Greg. I protested that she wasn't spending enough time with me or taking my feelings into consideration. I resented Greg for taking my sister from me, and resented Carl for leaving me.

"Feeling alone and abandoned, all I could think about was food. While I was falling deeper into my old habit, Brenda was working to normalize her life. It was frustrating that she no longer wanted to participate in eating sprees. She shot back, saying that she wasn't willing to risk her relationship with Greg and that I'd better not leave any evidence of my strange eating habits but keep the place presentable at all times.

"I argued that I had as much right to our apartment as she did, and the fact she had stopped purging was no reason to penalize me. Brenda was unswayed. She complained that if Greg stopped by unannounced and saw food scattered about the living room and kitchen, crumbs covering the rug, or splashes on the toilet, she would die of embarrassment. Greg had become the center of her life, and I felt jealous and frustrated.

"We argued constantly, and no compromises could be found. After a while, feeling terribly alone, I found a small apartment on the other side of town.

"The fourth domino came out of my loneliness without Brenda. Now I had only my three girl friends as buddies, and get-togethers with them meant indulging in lavish pastries and ice cream followed by purging. As for dieting, they pretty much looked to me as their guide, since I was the thinnest. We devoutly believed that slenderness would bring beauty and dates, leading to marriage and happiness. This was my paramount objective, and my girl friends supported this reasoning. I lost touch with reality, sliding into anorexic food rules and phobias.

"After shedding 30 pounds from my top weight, I hadn't been satisfied with being like the slender co-eds on campus — I needed to surpass them. In my mind, thinness had become my only avenue to love, marriage, and future security. It was my means to becoming acceptable and attractive. If this didn't work, I had no alternatives.

"When I'd slimmed down to 124 pounds, the weight I'd been in high school, I had still looked fat to myself, so I'd decided I needed to lose a few more pounds. Since I'd read that top fashion models my height were around 118 pounds, that had become my goal. But at 118 I was still dissatisfied and decided that losing two or three pounds might remove the saddle breeches on my hips. I always felt I'd look better if I trimmed down some more."

Anorexic Starvation

"Nothing was as important as thinness. My ritual of weighing myself increased to as many as ten times a day. I remember when I reached about 106 pounds I still looked bulky to myself, and though I was down to size five from size 14, I thought I still had at least 30 extra pounds that had to be shed.

"I was caught in a Catch 22, one step automatically leading to the next. First the desperate craving for food, then eating, fullness, vomiting, emptiness, and back to that desperate craving for food. I was listless and weary.

"I dressed for class in the morning but often was so exhausted I went back to bed fully dressed. As I lay there, I worried about what I was missing. Eating temporarily eased my worry, but after vomiting, I felt miserable again. The more I avoided life, the more I resorted to bingeing to temporarily forget my failure to meet commitments and responsibilities.

"I'd wake up in the morning feeling drugged, hazy from the bingeing and vomiting of the night before, depressed and lethargic. My eyes were yellow and hollow-looking. I hated to think the reflection was mine. The girl in the mirror looked haggard and lined, with puffy cheeks and broken blood vessels under her eyes, her skin pasty white. I didn't want to give up vomiting, but my store of health was running out. My hair became thinner, just like my body.

"Over the months my once clear complexion had become covered with blemishes, and the whites of my eyes had yellowed. My menstrual periods had stopped, although I looked at that with relief, glad to be rid of the pain and bother.

"I had so little padding that just leaning against a wall was painful. Every time I sat, I had to keep shifting my position. When everyone else in a room was complaining that it was hot and stuffy, I was asking for more heat. Cars were drafty, friends' homes were chilly, and school rooms were bearable only if I kept my coat on. I would have set the heat thermostat in my apartment at 80 degrees, but since I couldn't afford that comfort, I pulled on three or four sweaters plus long underwear under my slacks and two pairs of socks. I still felt chilly, and at times my toes and fingers became so cold they felt numb.

"I went through a daily routine of scrutinizing my body. I'd stand nude, facing the mirror, counting each protruding rib, front and back, checking my collar bones and shoulder blades. Next, I'd turn my attention to my pelvic bones, running my hands over them to feel their contours. I could discern the bones in my hips, and the more they defined themselves, the better I felt. I thought my pelvic bones accentuated my flattened tummy. Standing side-view and stretching my hands overhead, I'd suck in my stomach to see how close I could pull the front of my body toward the back, trying to turn myself into a two-dimensional figure.

"Strenuous dieting and exercising were taking their toll, but I thought thinness was worth the damage. I'd run my hands over my protruding bones, reassured that I had the appearance of a slim, sleek fashion model. Yet I always felt that if I could gather together more than a narrow pinch of skin between my fingers anywhere on my body, I needed to lose weight.

"I drank only calorie-free diet sodas as opposed to the one-calorie diet-cola brands, because even that one calorie added up; four cans a day totaled 1,460 calories a year! Lettuce had virtually no calories, nor did most raw vegetables. I allowed myself to digest small portions of these foods, rationalizing that I could get the calories off by exercise.

"Exercising was a regimented ordeal. During it, I'd work up a sweat, the dampness of my T-shirt indicating how strenuous a workout I'd undergone. I'd think, 'Quick, to the showers! If my skin dries, all the exercising I've done for the day will be cancelled, and it won't count.' I had to rinse off the perspiration before it began reabsorbing into my body, for I feared I would gain back what I'd worked so diligently to lose if the water seeped back into my pores.

"After exercising, I wouldn't eat anything more that day. Perhaps the next day, or the day after, I'd feel safe enough to eat some celery or cucumber or green pepper.

"As I lost weight, my family tried to convince me that I was eating inadequately and damaging my health. I hated their interference. I felt they were wrong and detested the fact they were trying to change me. I knew I must not believe them. When I was 104 pounds, my sister Lisa, repeatedly told me, 'You look dreadful! You're so thin your bones stick out everywhere.'

"Subsequent to confrontations with my family, I'd study my figure carefully in the mirror, asking myself, 'Do I really look as dreadful as they say? Whose idea of beauty is more correct, theirs or mine?' Fears and questions would race through my mind, but I clung to the idea that I wasn't thin enough yet.

"Their concern did have a small impact in that I searched through nutrition books in the campus library, reading about dietary deficiency diseases and looking at gruesome pictures of victims who were nutritionally deprived. I certainly didn't want to be like them, so as a solution, I laid in a store of vitamins and minerals, believing that if I digested them I could avoid ill health.

"For breakfast I took a multi-vitamin and mineral capsule plus extra iron, and vitamin C, B, and E. I repeated this routine twice more each day as my lunch and dinner. If I broke down and ate something before I felt the pills had digested, I vomited and then swallowed five more as replacements. I was proud of having discovered a 'healthy diet' with no calories — one that didn't even need a plate!

"As I became more fearful of digesting food, I graduated to vomiting after every meal. I only digested food when I was light-headed or frightened for my life. Eating had become distorted by deception. I vomited at school, at home, in public rest rooms, on dates by sneaking into restaurant bathrooms, at friends' homes, in gas stations' rest rooms — just about anywhere. I even remember sneaking off at a picnic and doing it in nearby bushes. I was afraid of calories, food, and fatness.

"Lethargy had long since replaced motivation. There seemed little reason to live anymore. I'd shut myself away from the world, closing my curtains and pulling the shades, hoping the place would appear deserted. By late October I had isolated myself so much that my life seemed pretty much bounded by food and the toilet.

"Mother sometimes invited me to have lunch with her on campus, as she'd done since I left home, but I turned her down to avoid comments about my weight loss, and had been reticent to talk with her when she phoned. Now sitting on my bed, I wondered, could she help? I thought alternately of death, of falling into a dream state that would offer relief from my misery. The vacancy of death seemed soothing. I was living from hour to hour; from that perspective there was no future to lose. Whether to take an overdose or call her — over and over, I ran these alternatives through my mind. Finally, I decided to call first and if that didn't work out, I could fall back on the other choice.

"When I called, because I had so rejected Mother and the rest of the family and felt I had made such a mess of my life, I didn't think I was worth helping, and thought that everyone would be better off if I were dead, including me."

Reality Distorted

At the time she returned home, Barbara lacked this overall perspective on the events that had led to her present fear of digesting food and her compulsion to purge almost everything.

To me, vomiting is miserable and to be avoided if at all possible, so I asked Barbara how she could stand purposely making herself throw up. As if explaining the obvious, she replied, "Well, when you do it right after you've eaten, food tastes the same. It's like having two meals for the price of one. A chocolate milk shake tastes as good coming up as when it went down." I was struck by the matter-of-factness of Barbara's response.

It was puzzling that in the same conversation she could be talking fearfully about almost suffocating because her airways had become blocked while vomiting, yet moments later defend her actions and chide me for worrying, saying, "Nothing bad has happened to me yet! I don't want to change."

To my comments that self-induced vomiting is unnatural and unhealthy, the most she would allow was that it did cause prolonged nosebleeds that were a nuisance. Though at times Barbara vehemently denied the dangers of vomiting, she was aware that her body was objecting to how she was treating it. In morose moods, she brooded about the pimples that plagued her once-clear complexion and her limp, thinning hair, accurately blaming these problems on her inability to eat. She complained that she was cold all the time and that her bones pressed uncomfortably against her flesh when she was sitting or lying down. She wondered whether she'd ever be able to have children and worried that if she did, they might be deformed.

She spoke despondently of wanting to feel well again and of her efforts to eat, commenting, "I've tried so hard to allow myself to digest an egg or a piece of cheese, but my mind won't let me."

Before she discovered vomiting, her weight had reached 150. In the months following, she lost a third of her body weight, returning home hovering near 100 pounds, which — for a woman who was five-feet-nine — was very thin. During her stay with us, she would not agree to my checking how much she weighed. I didn't press her for I could tell what was happening by keeping an eye on her belt size and the fit of her clothing.

Below a certain weight the body does not function properly, and the individual's ability to think declines.[1] As starvation progresses, lethargy sets in, and the dramatic changes taking place within the body can cause incoherent, illogical thinking. Barbara had become child-like in much of her behavior. If only she would *digest something* . . . .

Helplessness and Despair

During her first days home, Barbara was withdrawn, absorbed in an inner world of despair. She never smiled and described herself as being engulfed in a gray cloud that followed her every waking moment.

"I'm never happy anymore," she would lament. "I hate myself, and I hate the men I've met. College has no purpose, work has no purpose, nothing has any purpose for that matter. Life seems so desolate. I can't bear it anymore." She had developed an overwhelming preoccupation with death and dying.

She talked of having made a "mess" of her life and projected that she would fail at anything she tried. She dreaded graduation because she felt it would thrust her into the role of adult, and she didn't feel ready for that. The present seemed agony, and the future held no hope. Outside, the gray November rains echoed her melancholy. Incapable of taking charge of her life, her bottom line was, *"I can't . . . I'm helpless . . . I'm hopeless."*

Barbara saw no viable alternatives, nothing meaningful or satisfying that she felt she could achieve. Her talk turned to suicide. I found a note she'd written, "Death is not a threat. It will be a relief. It will take away the problems." I tried to control my own anxiety and concentrate on what might give her hope, but it wasn't easy. I felt helpless too, and she was relying on me.

When Barbara would talk of suicide, I'd hold her in my arms, stroke her hair, and assure her that she was a lovable, intelligent human being with a promising future. I told her that depression was part of her illness and that it would pass, trying to emphasize that in time she would once again enjoy life.

Desire for Escape

Nothing seemed to be working. "You're one of the dearest, most important people in my life, and I'd be devastated if you killed yourself. If you can't hold on for yourself, hold on for me. Give me some time to help you." I begged for time. She seemed to consent to giving me a "couple of weeks."

"Barbara, any time you feel despondent, tell me and we'll talk about it."

Struggling to find a balance between showing too much concern and too little, I felt it was best for her to decide when she needed me to listen.

When she spoke of the meaninglessness of life, it seemed like a plea, her silent message being, *"Please, somebody tell me life has a purpose. Tell me you believe in me and my future, because I don't. Give me reasons to live, because I see none. Please tell me I'll be okay and that life can be good again."*

Her pondering, regarding death, appeared to be not so much a wish for finality, *but for escape.* She spoke of wanting to drift into a "dreamless sleep" for a year, so that she wouldn't have to deal with life. This would be a mindless state from which she could be "reawakened and set gently back on earth to start life again."

A physical "depression" is hollow or concave: ironically, both terms fit Barbara back then. Listening to her, it was obvious that not only was she starved physically but also emotionally. Because I felt sure that at least part of her depression was due to malnutrition, I suggested that if she ate something she might feel better, but she countered that she did not need any food.

Depression is common in anorexics, even after extended periods of time. A follow-up study of anorexics (average 4.9 years elapsed since hospitalization) indicated that more than half reported depressive moods, and 45 percent reported phobias and obsessive-compulsive symptoms. More than a quarter still suffered from insomnia and feelings of worthlessness, irritability, guilt, worry, perfectionism, and lack of energy and concentration.[2] It was distressing to read that mortality statistics for anorexia nervosa not infrequently list suicide among the causes. How could I help my daughters?

Barbara's stepfather was swamped by the demands of his job and had little patience for her odd behavior. He discounted her talk of suicide. Having retreated from his announced rejection of her, he had accepted her back home again in her starved state. At first the two of them tangled over her problems, and he was adamant in his insistence that she should start eating again and get into the mainstream of life. He felt she should simply "snap out of it." Since she did not, they were at a standoff.

Though he considered it his duty as "head of the household" to have the final say in all family matters, in this instance he agreed to make an exception. He would avoid confrontations with Barbara and expected me to handle the situation.

It was frustrating and discouraging dealing with her while she was depressed and literally starving, for though I tried to provide reassurance and support, for the most part, her response was hostility and silent, stubborn defiance. Many times I felt exasperated and resentful, followed by guilt for being angry at her when she was so obviously miserable. In time I found the most helpful approach was to think in terms of just getting through one day at a time.

It wasn't until years later, when Barbara began dealing with her submerged anger, that we would learn of the relationship between rage, as well as unmet needs, and depression.

Measures to Take

Dealing with a depressed, starving anorexic or bulimic can be burdensome. If you find yourself in this situation, though you provide reassurance and support, your thanks may well be hostile, obstinate rebukes or stubborn defiance. It's reassuring to realize that depression is treatable and self-limiting. I found the following recommendations helpful.[3]

- Remove all guns, poisons, and potentially lethal medications from the area. (I hid all medications because Barbara had talked of taking an overdose.)
- Try to get the person to accept professional treatment.
- Be calm and supportive but not overprotective.
- Don't make demands or set unrealistic expectations.
- Provide hope and encouragement; point out the person's positive qualities and past successes.
- Reach out to the part of the person that wants to live.
- Focus on positive expectations for the individual's future.
- Know the phone number of the local crisis service and of the emergency services.
- Plan enjoyable activities for yourself so that the individual's mood doesn't drag you down, too.

CHAPTER 3

Professional Diagnosis

Back when Barbara returned home, anorexia nervosa and bulimia were not yet the popular media topics they are today, and I could find only two books on them, both technical. Few professionals had training in treating these disorders. Though I was vaguely aware of having read somewhere about the "skinny illness," I didn't associate it with Barbara's vomiting. I had no reference point from which to understand her peculiar behavior.

Our initial attempts to get professional help were decidedly unsuccessful, and I mention them to indicate the types of problems that arise, and to urge you not to become discouraged but to persist until you find competent medical assistance. When the individual with eating disorders resists medical care, those who are concerned about her need to get professional advice on how to appropriately intervene to see that she takes this necessary step.

Resistance

Barbara had stopped going to classes and sat slumped lethargically in the over-stuffed recliner chair in the window corner of the living room or lay in her bed sleeping. Now that she was home, my first objective was to get her to our family physician. Yet each time I mentioned professional advice as a logical step for her to take, she refused. Even in her weakened condition she was adamant, and several days passed while she continued to eat nothing. She argued that she hated doctors and their prying questions, but these excuses seemed to be defenses against her worry that a doctor might tell her things she didn't want to hear.

It would have been easier had she been underage, for in that case I would have just taken her to the medical center. But she was an adult, and though laws provide for enforced medical care for those who are in danger of killing themselves, I hoped not to take that route.

Though she knew she was slowly killing herself, she continued to resist medical care. Then, hoping to break the deadlock between her refusals and my requests, I switched tactics and instead of suggesting that she seek help for *her* sake, I urged her to do so for *mine*. That did it; she agreed to go if I'd go with her. My mind eased, thinking she would receive competent professional help.

Physician's Diagnosis

At the clinic the doctor gently questioned Barbara about her eating. Did she fear food? Was she afraid of becoming fat? Did she vomit? Did she have menstrual periods?

She recalled later, "I cringed with embarrassment at his questions, wishing I could disappear. But I answered truthfully, even explaining my dread of gaining weight. He listened sympathetically, then after his examination he told me, 'Barbara, you've expressed your distress over feeling too heavy, but obviously you're terribly thin. You're majoring in psychology and are a bright young woman, so I'm sure I don't have to tell you that your symptoms are indicative of something called anorexia nervosa. You must have already figured that out for yourself.'"

He didn't know any doctor in our area who could treat her but gave us the names of several therapists and referred us to a hospital nutritionist. He said he would instruct the nutritionist to put Barbara on a weight-gain program which she was to follow until she reached a "normal weight." As we walked to the door, Barbara hesitated, plaintively remarking to him, "I don't want counseling, because I might get over my problems and then I'd get fat," to which he replied, "You're putting up barriers already, aren't you?"

"Anorexia nervosa," I had jotted down on my pad. I wasn't even sure how to spell it, but at least we had a diagnosis and some vague idea of the problem we were up against.

He had prescribed no medication or any medical treatment for Barbara. If she refused counseling and persisted in not eating, he had no suggestions.

She had admitted to vomiting but hadn't told me or the doctor that after repeated episodes, she was racked by violent shakes, weakness, and profuse sweating. If I had known about these episodes, I would have asked the doctor about them myself, but Barbara had successfully kept them secret, leaving my concern focused on her starvation and talk of suicide.

Some time later, she would reveal the severity of the seizures she'd experienced when she repeatedly binged and purged before returning home. "I came to experience something I called the 'shakes.' The first sign that they were beginning was a buzzing sensation between my temples and a feeling of numbness, as though my head were being shot full of novocaine. Knowing what was ahead, I'd quickly lie down on the floor or collapse on my bed. My pulse would begin racing, and as my body heat increased, a cold sweat would spread throughout my upper body. This sensation gradually moved down into my lower extremities, and my hands would twitch and shake. I could feel the perspiration trickle down my lip and forehead, and sometimes I'd sweat so profusely that my sheets and pillow case would be wet next to my skin.

"I'd hang my head over the edge of the mattress, trying to make the throbbing in my head more bearable, for if my head were lowered, the dizziness seemed to lessen. My breathing was labored. Between gasps for air, I promised myself again and again that I'd stop vomiting if I could only be saved from my misery.

"Relief came when my rapid heartbeat slowed and the buzzing in my head turned to mild ringing. I'd breathe more normally then, and feel sleepy and depressed, thankful the episode had passed.

"The shakes lasted anywhere from 15 minutes to an hour, their duration and intensity dependent on the number of times I'd binged and vomited on that particular day. If I binged for two hours then vomited, and repeated the cycle five times in a day, after the last time I purged, the shakes would be almost unbearable."

Later I would learn that the convulsions Barbara called "the shakes" are caused by a combination of factors related to vomiting, including dehydration, and blood-sugar-insulin reaction, plus pH and electrolyte imbalances. Her convulsions were so severe they immobilized her (a sign of the danger she was in), particularly from an imbalance in the sodium-potassium ratio in her blood. The heart is triggered to beat by the muscles attached to it, and if there is not enough potassium available, then arrhythmia, in which the heart beats irregularly, may occur. This can progress to cardiac arrest and death.

I now know that a program for Barbara's physical care, including "refeeding," as well as counseling to help with her emotional distress, should have been established along with support for the family. I have also become aware, in the years since her return home, that her initial resistance to treatment is typical of self-starvers and binge-purgers.

Of course, if these eating disorders are present, *the sooner medical treatment and/or therapy is begun the better, because illness-related attitudes tend to become entrenched with time.*

Referrals

Today, most parents, relatives, and friends, as well as those ill with anorexia or bulimia, have a general awareness of these disorders. The growing epidemic has alerted those in the medical profession to the symptoms, so an accurate diagnosis is more likely. An increasing number of medical centers are specializing in treating patients with eating disorders, though it is still true that most therapists and physicians have little training in this specialty.

I should add that in spite of our early difficulties in finding appropriate professional help, a family physician may be a good place to start, and some campus medical clinics are excellent resources.

Also, in the years since we were looking for medical care for Barbara, I've learned that it's not a bad idea to talk with the head nurse as well as other nurses at a local hospital, especially if there is a department that treats eating-disorder patients. Who would they go to for such care? It's helpful to find out which local physicians and counselors they recommend as being the most knowledgeable about, and skilled at, dealing with eating problems, and then check this against the recommendations of local medical societies. There are also national sources that can supply referrals and information on anorexia and bulimia.

Anorexics and bulimics sometimes visit doctors on their own. However, they do so with considerable ambivalence, frequently disclosing only a symptom that is troublesome but doesn't seem too threatening, such as constipation or cramps, irregular menstrual cycles, depression, or insomnia. Because such patients are seldom straightforward in disclosing their full range of symptoms, accurate diagnosis at an early stage may not be forthcoming.

Months before declining into "the pits of anorexia," as Barbara later referred to it, she had been to an emergency ward for excruciating stomach cramps from an overdose of laxatives. At that time she'd been told that she needed to eat a better balanced diet to avoid further problems, but her secret anorexic starvation had not been diagnosed.

Nutritionist

Barbara balked at going to the nutritionist, insisting that she did not need to eat. Although she had been home more than a week, she'd only digested a few leaves of lettuce. Finally, at my urging, she consented to go.

At the hospital, the dietitian turned out to be a stocky, middle-aged woman. She interviewed Barbara about her favorite foods while filling in printed "Diet Exchange" forms listing menu variations for breakfast, lunch, and dinner plus two snacks daily. The woman was recommending a daily intake of 1600 calories. As she handed us the paper, I said, "Yes, but remember Barbara has anorexia nervosa. She won't digest 16 calories, much less 1600. How can she overcome her fear of digesting the foods you're listing?"

Patronizingly, she assured me that Barbara would have no difficulty following the diet plan and gaining weight. She simply advised her young patient to select foods from the menus until she reached a normal weight for her height. Feeling that the nutritionist had missed the point, I questioned, "But Barbara vomits all of her food — everything but lettuce. How can she get over her fear of eating?"

To my amazement and distress the woman casually replied, "You're worrying needlessly. I have a teenage daughter myself who vomits her food, but I know it's just a phase she's going through so I don't let it bother me. She'll outgrow it."

As we left the office, I thought, "How absurd!"

I remember the chill wind and my frustration as we crossed the parking lot, and my anger at the nutritionist's ill-advised remarks. I had so hoped that hearing about the dangers of vomiting from a health professional might have some beneficial impact on Barbara's thinking. Now this starving daughter was telling me, "You see, vomiting isn't dangerous like you thought it was!" The woman had not addressed her overwhelming fear of food or of becoming fat, and had only made matters worse by condoning her vomiting.

Months later I asked Barbara what her recollections were of the nutritionist. "Her comments about meal plans and daily requirements floated in one ear and out the other. I couldn't have cared less. She herself was plump, and I remember thinking she looked dreadful. Since I'd never allow my body to look like that, I certainly wasn't going to eat menus she recommended. What was important to me was that she said vomiting wasn't harmful."

In the following weeks, while the nutritionist's expensive diet plan remained taped to the refrigerator door, Barbara ignored it completely. Since she was determined to lose another five pounds (she was always planning the next five she wanted to lose), she saw the weight-gain plan as ludicrous.

When I broached the subject of the human body's need for nourishment, she would get angry and say, "I'm not like other people; I don't need to eat!"

Sometime later, thinking a more enlightened nutritionist might be able to help Barbara, I located one who specialized in eating disorders and taught college-level dietetics. She made an appointment for both of us.

After an hour or so of technical jargon, interwoven with talk about food being "more than fuel to stoke the furnace, it's emotional nourishment as well," this nutritionist turned to comparing Barbara's eating difficulties to her own! She revealed that she couldn't eat when she was either "very happy or very low," and that at times she went for days without being able to force herself to put a bite of food into her mouth. She had recently put on weight, she said, because "I was aware I was looking scrawny."

When I asked how she'd gained weight, she explained, "I ask a friend or neighbor to come over and prepare food for me with love, and then if they listen to me, I can sometimes get a few mouthfuls down while I'm talking and not thinking too much about what I'm doing." She mentioned that she and her husband had converted to a religious sect that emphasized femininity for women and that she'd changed her behavior and wearing apparel (frilly pinafore that day) to conform to the teachings of her guru.

During the ride home, Barbara's reaction was surprise that a nutritionist would have difficulty eating. She wondered aloud whether the young woman's abrupt change to overly feminine behavior had anything to do with her eating problems.

Detours and Discouragements

Six months before returning home, Barbara had arranged to get weekly counseling at the local mental health clinic. Subsequently she wrote, "I spent each hour explaining my confusion and unhappiness, but after each session I'd feel no better than before. I was scared of the future, unsure in dealing with teachers, people at work, dates, authorities of any kind. When I'd ask, 'How can I be happy?' the counselor had replied, 'Happiness must come from within.' Yet when I looked within, there were only feelings of loneliness and depression. I changed counselors, but got no relief. I didn't tell either of them about my peculiar eating habits, afraid that they'd censure me, or try to change me, which meant I'd get fat."

Still, our family doctor had recommended counseling, and the next logical step seemed to be for Barbara to get to a reliable therapist who had experience in dealing with anorexics. But any time I suggested this, Barbara's response was, "That would be like admitting I'm crazy! Besides, if I honestly said what I think, they'd probably lock me away!" She had been to two counselors, revealing nothing of her vomiting, viewing it as her secret protection against fat.

We were into Barbara's second week home, and her weight was continuing to drop. I suggested seeing a counselor who might be able to help her find ways to feel better. One afternoon, terribly depressed, she agreed to try one of the counselors recommended by our doctor if I went with her on the first visit. I remember sitting together in the waiting room of the campus clinic, hoping that Barbara would at last be in the hands of someone competent to treat her illness.

After a long wait we were finally in the therapist's office. He was a gruff-looking man seated in an imposing black leather chair behind a massive desk, who motioned for us to be seated on a straight-backed bench to his right.

"So you have anorexia, do you?" he questioned, staring at Barbara. Pausing for effect, he leaned forward and pointing at me queried, "Why then, is she here?"

"I want her here. I asked her to come with me."

"You're an adult; why do you need to have her here? Patients come here by themselves, not with their mothers! Tell me, do you really need her here?"

Barbara nodded a silent yes.

Next he turned toward me. Sarcastically he asked, "Well then, Mother, do you have anorexia?"

I shook my head, no.

Grinning triumphantly, he declared, "Well, I guess that settles it; we don't need you here, do we?" He then launched into a derisive lecture, denouncing me for interfering in Barbara's life, arguing that her anorexia was no excuse. Then he pointed to the door, indicating he wouldn't continue the session until I left.

Half an hour later, Barbara emerged from his office crying. She wiped hot tears from her cheeks, while she talked of her session.

"He commented that he knew all about anorexics and that it's ridiculous for girls to starve themselves. He also said he had absolutely no respect for girls like me and asked whether I vomited and how often. When I told him, he shouted, 'I know your kind! You're lying to me! Anorexics are confirmed liars, so you can't fool me!'"

Shivering in the cold as we walked to the car, she continued, "It was so scary, Mom. He criticized everything I said. I remember his saying I'm stupid for vomiting and that my behavior is disgusting and irrational. He called my actions contemptible.

"I hated the way he kept referring to me as a patient, so I tried to stand up for myself by asking him to please call me by my name. He answered by saying, 'Young lady, you're in a mental clinic. I'm calling you patient, so you'd better get used to it. Frankly, your kind are virtually untreatable.' I sure pity others who go to him."

He had not told her that she was a capable young woman with a curable disorder, nor had he expressed any commitment to helping her. I agreed with her decision not to return.

Later Barbara wrote, "I can see how other girls like me would reject the world of cure. If this kind of treatment was supposed to be a route out of my 'diseased state,' I preferred to remain sick. That session was worse than my symptoms."

I resented the therapist's gruffness, lack of compassion, and his insistence that he not call Barbara by her name. Since identity and self-esteem are key issues for anorexics, why hadn't he been willing to concede this small helpful gesture rather than labeling her a mental patient. His statement that she had little chance of recovery seemed ill-conceived, a classic self-fulfilling prophecy.

A short while after Barbara came home, another young girl in town, who had been living alone, was found dead of anorexia. No one had intervened, though the news story the next day mentioned several people who had known of her determined self-starvation and weakness.

When Barbara was in the starvation phase of her illness, I was desperately searching for answers yet could find no resources in our area that could provide them, so we were thrown back on our own resources to figure out ways to increase the likelihood of her recovery.

I will mention that months later, when Barbara again wanted counseling, she located a psychiatrist in a neighboring state who specialized in the treatment of anorexics. She phoned long distance three times to arrange a conference, and eventually I spoke with the woman to confirm the appointment. Barbara wanted me to meet the therapist, so together we traveled by plane and then through congested metropolitan traffic in a rented car to reach the psychiatrist's office. When we arrived, there was a note on her door saying she was cancelling all appointments for the afternoon because she was ill.

Discouraged that we had come so far for nothing, we sat for 45 minutes in the empty waiting room trying to decide what to do next. Suddenly the psychiatrist swished into the room, apparently startled to see us still sitting in her office. Without a word she strode past us, grabbed the note off her door, unlocked it, and slammed it behind her. Obviously she hadn't expected us to linger as long as we did. Shortly thereafter, an anorexic girl entered, evidently for counseling with her.

We never found out why she had so unceremoniously cancelled our long-distance appointment. That day was a low point. I mention it for those of you who have made unsuccessful attempts to get professional assistance. You are not alone. But I want to point out that eventually we found a gem of a counselor with a "good track record" in his practice who helped Barbara better understand why she had been vulnerable to anorexia.

In recent years, social pressures that encourage problematic eating among women are ever-present, so a healthy, supportive environment becomes particularly important. For those with eating disorders, a *cohealing network* of family, friends, professionals, and self-help–group members can be enormously helpful. It takes more than one approach and more than one person to support an individual in recovery from addiction, a matter we'll get into later.

Success rates are low for many therapy programs, and finding competent help is not always easy. The point is not to let discouragements keep you from persisting in your attempts to find reliable professional guidance, but to keep at it until you do.

CHAPTER 4

Pitfalls in Helping a Compulsive Eater

Here's what Barbara wrote about her first days at home.

"The first thing Mom wanted to know was which foods I'd digest. 'Just lettuce and diet pop,' I recall telling her.

"She didn't seem surprised. 'Okay, we'll start from there.'

"She never forced food on me; in fact, quite the opposite. If I started to reach for food other than lettuce or a non-caloric drink, she'd ask if I was going to keep it down. If I answered, 'Yes,' we both knew I was lying.

"Mother requested that I not vomit the food she bought, but since I didn't see food as digestible and I wanted to eat, it became my routine to slip morsels of food into my pockets when no one was in the kitchen, and then conceal them in my bureau or slide the small packets under my bed. Like a pack rat, I gathered food whenever I could and sometimes collected quite a cache.

"I felt really guilty about this, sure that Mom was aware of my secret raids. Though I was cautious not to give myself away, a few days after my arrival, she eliminated all sugared foods and all snack items from the kitchen cupboards, shelves, and refrigerator, a sign that she suspected me and wanted to end my bingeing."

Reducing Temptation

There was no way we could force Barbara to eat or prevent her from upchucking, but we could drastically change her environment. In her apartment her pattern had been to continue eating, interspersed with vomiting, until exhaustion led to sleep. That was not to be the pattern at home.

To increase the likelihood that she would not spend her time in runaway binges, and to cut back on her vomiting, I stripped the kitchen of foods she had habitually abused, including cake mixes, sugar, flour, and anything else that could be baked into sweet treats. In addition I got rid of all crackers, granola, potato chips, nuts, raisins, and other snack items.

I kept foods on hand that Barbara said she didn't crave, such as limited quantities of fresh fruits, vegetables, and meat, along with cheese, milk, and a few other basics. I made it clear these were for family meals and she was not to pig out on them. A bunch of celery was not as likely to trigger her compulsion to stuff herself and vomit as might a bag of doughnuts or a gallon of pistachio-nut ice cream.

So that she wouldn't be tempted to write checks on nonexistent funds, Barbara gave her unused checkbooks to her Dad, which meant she had no ready means of obtaining food other than what was in our kitchen. Denied her binges, Barbara felt thwarted and angry and began scapegoating me. At times I found this tough to take, but reminded myself that *the objective was for her to regain control of her life. I was not seeking her seal of approval.*

Barbara had been substituting food for human nurturing, cutting off her lifelines to those who cared about her, but now that she was no longer engaged in marathon bingeing, family members began filling her hours by listening and sharing time with her.

Reducing the temptation to binge helped release Barbara from feeling that she couldn't resist food. She didn't empty the cupboards or raid the refrigerator until it was bare, as she had done at her own apartment. We later learned that disruption of the eating-vomiting cycle is recommended. A respite from it can motivate the binge-purger to relinquish this pattern.[1]

Feelings of Helplessness and Distress

Trying to help starvers and stuffers can be frustrating, discouraging, aggravating, and profoundly distressing.

Superficially, the solution to recovery appears easy. As the father of a bulimic daughter commented to me, "It seems like all I should have to do is tell her, 'There, there, honey, eat right and just don't vomit anymore, and you'll be fine!'" But we all finally realize that *these young women cling to their starvation and purging as if they had no freedom of choice to do otherwise.* It's no wonder that we feel such pain, loving someone with these eating problems. I recall the mother of a 21-year-old binge-purger who said, "It's such a ridiculous situation. How can I help my daughter overcome her feelings of helplessness when her illness makes me feel so helpless myself?"

It was this sense of uneasiness and distress that shadowed me the first days Barbara was home. *I felt so alone.* If I'd had a supportive, close relationship with my husband, maybe being able to talk the situation over with him would have helped. Some couples develop greater closeness by facing a crisis together, but with us this was not the case, and there were no eating-disorder self-help groups back then as there are today. Fathers can be instrumental in the cohealing process, giving invaluable support to an ill daughter, as can husbands to a wife with eating disorders. As it was, however, I faced the situation on my own, trying to figure out what to do one day at a time.

When a loved one is starving or purging, it is not at all uncommon to feel anger and resentment, emotions that can provoke an energizing response; but during the stress of Barbara's deepest illness, though at times I felt angry, my overwhelming sense was of distress and a feeling of helplessness.

When I was feeling desperate and aching with distress, if Barbara wasn't around, I would stand in the kitchen by myself trying to hold back the tears and fight the tightness in my throat, often breaking down and sobbing. I recall thinking, "I feel so *helpless.* If only there was somewhere to turn for direction." (This book is aimed at giving the very type of help I wanted so much back then, but which was not available.)

In the beginning, I found myself silently and repeatedly denying I'd had any part in Barbara's becoming ill. Defensively, I'd think, "Hadn't I done my best to be a loving and devoted parent?" But after awhile, I started feeling enormously guilty and wondering what I might have done to contribute to the situation. It seemed even more discouraging when I eventually learned that ours was a rather typical household among those struggling with eating disorders.

The arrangement we made when Barbara first came home was that she would stay with us until she felt well enough to make it on her own. She would not pay for room or board, but she was to repay the money we put out to cover her past indebtedness, and she was not to take food she didn't intend to digest. Little by little other specifics were negotiated.

Avoiding Rescue

I was not out to "rescue" Barbara and tell her how she should live her life: she needed to become responsible for herself.

When Barbara came home starving, confused and discouraged about her life and asking for advice, instead of advising her, I turned her questions back to her, saying, "What do *you want* to do, Barbara?"

"I don't *know* what I want. If I knew I wouldn't be asking you!" When she saw no viable solution, I encouraged her to consider alternatives — what could she do next, and what might result?

She needed to become responsible for herself. To have let Barbara push her decision-making responsibilities on me would simply have perpetuated her feelings of helplessness. She didn't need parental prescriptions but permission to make her own choices (with the exception of those that would harm her). Real help, as I saw it, was allowing her to be responsible and accountable while working through her own problems.

I remember later reading that daughters tend to be more restricted than sons because of cultural expectations, and that excessive parenting hampers the formation of a strong, self-determined identity. Undue control inhibits a child's growth toward independence and can contribute to continuation of anorexia.[2]

Anyone with a loved one who is feeling helpless, frustrated, frightened, hurting, ashamed, needy, upset, troubled, knows that the situation is ripe for rescue. If we feel the compulsive eater isn't acting responsibly, it's like a baited "hook" inviting us to rescue her; but we need to resist the urge to take over her responsibilities. It's important to continually guard against becoming obsessed with her problems and trying to control what she does. We have the difficult task of finding a balance between obsessive overconcern and inappropriate lack of concern. We especially want to remind ourselves to avoid judging and finding fault, for in so doing, we would only compound the problem.

Real Help

Real help is a matter of choice rather than being locked into feelings of duty. One of the features that distinguishes real help from rescue is that it is based on choice, not sacrifice. Sacrifice involves doing something that you do not want to do, whereas choice means doing something you do want to do.

Family and friends who want to provide real help need to think in terms of being noncoercive. The compulsive eater needs to be encouraged over time to act responsibly on her own behalf. Remember that though we may facilitate her recovery by being cohealers, the personal changes are up to her.

Real help is based on asking for what we really want and on doing what we've agreed to do. It is based on saying such things as, "Here's what I'm willing to do . . . and this is what I'm not willing to do." It entails stating such things as, "Here's what I'd like from you . . . and I'd like to know what you want and are willing, or unwilling, to do . . . ." This is open talk, real and honest. It says, "I want to hear your reservations now because I know that if they're not dealt with, we really have no agreement at all." Accountability and commitment are part of such authentic transactions, as is the responsibility to act on our agreements.

This type of interaction involves asking what the individual wants from us and deciding what we are willing to give, and on what basis. Will it be *quid pro quo* so that we are not sacrificing on the other person's account?

Commonly, those with addictive problems have been keeping a large part of themselves so hidden that they feel no one truly knows or understands them. Frequently, they feel both distant and different from other people. In family systems with compulsive disorders, unstated rules often inhibit free expression and discussion of problems and feelings. Given this setting, the cohealing process needs to include gradually developing attitudes and skills that promote authentic communication within the family, since this is essential to establishing healthy ways of interacting. Negotiation of needs and wants between family members assumes utmost importance.

For instance, when an adult daughter like Barbara returns home, defining the expectations of everyone becomes appropriate, and it is well to discuss and agree on living arrangements. Will she be paying for room and board? What are her "areas" in the house? What amount of noise or music is acceptable, and at what hours? What about her friends coming over? What household responsibilities is she to share? What is each family member willing to contribute to make this a mutually beneficial, cohealing situation? It may even be a good idea to set a tentative estimate as to how long her stay at home is expected to be (though this can always be renegotiated). With Barbara, when she first returned home, we chose to leave this open-ended.

Deception

A bulimic or anorexic, or anyone who is suffering problems of addiction for that matter, is often bent on deceiving others into thinking she's recovering when, in fact, she has no intention of giving up the security of her illness-related behavior. She may use fibs and other tactics to avoid detection or weight gain. For instance, bingers sometimes stock food in secret hoards, as Barbara did, for later clandestine eating to be followed by vomiting when no one else is around.

It's natural to feel hurt and even betrayed when you find that a loved one is stealing or lying. Your immediate reaction may be to unload accusations, threats, and blame, but this behavior can be put in perspective by realizing that it is related to the illness and to a desperate urge to binge.[3] From this standpoint, you have a better chance of assuming a calmer, more considered response to the situation.

During the months Barbara was becoming anorexic, she had increasingly hidden more of her life. She was afraid people would think her weird if they knew about her abnormal eating. The thought haunted her that one day she might pick up the campus newspaper, and there on the front page in banner headlines would be a story revealing her bizarre secret behavior.

Lies seemed necessary — lies explained her intermittent work attendance until she didn't have the strength to make it to her job any longer. Lies had placated instructors for missed exams and excused her failures to keep commitments with friends. Lies gave protection. "I told people what I thought would keep me safe, and truth really didn't have anything to do with it. But life kept getting more and more complicated as I tried to keep track of what I'd told different people."

Each secretive day she'd spent bingeing and vomiting added to the sense of shame that dug her deeper into isolation.

Months later she wrote, "I felt unworldly, afraid, incapable, and insignificant, but I hid my insecurities. I realized that others considered vomiting disgusting and abnormal, and I was terrified of being found out. I knew people were being taken in by my deception, and at heart I felt I was a fake."

At home Barbara tried to disguise her vomiting, explaining later, "I realized that slipping to the bathroom to 'dump' after eating would upset my parents, but it was easier to live with my shame and guilt than deal with the fear of becoming fat."

For me, it was helpful to recognize that *deception was part of the illness, not a moral issue.* But realizing this didn't solve the problem of how to deal with Barbara's reliance on dishonesty. I chose not to question her on whether she was sneaking food and vomiting it, since she would simply deny having done so and I didn't want to corner her into lying. On occasions when I came across hidden food, such as vacuuming under her bed, I left it and didn't comment on my discovery. Gradually Barbara began sharing her fears. When this happened, we discussed *how everyone has private thoughts they don't reveal but that the more we fabricate and deny, the more we are taxed emotionally.*

Later on Barbara wrote, "When first home I lied, and Mom seemed to believe me. I thought, 'Ha, ha, ha, I sure fooled her!' But by being so closed to everyone, I felt terribly alone. In time I discovered that whether I upchucked or hid food, she didn't seem to think any the less of me. So I stopped trying to outwit her."

We can communicate to the anorexic the following: "I know that you are really an honest and truthful person, but I also know that your illness may compel you to do things which are not in your nature, especially when you become anxious about putting on weight."[4] This is helpful advice for it places the focus on deception as an illness-related problem.

In our case, it also proved helpful to talk about the fact: people who are *emotionally congruent* — that is, who feel good about themselves and therefore do not feel compelled to keep a large part of themselves hidden — are less stressed in social situations because they can be natural rather than evasive and defensive. This gave Barbara a goal that she could work toward over time.

Overcoming Guilt and Self-Blame

For parents, anger may not only be directed at the daughter for damaging her health, but also at each other for anything that seems to have been detrimental to the situation. As for feelings of self-blame and guilt, many psychiatrists give family members little consolation. Therapists with traditional sex-role biases tend to fault the mother. However, there are therapists who cite fathers or blame both parents.

Fortunately, some professionals have the good sense not to censure anyone. William Nolen, a physician, notes, "When psychiatrists or psychologists attribute behavioral disorders in children to some defect in the parents, almost all parents can, with a little effort, find something in their behavior for which to blame themselves. These guilt feelings are unproductive and very frequently unjustified."[5] Suffering such pangs of guilt is useless, a waste of time and energy.

The following are some reassuring thoughts to offset self-blame:
Almost without exception, as parents, we find that our sons are not having compulsive-eating problems. Only a very small percent of anorexics and bulimics are male. Thus, for the most part, we've raised sons who eat normally, so we must look to a variety of social factors that affect females for clues as to why in recent years record numbers of our young daughters are falling prey to these devastating disorders.

Self-blame can also be diluted by recognizing that these illnesses have become epidemic, so we parents have a great deal of company! There are literally millions like us facing these problems. It's well too to consider that in nations plagued by food shortages these eating disorders are virtually nonexistent, a fact that underscores their social context. From time to time it can be helpful to remind ourselves, "I'm not responsible for fashion's reverence for angularity in females, and I didn't establish a cultural norm in which women's looks and desirability are judged on a scale of one to ten with a ten given to women who are almost hipless."

If self-reproach lingers and is perhaps kindled by a spouse, psychiatrist, or daughter, remember that each child makes her, or his, own choices between life's innumerable options. We did not make the choices along the way as to how our daughters would react. They made the day-by-day decisions that led to becoming ill.

When we're feeling guilty, we can further remind ourselves that authorities in the field confess their ignorance as to the specific "cause of eating disorders," admitting that no simple predictors have been identified.[6] Parents both reflect and perpetuate cultural patterns as well as family systems. As primary nurturers, we parents have a profound effect on our offspring, but these eating disorders are based on interactions between many influences in our daughter's lives.

Perhaps the best way to get a perspective on the situation and not wallow in self-criticism is for us to recognize that most of us do the best we can with what we know at the time. As parents, we may resent a daughter for casting a negative reflection on our parenting and feel, "How could you do such a thing and hurt me so?" I know that when Barbara and Brenda were first so ill, I felt angry that they were damaging their health and flirting with death. "Why were they doing this to themselves?" I actually experienced their illness as an aspersion on my parenting and found myself defensive and resentful, yet also deeply involved in trying to do whatever I could to help each of them recover (though at times, it seemed like an almost hopeless situation).

Put-upon by the strains of a loved one's illness, we may also harbor a wish for her to feel just a bit guilty and penitent for all the worry and extra expense she's creating for us. But these troubled young women certainly don't need the additional burden of our blame, and they are also better off if they don't condemn themselves.

The lean look that so many women are diligently striving to maintain may not be compatible with an individual's genetic heritage. Sometimes dieting problems are due to wanting a reed-like shape that simply isn't natural or healthy. Unfortunately, today's young women inherit a value system in which styles for females have been excessively slender. We can be sure that if fatness in females was thought desirable, they certainly wouldn't be obsessed with dieting nor would they be purging to rid their digestive systems of food!

As each family member faces the daily task of trying to determine what to say, or do, to support the anorexic or bulimic in recovery, it's seldom easy to feel certain or confident that the choices being made are appropriate. There is an air of uncertainty, even confusion, and of trial and error. However, as progress is made, the direction becomes clearer, and it becomes easier to determine what might help. Cohealing takes courage and determination as well as an open attitude toward life's possibilities, but the personal rewards alone can certainly be worth it.

At times it is natural to feel despairing, utterly frustrated, helpless, and angry. But we need to strive overall to maintain a sense of balance and self-control, concentrating on getting through this hour, this day. Balance comes with realizing that the greatest power of healing is love, and that this current crisis will pass.

So, think in terms of dealing with the problems one at a time. Don't try to go it alone. Seek the support of friends and family, as well as of cohealing self-help and therapy groups, professionals, and your religious denomination, if you have one. For now, just try to do the best you can and not become bogged down in despair and helplessness. It's important to stay involved in meaningful activities you enjoy and to know that, in time, you will get through this.

Looking back, I can see that my commitment to recovery was an intuitive act of trust; trust that, somehow, answers could be found to the girls' eating-addiction problems. It was during this period that I slowly began admitting to myself how much I was hurting and that I needed my own healing as well. It was not just my daughters who needed to make substantial changes, but me as well. Unknowingly, we had set out on a path of shared exploration toward recovery and wholeness.

Distress is strong motivation for self-examination and change. By understanding our own pain and working on healing ourselves, by being open to making positive changes in our own lives, we become part of the process of growth. By sharing the path to greater satisfaction and actualization, to greater awareness and growth, we improve our lives and avoid the pitfalls of trying to rescue someone else and "fix" their problems. This cohealing approach avoids blaming others and circumstances for our, or their, personal problems. It instead fosters personal responsibility, a positive identity, and self-direction.

As cohealers, we need to accept the individual with eating disorders or other addictive problems as being okay, as a reflection of our loving approval of them for who they are.

Since helping someone with compulsive-addictive problems requires a balance between overconcern and under-involvement, and patience when patience wears thin, plus judgments as to what actions are appropriate and warranted, even when nothing seems to be working, I share some additional thoughts on this subject in the section titled "Helping the Compulsive Eater" at the back of the book.

CHAPTER 5

Dual Personalities

Months before Barbara returned home, her sisters had told me of their concern when she seemed "like two different people." Her own account of her first days at home reveals her conflict between clinging to anorexia and wanting to recover:

"Mother would ask, 'Wouldn't you feel more at ease with people if you knew you didn't vomit anymore?' I could feel my resistance to her words in my neck and stomach. 'No,' I'd think to myself. 'I have to continue as I am. I don't *want* to be like other people. If I'm just like other women, I won't be special anymore.'

"Mom would say, 'You won't eat and you're slowly killing yourself. Don't you want to get better? I know you do because you called me late one night asking for help, and sometimes you say how much you wish you felt normal.'

"I'd chant to myself, 'Don't listen to her. Don't let her change you, and don't back down. Resist! Resist! Resist! WILL that she'll never win. She has no power to destroy the rules. She's wrong!'

"She'd question me, 'You say you want to travel and fully experience life, fall in love and marry. How are you going to have the strength and energy to do these things if you lie in bed all day and don't eat?' Part of me saw the logic of this reasoning, but another part didn't want to be cured because I might lose control and become fat.

"My more rational self could see the reality Mom conveyed, and it lingered and nagged at me. That was the self I usually tried to smother, but Mother, recognizing that she was reaching me, became even more persistent."

Barbara often became so absorbed in daydreaming that she was unaware of anything going on around her and unresponsive when spoken to. When I asked what was on her mind, she reported that she was thinking up ways to be discovered by someone with Hollywood movie connections. Seeming serious and intent, Barbara spoke about using her will power to bring her dreams into reality, envisioning a future of public appearances, adoring fans, world travel, and marriage to a suave millionaire.

This vivid fantasy world contributed to Barbara's confusion. In the same hour she might tell me how she was going to be rich and famous, and a few minutes later lament, "I know I'm going to end up being a poor old woman in some forgotten town."

The "Anorexic Self"

One afternoon during her third week home, I questioned her while we waited together for an hour in the car.

"Barbara, it's puzzling to me that you flip back and forth between saying you're *uncomfortably thin* and saying you're too fat; between asking for assistance and rejecting it. One moment you're predicting a future of poverty and the next you're positive you'll marry into wealth."

She leaned back against the car door trying to decide whether or not to share her inner world.

"Well, it seems to me I have two selves. Part of me wants to get well, but part of me rejects that because I don't trust myself not to balloon up and become fat again. Part of me believes I can marry a millionaire, but part of me doesn't. The part of me that fears I'm killing myself wants your help, but the part that panics every time I even think of digesting food can't listen to you because you might change her."

I was impressed by Barbara's awareness of her inner conflicts.

"You say 'part of me'; which part are you now?"

"Right now I'm the one who feels terribly afraid and wants your help. My other self wishes I'd disappear. She hates me and thinks I'm pitiful." Pausing, she added, "She's the one with the big schemes of marrying a millionaire."

Why had she described herself as "pitiful"?

"Well, for one thing, I can't stand up to other people. I don't know how to be friendly and yet protect myself. I'm always getting hurt. She can be cold and mean, and she hates it when I'm sweet."

It seemed strange sitting there listening to Barbara describing another set of feelings within herself *as though they were those of a separate person*. But since this was her own interpretation of her internal experience, I felt I needed to accept it. Intrigued by the comment that it was the other part of her who wanted to marry for money, I asked, "How about you; how do you feel about being rich and famous?"

She chose her words carefully. "The other part of me is heartless and ambitious. *She* doesn't love people as I do. She thinks she can't get the things she deserves — that's why she lies. *She's* the one who stole the clothing last year from the department store. She felt she had to be glamorous to feel good about herself. *I* never meant to steal or be promiscuous, and I feel bad that she's so unkind. All I wanted was to be loved."

Trying to understand what Barbara was saying, I asked what she wanted for her future. At this she drew a blank. She could think of nothing worthwhile that she felt capable of accomplishing. Since she expected to fail, why plan? When I reminded her of career possibilities she'd considered back in high school, she brightened noticeably and began talking about possibly wanting to work at a nearby animal refuge. I felt we were making some progress until several minutes later when I was taken aback by her unexpected turnabout.

"I don't want you talking to me when I'm like that!" she said angrily. "I can't have that kind of thinking if I'm going to succeed. I try my best not to let her take control, and I don't want you encouraging her!"

Suddenly she seemed the opposite of the daughter who minutes before had described herself as loving and not wanting to hurt anyone because she knew how painful that could be. Now I was hearing, "I hate it when I'm sweet like that because I'm always getting hurt."

When I asked how she felt about having shoplifted clothing, she replied, "It was fun. It didn't bother me at all. Once I had the clothes, they were mine."

Breakthrough

Recalling her childhood, she talked about having been "dumb, plain, and unpopular." Her dreams were of being discovered and whisked off to admiration and power. Like Cinderella, one day everyone would realize how special she was. The Ugly Duckling would become a swan. This side of Barbara wanted to be perfect. Thinness was to be her salvation, her ticket to stardom and wealth. There could be no room for alternatives.

Was the pretentious side of Barbara's personality a smoke screen for the feelings of inadequacy which the other side so readily admitted? Since she had refused therapy, I asked how she'd feel about outlining what she viewed as her two selves. She said okay, and after considerable thought the following list developed, titled, *"My Two Different Personalities."*

Personality #1

I should be: Super thin, made-up, stylish, so men will like me.

I want: Possessions, luxury, to be envied, to be superior, not to be seen with anyone who is beneath me.

Appearance: Being beautiful is extremely important.

Self-centered: I can be cold and use other people.

Future: I want to be a model and a famous movie star. I want to marry a millionaire who is famous and extremely handsome, and I'm sure I can make this happen.

This personality is perfect, and counseling would ruin it.

Personality #2

This personality cares about people.

I could be happy in a cabin with a man I love, maybe with two children, a vegetable garden, and a cat that would sit on the doorstep.

Wealth and fame aren't important to me. I want to be warm, outgoing, and kind, but I feel I'm boring. I don't know what to say to people. I feel I have no personality.

I want to be open, but I don't know how without being vulnerable. I want to learn how to enjoy things, but life isn't fun anymore.

This part of me thinks maybe I should end it all and then I wouldn't have these problems. This is the self that wants help.

The bottom of the second page dealt with daydreams. "They are a separate world I create in my head that is an escape from my problems."

Just as with food, grandiose fantasies provided Barbara with temporary relief from the stresses and disappointments of life, and at the same time afforded pleasure. Fantasies can be rehearsals for constructive action, but Barbara used them as an escape rather than as a basis for taking action.

Having this awareness of Barbara's "anorexic self" (which defended her anorexic behaviors with a vengeance) helped me spend less time in frustrating, unproductive discussions with her and reduced antagonism between us, such as when she was belligerently denying her need to eat. Anything that might promote recovery was seen as a threat when she was her "anorexic self." It was best to reserve discussions of any type for times when she was nondefensive and more in touch with reality.

Recognizing the Split Self

Anorexic girls sometimes confide that they feel they are "divided" like "a split person or two people," as noted by Hilde Bruch,[1] an authority on anorexia. She pointed out that most of them are hesitant to discuss this split.

Several years later I went to a workshop by eating-disorder therapist, Jean Rubel, who commented that these women present a duality, with one reaction being, "Go away! Don't change me. Look at how pure and ethereal I am!" Yet their other reaction is, "Please take care of me and help me. I'm frightened." One half of the self feels powerful and proud, while the other feels frightened and is crying out for help.[2]

It was as though she was describing Barbara a few years earlier. It all sounded so familiar when she explained that an anorexic woman will sometimes declare that she is perfectly healthy and happy and feels good, denying being thin, cold, fatigued, or hungry. She also mentioned that the same person in the other half of her reasoning will say, "I see no reason for living. I'm a failure. I'm depressed, sick, and dying." These women can be accommodating and people-pleasing, or they can be snappish, sulky, defiant, and defensive.[3] Such exasperating, conflicting messages may make others feel as if they're dealing with a split-personality.

Eventually, as we better understood the confused interactions between what Barbara viewed as her "two selves," we would see how this related to her feeling that a commanding voice spoke to her, demanding she vomit after eating, and to her feelings of helplessness to disobey the voice even when she felt she needed to digest something.

Stealing and Alcohol Abuse

Subsequently, I learned that anorexia nervosa and bulimia are frequently associated with stealing and alcohol abuse. Those who steal were often older and not living with parents when they became ill. They are more likely to lie extensively while ill, be more active sexually, and both binge and purge.[4]

Unlike Barbara, when she first became anorexic, who had stolen some clothing in an attempt to feel more acceptable, money and food are the things most often stolen by sufferers of eating disorders. A disintegrating life combined with starvation often plays a role in this behavior.

I gained perspective when I read in the literature on such disorders that "Stealing is probably a far more common and important feature in . . . these conditions than has been generally recognized."[5] For example, a study of such patients revealed a "very high prevalence" of stealing, with 52 percent evidencing theft. This study also found that individuals with eating disorders are among those who "are particularly vulnerable to alcohol abuse and eventual alcoholism."[6] During the later years of her bulimia, Barbara did go through a period in which she relied heavily on alcohol when stressed.

Obviously, stealing and alcohol abuse add to the guilt associated with bingeing and vomiting.

CHAPTER 6

Body-Image Distortions

Like many women, Barbara engaged in futurist thinking that "someday, when I'm thinner, my life will get better." She talked about her body as though it were an enemy that she was fighting to subdue.

Denying her hunger was proof that she was winning the battle over her body's attempts to defeat her social life. It had been easy to justify drastic and damaging measures because the body was no longer something to protect. She felt ineffective in other areas of her life but controlled her size and shape with an iron will.

In the process of slimming, Barbara had lost sight of the fact that *a weight-loss diet needs to have a beginning and an ending* and that when she'd reached her preset weight goal, she should have stopped. A competition had set in between Barbara and her anorexic friends, each trying to become thinner and "better" than the others. None of them wanted to be outdone. Self-improvement had become synonymous with losing weight, and every pound lost became a reward in itself.

Now, thin and pale, she sat bundled in her bathrobe trying to keep warm, telling me, "When I lose weight, I mentally pat myself on the back. If I were to gain a pound, I'd be furious with myself. For me, gaining weight would seem quite unnatural and backward."

For many people, the scale is an indicator of how they feel about themselves. Barbara had carried this to extremes, weighing herself nine or ten times a day. Because of her penchant for judging herself according to the scale, I removed it from the bathroom so it wouldn't be available as a reinforcement for weight loss.

Fluctuating Body-Image

Like other anorexics, as the pounds had dropped away, her mind hadn't adapted to her decreasing size.

I found it puzzling that Barbara thought that her body fluctuated quite rapidly in size: "In the morning I may wake up looking thin to myself, but by afternoon my entire body can swell like an inflating balloon. Sometimes by night I could swear I weigh 160 pounds."

"There are times when I'm standing squarely before a mirror and see skin hugging my bones, and I think, 'Yes, I'm thin. Perhaps Mom's right, too thin.' Then hours later when I pass the mirror I do a double take and see fullness that wasn't there before. I don't understand where it comes from because I won't have eaten anything. Yet no matter how I analyze myself, my image looks heavy. It's agonizing waiting until my body shrinks back again."

Surprisingly, she tended to see her body as more slender when she was wearing clothes. Barbara explained that if she were to eat, afterwards she'd appear fat to herself.

Many women report that their frontal view looks broader to them after they eat, especially after consuming carbohydrates; this is particularly true of anorexics. Subsequently, she would recall her puzzlement over this fluctuating body-image, remarking, "My body seemed to change from looking thin to looking obese instantly. From hour to hour I never knew what to expect. When I looked fat to myself, I felt fat. Was it the vegetables I'd had for lunch? The apple I had for dinner? It didn't seem logical that I could gain so much weight after eating such a small amount of food, yet I could feel the fat on me. An hour later I'd be thin again, and could feel and see the bones once more. It was a mystery where the fat had gone."

One evening I heard Barbara crying in her room, and when I asked what was wrong, she indicated she'd ballooned up. She was sure her arms were grossly large, and hesitantly asked me, "Do I look much heavier than I did an hour ago?"

"You look the same to me, Barbara. You looked thin then and you look thin now." I suggested she grasp her fingers around her upper arm to measure it. Barbara never seemed to think of her hands as changing size, and since her fingers still reached around her arm, she realized it must be her *perception* that was changing, not her body.

Barbara liked to study her reflection in the mirror, so I thought to ask her how she looked to herself. This was revealing, for I discovered that she could describe her body above her waist with much greater accuracy than below. Between her waist and knees she saw ugly, puffy bulges, and I watched in amazement as she indicated with her fingers that she wanted to cut two inches off each of her hips. I protested, "But honey, that would be cutting through your bones!"

She put a chair in front of the mirror and inspected how her thighs looked when sitting on this hard surface. She said that in this position she could judge whether she'd finally gotten rid of the fat. She did not view her body as a whole, but instead analyzed herself as divided up into sections, like a side of beef, with each part — chest, back, waist, hips, thighs, calves — needing to meet certain qualifications in order to pass inspection. "It's like in beauty-contest judging," she said. "My girl friends and I used to say we had to be USDA Prime, for Unsurpassed Skinniness Desired in America."

Barbara intended to lose weight until she consistently looked thin to herself. Like other anorexics, she needed to realize she was too thin so that she could see a rationale for restoring some of the weight she'd lost. But how to accomplish that?

To help her gain some perspective on how her feelings toward her body had changed, I got out photos taken of her in high school. Studying them, Barbara was surprised at how "fat" she looked in them. This gave me an opportunity to point out, "Before anorexia you thought you looked good in these snapshots. Now you weigh far less than in those days and yet instead of being satisfied, you say you're fat."

String Test

I asked if she'd be willing to test how accurately she could judge her size. She agreed, so I handed her a piece of string, suggesting she lay it in a circle on the floor that matched the size she thought her hips were at the widest point. Barbara spent considerable time mentally calculating the shape and circumference the circle of string should be to represent her hips.

When she'd decided that the shape on the floor was accurate, we used a measuring tape to determine the length of the string in her circle. Then we measured Barbara's hips, and to her surprise she found they were actually nine-and-a-half inches *smaller* than what she'd estimated with the string! I observed, "You've been trying to lose nine-and-a-half inches that don't exist."

Next she laid out a circle the size she felt was equivalent to her upper thigh. Again we measured the length of string in her circle and then measured her. Her own thigh was four-and-three-quarters inches *smaller* than what she'd estimated with the twine. She acknowledged that this four-and-three-quarters inches of bulging fat must exist only in her mind.

To further help her picture how thin she was, we formed two twine circles on the floor *that matched the actual size of her hips and thighs.* Barbara was astonished to see how pathetically small they were. *The "string test" provided the first concrete evidence to her that she was substantially overestimating her body size.*

Detecting Distortions

Skipping ahead, months later, when Barbara had reached 114 pounds and had left home, I suggested that we each make a sketch of her and compare them. Neither of us looked at the other's sketch while we were drawing, and we both laughed when we compared our impressions. From our sketches no one would have guessed they were of the same person! Barbara had drawn herself with no facial features, and a retracing of lines emphasizing bulges in the region between her hips and knees which she had labeled "always gross — obese, uncontrollable."

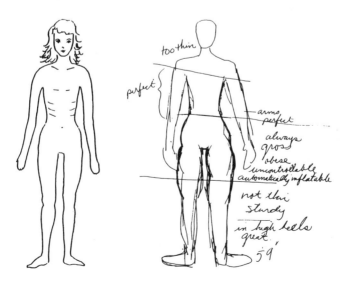

We also discovered that the most effective way for Barbara to perceive herself as thin was to view herself on television. A friend filmed Barbara in motion: lifting, stooping, bending, and walking. Technicians showed us the video cassette on a closed-circuit color TV camera. Seeing herself on video from all sides, wearing shorts and a T-shirt, she repeatedly commented, shaking her head, "I can't believe that's me! I look so thin! No wonder people keep telling me I'm too skinny!"

At that time she had regained to 116 pounds. Barbara commented that she saw herself on video as a "whole moving person" rather than section by section, and that seeing her body movements from a distance gave her an overall perspective on herself that she'd lacked before.

Anorexics can sometimes more accurately assess their size in snapshots or video pictures if their facial features are covered. Probably this distances them from their own identity, with the result that they can be more objective in their self-appraisal. It's well worth a little effort to video record the self-starver so that they can experiment with this means of feedback.

Perfectionism Versus Function

Barbara thought of her physical being as something that had to be molded and groomed into an object that would draw the awe and respect of others.

Since she seemed to think solely in terms of looks, to the exclusion of the body's basic function of survival, I talked about how her body was serving her in spite of her abuse of it, saying, "But if you continue to starve it day after day, as you are doing, you will no longer have a body that can support you in being alive."

I tried to remind her that the healthy human body has the capability to do everything it needs to sustain life. Matching the current ideals of the entertainment and fashion industries is not its essential purpose.

Her talk of wanting a perfect body led into a discussion of a cat basking in the sunshine warming its fur. In every sense it's doing "cat" perfectly. Unlike people, it's not self-critical. It isn't wishing its fur were a different color or its stomach flatter, its thighs skinnier or its tail longer, to match this year's fashions.

Barbara was intrigued by this idea that animals are unselfconsciously content with themselves. Many months later, during a walk, we watched as a sparrow bathed in a puddle, flipping water onto its feathers, intent on its grooming and quite unconcerned about our presence. Barbara was touched and reflective. Suddenly she felt connected with nature's small creature, learning from its self-acceptance.

Self-Talk

Listen to females gathered for just about any occasion, and chances are that talk will get around to weight and dieting. *Few of us are ever satisfied with our shape or weight,* and it seems quite natural to hear the sharing of self-deprecating comments on what we'd like to change about our contours.

Barbara vacillated between pride in her boniness and misery over feeling too fat. Unfortunately, her expressions of self-depreciation far outweighed those of self-approval. If she were ever going to want to take care of herself, she needed some strong doses of "self-like."

To her worried remarks about how fat she looked, I found myself asking, "Isn't there *something* positive you can say about yourself? If you had a roommate who disparaged you the way you do yourself, you wouldn't put up with her! You'd find someone else who treated you better. I know you'd never harp on a friend the way you're continually harping on yourself. *You need to become your own best friend.*" Obviously, Barbara needed to learn how to celebrate herself and delight in being alive.

For her body to function well she needed to take care of it, not hate and deprive it. Gently I repeated the thought, "The hunger and distress your body relays to your brain indicates its needs aren't being met."

It wasn't until months down the line that she made the comment, "You kept telling me that I judged myself too critically and needed to look for something upbeat to think about myself. At first it seemed hopeless. But I tried to think up something supportive to tell myself. I began repeating 'I'm okay — *more* than okay. Yes, I am a beautiful person,' and tried not to get hung up on what I thought were my flaws. In time I felt better about myself."

Subsequently I learned that Barbara's body-image distortion was typical. Though emaciated and hungry, anorexics have such distorted self-perception that they struggle to lose chubbiness that doesn't exist.[1] Even if they regain some weight, cure cannot take place until body-image distortions have been corrected.[2] (Interestingly, many young women think of themselves as larger than they really are, particularly ones who tend to be overweight.)

Later, we would learn that disassociation is a way of *detaching from reality*, a way of escaping "confusion and emotional pain," a defense against feelings of inadequacy and alienation.[3] Disassociation can result in a split self and may also be related to gross distortions in body-image perceptions.[4]

Some girls, particularly anorexics, are "skin and bones. Yet they will look at themselves in the mirror and say 'I'm so fat, the fat is just rolling off of me,'"[5] comments Frank Putnam, a psychiatrist at the National Institute of Mental Health. "How can this be? Well," he reports, "we think disassociation contributes to that."[6]

CHAPTER 7

From Inertia to Action

During the first couple of weeks after her return home, Barbara brooded about her problems. She seemed exhausted, mired in inertia.

Except during our unsuccessful attempts to get professional advice, she remained at home curled up in the living room recliner, staring blankly out the window or catnapping under piles of covers in her bed.

In part, her inactivity stemmed from fear of failing; since she felt incapable of managing her life, why even try? The words "I can't!" came automatically to her.

She wanted desperately to be perfect, or at least to appear so. Failing this, everything seemed hopeless to her.

(I should mention that many of the events discussed in this and previous chapters were going on concurrently, thus my attempts to understand and react to her talk of suicide, resistance to eating and professional care, talk of being a failure and her frightening body-image fluctuations, conflicting "selves," and other problems mentioned so far, were interwoven during her first days and weeks home.)

Overcoming Being a Recluse

She explained to me that before coming home, "Because of my peculiar eating rituals, I couldn't feel good about myself with other people, so I spent my time with other anorexics because they shared my reality and weren't disgusted by my vomiting.

"On campus I tried to act normal, but I was always on guard, afraid I'd slip up and give myself away. I worried about the possibility of being caught vomiting in a public restroom. I kept running back and forth between these two realities, and when the strain became too great I holed up in my room, shutting myself away from the world, closing my curtains, and pulling the shades. As evening would approach I'd turn on a small desk lamp, so that the place would appear deserted. If the doorbell rang, I'd sit silently until the unknown visitor left."

Barbara talked of being fearful of dealing with people, even by phone. When I questioned her, she said that before coming home it had been progressively more upsetting to leave her apartment, though it might just be to go to a grocery store.

She said, "It would be terrifying to ask for things or make people listen to me. I can't enter a store and ask where the toothpaste is or sit in a cafe and ask for salt and pepper. I guess I tried so hard to ingratiate myself with others, by giving in to their needs, that my confidence evaporated. Somewhere along the line, I lost my sense of who I was and what I wanted or believed, and now I feel powerless to stand up for myself."

Although she was worried about the classes she was missing and about being fired from her campus job, she did nothing about either. With only five weeks until finals, time was running out for her to try to catch up. So toward the end of her second week home, when she seemed relatively relaxed, and we were sitting together on the sofa, I asked what she wanted to do about her classes. "By not attending, you're losing by default and you'll flunk out. Would you like to finish the semester or perhaps officially withdraw?"

At first she talked in circles about not wanting to continue yet not wanting to drop out because she'd feel like a failure. Since she could think of no positive options, I began asking how she'd feel about discontinuing her education and trying something else. What jobs might she like to try? What experiences would she like to have? Could she catch up if she wanted to stick out the semester? I felt it was important that she make up her own mind about what she wanted to do, and the questions prompted her to evaluate her options.

Within an hour, she concluded that she wanted to finish the quarter, but she saw one obstacle after another standing in her way. She was too weak to get to campus so I offered to drive her until she could make it on her own. She'd sold all her textbooks for money to buy food. I offered to lend her money to buy them back.

One after another, we discussed the hurdles and worked out solutions. These included the decision to request free math-department tutors and borrow professor's notes.

Since she was so afraid of talking with people, we rehearsed conversations she planned to have, role-playing how people might react. In each instance, I took the part of people responding to her questions and requests, with her deciding how she'd like to handle various eventualities. When she felt ready, Barbara made the actual contacts and in small stages began taking social risks again. It was a simple, straight-forward process that quickly produced positive results.

Taking Responsibility

As with other purgers, Barbara's vomiting was a way of *not taking responsibility* for the calories ingested, and this attitude had eventually expanded into other areas of her life. The more things had gotten out of control, the less capable she felt and the less responsibly she acted. Therefore, *regaining responsible eating patterns needed to be tied to developing responsible actions in other areas of her life.*

In the beginning, after I'd driven her to campus, she still felt too depressed and frightened to walk to classrooms on her own, so I walked with her and returned to meet her after class, but within a few days she managed this on her own.

Because bingeing no longer consumed her waking hours, she had time to devote to her studies and became intent on catching up on missed exams and homework assignments. From her first day back on campus, she was too busy handling practical day-to-day matters to brood about being a failure.

By getting back to her studies and campus job and by deciding "Today I will . . . ," she began breaking down what she'd referred to as "the total blackness of eternity" into small intervals which seemed more manageable. And by involving herself in activities that absorbed her concentration, she had less time to obsess about food. She was again taking practical steps to reach her goals.

It was slow going in the beginning, but she never talked about giving up or about flunking. She just kept plugging away at her backlog of school work, and by her second or third week on campus began interacting with other students again.

Self-Assertiveness

I was surprised that she complained that she had nothing interesting to say. "If I only had opinions and could carry on an informed conversation, I think people would respect me and want to talk to me."

It seemed odd that Barbara felt she had no opinions, but this was how she experienced herself. "Having mirrored everyone else's opinion for so long, I have none of my own." Three years down the line she would write, "I'd made it a habit of saying what I thought people wanted to hear. I never questioned an unreasonable class or job assignment, an unfair grade, or an incomprehensible lecture. Even with family, I seldom found the courage to disagree."

Barbara hadn't read a newspaper or listened to television in months and had little idea of what was going on in the world. On a hunch, I encouraged her to read the evening newspaper. At first she would read a story and say helplessly that she had no opinion. So we would talk about the key issues, looking at them from various standpoints, political, social, ecological, religious, and the like. The point of these news discussions, which at times became quite lively, was for her to develop her own positions and become comfortable voicing and defending them.

Later she wrote, "Eventually I was defending my opinions on campus, and people were telling me I expressed myself well. I began gaining confidence. I was still too sensitive to criticism, but instead of always rushing to agree, I began defending what I believed."

As Barbara started standing up for herself on political and social issues with friends, she became more forthright and honest in other ways. After a while she could tell the family, "No, I don't want to go to the movie, but thanks anyway." In the past she would probably have gone with us but been resentful. It was important when she stated her preferences that we accepted them.

The process of defining, "Yes, I want this," and "No, I don't want to do that," indicated Barbara was beginning to work on pleasing herself, and that was good.

Reducing Mealtime Tension

Family mealtimes can become a battleground where Mom and Dad struggle to get their recalcitrant daughter to eat while she resists their efforts. When the children were young, their stepfather had been a stern disciplinarian about table manners. There'd been reprimands for forgetting to put napkins on laps, eating too fast, not sitting up straight, talking too much or too little, too loudly or too softly. This was no longer the case.

Barbara's illness had brought her under our roof again and focused concern on her problems. It would have been easy to make her the center of attention around the house, but this wouldn't be good for her or for us. We discussed that we didn't want to reward her illness-related behaviors, so we worked to minimize the attention given them. For example, by agreement, at the dinner table the family never commented on Barbara's unadorned plate of lettuce.

It seemed important *not to let her eating and thinness become topics for mealtime conversation by her or the rest of us.* This agreement among family members avoided nonproductive verbal confrontations and proved to be a very good choice. Still, her refusal to eat did need to be addressed at other times.

For Barbara there was unknown peril in a sip of milk, overindulgence in a sliver of cheese, untold fear in a spoonful of scrambled eggs. Prior to anorexia she had understood the basics of nutrition, but somehow that knowledge had vanished. It was as though she wore "anorexic blinders" on her mind, blinders that cut her off from basic nutritional realities. I can remember thinking it would have been easier to teach them to a five-year-old than reacquaint Barbara with this information.

Denial

In diary notes to myself I wrote, "Hunger that others would find intolerable, gives Barbara a feeling of safety and of being victorious. My words of concern over her health are cut short with statements like, 'Mother, you're wrong. I don't need to eat!' Or 'I don't want to hear it!' Hunger is her friend, an empty stomach her insurance against getting fat."

In my diary I also noted, "It seems so unreal to be listening to Barbara talking about having to floss her teeth because she might have particles of food caught between them and can't stand the thought she might accidentally swallow them!" Barbara was sure that digesting food would put her back on the road to uncontrolled weight gain. She feared me because she knew I wanted her to eat.

She later wrote, "When Mother said, 'I want you to be healthy,' I interpreted that as, 'I want you to get fat'!"

Impending starvation didn't seem to have any impact on Barbara's anorexic reasoning. She insisted that her body did not need calories and that anything she ate would be extra and turn to fat.

When I disagreed, she insisted, "I've experimented with not eating and find food isn't necessary to make the body work, people just *think* it is. Actually, the body is self-sustaining. It's rather like a chair. You don't need to put food into a chair. It just *is*."

It was bewildering to hear this intelligent daughter (who'd been a straight-A student) comparing herself to an inanimate object.

"Barbara, a wooden chair was once a living tree that needed nourishment. After being chopped down it doesn't need nutrients anymore. As long as you are *living*, you need nourishment."

It seemed strange indeed that she persisted in comparing herself to a chair in order to bolster her argument that she didn't need food. I found myself responding, "A chair is dead just as you'll be if you continue to persist in believing you don't need to eat. You're *not* made of wood!"

Reality Checks

For the first couple of weeks I couldn't get through to her. She would say, "I don't need food. I've proven it to myself."

"But you are *very* ill. You're wasting away by living off your body's tissues. This can't go on indefinitely."

I used an example: "If a naive millionaire continually made overdrafts from his bank account, believing there were unlimited funds, one day he'd find that his resources were exhausted. For 21 years you've had a bank account of good nutrition, but by believing you can draw upon these reserves endlessly, one day your body will be bankrupt. And that time isn't far off.

"The reason you're cold all the time is because you've lost so much body fat. The calories you dread are nothing more than units of energy that are a way of measuring the fuel your body utilizes to sustain itself. Every heartbeat requires calories, and only the excess above what our body requires is stored as fat."

"It doesn't make sense that calories would go to my heart. I know where they go. They go to my hips and thighs!"

Barbara needed consistent reality-checks in response to her startling misperceptions. I showed her charts indicating how many calories are required for basic life functions plus how many she'd burn if she were to participate in her favorite sports. This repeated the theme that the human body needs calories to function.

Since iceberg lettuce was the only food she'd digest, in order to vary her salad plate, I bought other types of lettuce, endive, butter lettuce, romaine, etc. This was a small change, but it gave Barbara's plate a more varied appearance and established that she *could* digest something other than iceberg lettuce.

It seemed logical to begin with foods she feared least, so when she prepared her lettuce I might comment, "Would you like to use the grater to put a few sprinkles of raw carrot on your salad?"

Once minor amounts of carrot had become acceptable, I mentioned that celery had almost no calories and perhaps she might like to try a few crunchy slices on her salad.

From this she moved to tiny chips of red cabbage and began asking, "Do you think it would be okay if I ate this much celery?" or "Do you think this would be too much cabbage?" testing to see whether I thought her choices were safe. Next she added bits of green pepper, and on her own initiative, she tried cottage cheese and bits of well-blotted canned tuna on her salads.

Once she had established this minor foothold on digesting food again, I discussed "food exchanges." It made sense to point out that since she felt the calories in a carrot were safe, she could exchange those calories for ones in some other type of food. As it turned out, it was this reasoning that made it possible for Barbara to accept adding variety to her diet.

First Meals

Years later she wrote, "I was used to unlimited quantities of sweets. Meager salads in no way compared with the foods I liked best. Mother suggested that I replace my binge-purges with small portions of food to be digested. It seemed so irrational — why would I want to limit myself to a few paltry calories when I could enjoy 40,000 and more calories daily, eating anything I wanted!"

I picked up government nutrition booklets from the county extension office so Barbara could make food choices based on facts rather than on her anorexic fears. These charts listed minimum daily nutritional requirements and the percentages of basic substances in common foods. During meal preparation, I would comment on them.

Later she remembered this and wrote, "Mom would review the food in the refrigerator, talking to me about it in terms of health. She would point out how much a quarter of a cup of chicken would provide in the way of minerals, protein, and other nutrients, and what it would do for the body."

By initially experimenting with a few low-calorie foods, Barbara found that her clothes still fit. When she saw that she was no larger, her fear of digesting diminished. However, the real payoff came when she began feeling better. This led to her increased acceptance of digesting and to her adding new foods to her salads including bean sprouts, cauliflower, grated cheese, hard boiled egg, thinly sliced meat garnishes, and diluted diet dressing.

Within three weeks she progressed from the first gratings of carrot on bare leaves of lettuce to chef's salads. She found these more pleasurable and began digesting them. Sometimes she panicked and hurried off to the bathroom to vomit, often returning to the kitchen to make herself another smaller salad in an amount she'd feel safe digesting.

Some days Barbara seemed comfortable digesting food. Other days it appeared she vomited everything.

Brenda's Example

During this fragile period of tentative improvement, it was helpful for Barbara to talk with Brenda about her recovery, because Brenda was again eating well-balanced meals and returning to a normal weight.

At one point Barbara wrote, "It was difficult for me to believe the changes in Brenda. Only weeks before, she'd been pale, her hair and nails brittle, her neck glands swollen. When she began eating regularly, she looked different and people were telling her she was beautiful. She urged me to eat saying, 'You can digest at least 1600 calories a day and not get fat.' For a good while, this seemed too frightening to try, but eventually, knowing we'd binged and vomited together, I was influenced by her talks and her example."

It can be helpful for those with eating disorders to talk with others who have made progress in overcoming similar problems (such as at a clinic or therapy group), and Barbara was fortunate to have a sister as an example to which she could relate.

As the weeks went by, I encouraged Barbara to read nutrition books. She recalled, "It was a shock to me that an elderly person sitting all day in a nursing home needs at least 1,000 calories daily just to survive. It blew me away! All of a sudden I thought, if that's what they need just vegetating, maybe I can eat more than I thought I could!"

Initially Barbara ate only at dinner time, but as she reacquainted herself with the need to eat, I'd find her in the kitchen at other times making herself a small salad when she was hungry. The same broccoli, chicken, and other salad garnishes that Barbara had come to feel were safe on a bed of lettuce were taboo if eaten separately and had to be purged.

Her fear was diminished in stages. First she ate a carrot separately, then a spoonful of cottage cheese, then a small piece of chicken. In time these foods gradually became acceptable in non-salad dishes. With this progress I began accommodating our dinners to her food preferences so that she could eat meals prepared for the family.

Barbara had to relearn a sense of *completion* after having eaten. For months she'd consumed food compulsively. It was easy for her to slip into making one salad after another, which she'd secretly upchuck. It worked best when she served herself just the amount she planned to digest, placed her empty plate in the kitchen sink when she'd finished it, and moved on to other activities that would take her attention off food. This reduced her temptation to continue eating.

Refeeding

Barbara subsequently recorded her feelings about "refeeding."

"At first, I flipped in and out of two opposing realities. If I was listening to Mom while deep in anorexic thoughts, she sounded foolish. Yet when I could grasp her words, the weirdness of habits I'd fallen into became clear. I'd felt like two separate selves, but gradually my personalities began meshing into one and I was spending most of my time in the real world rather than in 'anorexic thinking.' Then I began to see how digesting made sense and vomiting everything didn't. Most important was that Mom provided a consistent and dependable outlook. I had to test my family's world. The day I first ate a piece of chicken and learned I could be safe, I held onto that realization in amazement.

"I knew Mom worried about me, so I felt guilty when I secretly vomited. Sometimes I wished she'd disappear from my life. At other times I felt she was the only person in the world who could help me.

"I hadn't realized the relationship between lethargy and starvation, but when I began digesting, I could feel my energy rebound. Eventually I was able to see how my depression returned when I starved myself. If I became upset with weight gain and vomited for several days, I sank back into feelings of sadness, helplessness, and despair. When I started digesting again, depression lifted. Finally I'd ask myself, 'Is it better to be thin or depressed?' If worries about becoming fat were getting the best of me, I would put up with a few days of depression until my weight dropped to what I considered a safe level."

Pleading, threatening, or bargaining with Barbara to gain weight might have led to her feeling coerced. That could set a pattern in which she might try to control me with demands or threats of her own. In a battle of wills, with her refusing to eat and my insisting she do so, both of us would inevitably lose.

During the three months she was home, we supplied the foods she would digest and she made the choices of what she ate, how much, and when, keeping in mind that the goal was for her to regain control over her eating, not to relinquish that control to someone else.

Months later Barbara commented, "I kept expecting you to react resentfully to my stubborn resistance, but you didn't. Looking back I can see you were reinforcing anything I did that was directed toward wellness. You'd give me reality checks when I was off base. I needed this, though at the time it infuriated me."

"Refeeding" programs often include high-calorie foods in frequent, relatively small meals, combined with therapy aimed at resolving psychological issues.

High-calorie foods are, of course, preferable for refeeding, but initially Barbara refused to consider digesting them. Since she still had a dozen or so pounds between her and hospitalization, there was time to gradually reintroduce her to eating.

Starting with the foods she found least threatening reestablished her digestion of food again. Within a few weeks she progressed from lettuce to sharing family meals. Though it is discouraging watching an anorexic resist eating, when improvement does begin, the progress can be remarkable. Barbara's weight leveled out at 115 pounds. At five-feet-nine inches, this was still slim, yet she worried over her increased weight and the feeling of fullness she experienced after eating.

I'd find her gazing at herself in the front-hall mirror, distressed that she could no longer wear the tiny clothing sizes she could fit into before. Since she was disturbed over her increasing size, I decided not to praise her on her weight gain. Instead I found it best if I kept my comments to such things as how much clearer her skin was and how much better she was looking generally. I'd also mention how delightful it was to hear her laughing and singing, a reminder of the progress she was making.

She enjoyed the good feeling of being warm again, with enough padding on her bones to sit comfortably. Most of all she commented on how nice it was to wake up looking forward to the day, rather than dreading it. When she recognized that these improvements were related to digesting food once more, I could see that we were making some real progress.

CHAPTER 8

Male Rejections

Hurtful rejections, by men Barbara had dated, had left her feeling abandoned, miserable, and confused.

In the past she had always asked herself what she'd done wrong. Why had she been cast aside? What could she have done differently? In terms of dating, Barbara had moved from disappointment to disillusionment, to despair.

Later, recalling this progression, she wrote:

"As my sophomore year progressed, I had experimented with various fad diets and managed to drop some unwanted pounds. Since more than ever I wanted a man in my life, I set about meeting men I considered possibilities.

"By winter quarter I was intermittently dating several campus athletes, hoping that one of them would choose me for his steady. I did everything I could to please them, not realizing how naive I was. Weeks later their phone calls stopped. I couldn't understand why men rejected me, since I tried so hard to please them. How had I fallen short?

"I'd hoped that if a man made love to me, he would learn to love me. In the process I lost the ability to tell the difference between emotional caring and physical sharing. On the one hand I thought of myself as alluring, and on the other, I felt used. During the winter quarter, strangers began appearing at my door saying they were friends of men I'd dated.

"'Jim tells me you can show a fella a good time. How about inviting me in? I'd really like to get to know you. Let's have a good time.' Their breath smelled of beer, and their actions frightened me. Occasionally,

I'd invite one of these strangers in, saying I was not interested in anything physical, but willing to start up a friendship. In no time, fingers, hands, and arms would begin sliding around my body, and as a last resort I'd threaten to call the police. When this harassment turned into obscene phone calls and midnight callers pounding on my door, my dream of a 'Prince Charming' crashed.

"In time, I realized these young men didn't give a damn how I felt or what pain they caused me. In their eyes my function was to be enjoyed and discarded. I was crushed, deflated, and bitter. I wouldn't be the innocent any longer. They would have to find another victim. I began hating men because of these experiences. Their drunkenness, yelling, and raucous laughter left me angry and filled with emotional poison. And they frightened me.

"Dad had described marriage as the cure-all for women — as providing protection, security, and love. He expressed his expectations frequently by saying, 'When you find a man . . . When you settle down and get married . . . When you have children of your own . . . .'

"Yet many times in the same breath, he had also warned me, 'Don't trust men because they'll take advantage of you. Lock your doors, or you'll be raped.'

"Time slipped by, and I finally met a young man who showed genuine interest in me. For the first time in nearly a year I went on real dates, dinner and dancing, fun and sharing. He took me to concerts and parties. Sometimes I'd come home from class and find a bouquet of roses on my doorstep with a note of affection slipped between the petals.

"At last someone cared. As my confidence began to return, the world looked hopeful again. It was wonderful knowing a man enjoyed being with me and felt I was worth his time and company.

"Three months later as we sipped wine, during an evening dinner, his words began to spill out, telling me I was too sweet, too nice, too virginal, too proper. Why wasn't I sexy like the other girls he had dated? Why didn't I phone him and show myself off around the fraternity? The girls he'd dated had slept with him, he said, remarking that I was innocent and unaware.

"He then told me he had recorded our telephone conversations so the men in his fraternity could laugh at them over a cold beer. His letters and cards had been a joke. Obviously the joke was up now. He was tired of the game he'd been playing at my expense.

"I was uncomprehending. I couldn't hold back the tears. They made their way down my cheeks and onto my hands, and I was embarrassed, for they showed how much I had cared for him. I wanted to run away, disappear, escape.

"His manner was clipped and unemotional. Abruptly, he said, 'Let's go.'

"I thought to myself, 'Should I tell him my past so he won't think I'm such an innocent virgin? Would that give me back credibility in his eyes? If I'd acted sexy and sensuous, would he still have dumped me?' I was confused and wanted to remedy the situation. I hated the idea that he was dissatisfied with me, and that he had been telling his friends about it.

"We walked to his car. He commanded me to open his door, and I did in a dazed silence. Grinning, he leaned over to the passenger side, locked the door and started the engine. I just stood there and watched as he honked his horn and waved good-bye. Then I turned around and crossed the field adjacent to the parking lot and started home.

"I was too shocked for more tears, but my body trembled, and my hands were cold with sweat. I couldn't believe he'd left me and that he'd enjoyed the idea of it. I said over and over to myself, 'This can't be happening to me. I don't believe this is real.' After walking miles in my flimsy high heels, I finally reached my doorstep. Then the tears really hit.

"I felt men were more trouble than they were worth, and temporarily I stopped dating. I felt better that men weren't using me, but there was no denying my loneliness. When March brought cold, brisk winds and endless rain, a combination of sweets and television became temporary balm for my sagging ego and relief from hours of studying.

"Just before my first vomiting, I was in this period, feeling very deprived and lonely. I'd struck out with men. I was working eight hours a day earning minimum wage at a job that was a tedious, menial bore. From day to day I was living my fear of being a powerless nobody with no change in sight. I ate treats to make life bearable, and the pounds crept on, eroding my visions about my future.

"In the beginning, a basic reason for vomiting was that I ached for a loving relationship with a man and was determined to get myself thin because I felt this would increase my acceptability and my chances."

Platonic Friendships

While anorexics are often adolescent girls who may or may not be dating, bulimics frequently are older and sexually active. For many binge-purgers the search for a male partner is a central issue, and they can identify the onset of their illness as having occurred after a particularly painful male rejection. Just prior to becoming ill, Barbara's disillusionment with dating had been compounded by the trauma of the rape she experienced at her campus work-study job, discussed in a later chapter.

When first home, lethargically sitting in the living room recliner under mounds of blankets, she had repeatedly commented on how she longed for a loving relationship with a man. Yet, at the same time, she'd talked of fearing and hating men. She now spoke of wanting to marry someone who'd be a husband, lover, and father figure, all rolled into one; a man who would protect and take care of her and be a companion at the same time. She often expressed a sense of being cosmically adrift and alone, afraid she might never find a man she wanted to marry who wanted her.

With no close male relationship, Barbara had felt starved for affection and recognition. No amount of bingeing on sweets had been able to fill this *hunger for intimacy*. It was apparent that recovery would have to be based on Barbara's filling the emotional voids in her life. This would need to include developing a trusting connection with people she cared about. She wanted male companionship most but was immobilized by dread of being hurt again.

Platonic friendships might be a way to include men back into her life without fear of romantic rejections, so I suggested this and asked if she might want to drop by her brother's fraternity house on her walks home from campus. The thought appealed to Barbara, and over the following weeks she gradually developed friendships with two members of Roger's pledge class. At last she seemed to be having fun. Before this, Barbara had looked at men as either having dating potential (with marriage in mind) or not worth her time. It's interesting that neither of the men she chose to pal around with were ones she'd have considered "marriage material," though as friends they were outstanding.

In the past she would never believe praise. Now she was no longer as guarded. A bond of caring trust had developed. She reported that with these new male friends she was comfortable being assertive and later wrote, "It was a revelation to get an inside line on men. They'd been deceived and rejected by dates and were hurting and cautious in dealing with the opposite sex. I found they weren't all that different from me, so I stopped being scared. I grew closer to these men by just being their friend than I'd been to any man as his girl friend, and I realized that my problems with men had basically stemmed from gender stereotypes and associating with men who weren't good choices."

By forming a trusting bond with these men and recognizing that, just as with her brother, she greatly admired and trusted them, Barbara could see that stereotypes are often the basis for inequities and injustices that handicap both genders and that she needed to distinguish between men in general and those with whom she'd had distressing experiences.

She also saw that looking at a man as a marriage prospect opens the possibility of heartache. Without such expectations of male friends, Barbara could be at ease, neither predicting nor dreading the future. She was now stepping outside conventional roles of male dominance and female dependence. Herb Goldberg, in *The New Male*, describes her previous attitude: "The gender fantasies we have all been raised on of establishing a 'happily ever after' relationship between Miss Passive-Delicate-Fragile-Emotional Female and Mr. Right-Successful-Rational-Dominant-Powerful-Strong Male are, from a look at their psychological underpinnings, an impossible dream."[1]

Barbara gradually learned that courting rituals foster the presentation of only one's most pleasing attributes, attempting to conceal shortcomings and down-playing differences. Realism is often less in evidence than illusion, as two people attempt to match the image of what each other desires in a mate. She remembered how the use of flattery, formality, temptation, and solicitation were often the foundation of her former dating experiences.

She had felt hollow back then because she had lacked true intimacy, which is based on familiarity and the sharing of innermost feelings. It rests on being real in matters personal and private, and she had not experienced this. Barbara had wanted to be endorsed unconditionally, not measured by virtues, accomplishments, or conditions. Knowing that what she honestly felt and thought was accepted by her new male friends helped reduce her self-criticism and bolstered her confidence.

In time she made other friends and began accepting invitations to campus social functions. The crisis of her self-imposed isolation had passed, but a critical period of social testing was still ahead.

PART II

A Cohealing Response to Bulimic Binge-Purging

CHAPTER 9

To Get Well
or Not Get Well

During Barbara's first three weeks at home, I spent considerable time with her, but by the end of that period she was again
attending school and back at work. This meant that our shared
time became pretty much limited to the dinner hour and evening
chats during her study breaks.

Since she was again digesting healthy foods and had regained to
a more normal weight, yet still purged "overindulgences," she had
begun thinking of herself, not as anorexic anymore, but instead as
bulimic. She knew that she was not yet out of the woods.

Barbara had arrived home in early November. By spring, she
felt ready to try living on her own again, having made the decision
to find an apartment to share with her sister, Lisa. Because it had
been a relatively short time since she was so ill, I worried whether
she was ready for this step. But because Barbara's becoming self
reliant had been one of our major objectives, wasn't her wanting to
be independent an indication of the progress she'd made since returning home? I felt I should be supportive of her move toward
responsibility, though I was concerned it might be premature.

She searched the newspaper classified section, drove around
looking at rentals, signed a contract, packed her things, and re-
settled herself in a new apartment. I was encouraged by the remarkable contrast with her condition months before when she'd
been unable to gather her own belongings to return home.

And what of the progress she'd made over the previous months?
Physically, Barbara was greatly improved. She'd regained to 115
pounds, a low weight for her height, but no longer emaciated. She
insisted she needed at least a ten-pound "safety margin" below

what she considered a normal weight for her height. She was energetic and no longer complained of feeling cold, tired, or weak.

The vague, haunted look of depression and lethargy was gone. She 'd landed a new campus job that she liked, and was responsibly handling her finances. She had completed the remaining weeks of the fall semester with honor grades and was continuing with excellent marks in the winter quarter. Instead of retreating, she was seeing friends regularly and going on dates with men.

Though she was eating and digesting a healthful diet, every meal was still based on juggling her food phobias. At least her body-image had become somewhat more accurate, though she continued to judge herself as heavier than she actually was. Having once experienced a period of uncontrolled weight-gain, she feared it might happen again.

At times, she splurged on sweets in mini-binges, which might consist of a bag of sugar-frosted cookies bought with spare change, or a can of pre-mixed vanilla frosting. This was food intended solely for pleasure, eaten with the expectation of vomiting it. She continued to mentally separate food she intended to purge from food she intended to digest for health. But sometimes she vomited food she'd intended to digest, fearing she'd consumed too much.

Progression and Regression

For several months after leaving home, Barbara continued making progress, but gradually her momentum slowed. When we got together, she was again expressing frustration and anxiety over the burden of supporting herself while at the same time maintaining her regular college-class schedule.

Under this stress, her unsureness had increased, and she reverted to trying to impress and be pleasing to others, rather than doing what was in her own best interests. Even though she didn't resort to starving herself, at times she let her weight dip below 110 pounds. When this occurred, her depression and troubling physical symptoms would return until she allowed herself to return to a more normal weight.

Improvements were counteracted by setbacks, setbacks by improvements. Barbara later commented, "To others I look recovered, but the craving to fill some emotional void with food continues. I need to vomit or I'll get fat again. I still don't want to be cured though I want to feel well."

Barbara's eating problems progressed and regressed, depending on how her life was going. For two years, she dated a man several years her senior. They were talking of marriage, children, and a future together, when she discovered that he wasn't monogamous and had no intention of ever being so. This was a devastating blow. When conflicted and under stress, she again moved into what she referred to as an "automatic mode" in which she felt helpless to resist the urge to overeat.

Barbara was an avid reader of self-actualization books and had gradually gained insight into her problems. But understanding was one thing, changing quite another.

"I was stunned that I had virtually every 'erroneous zone' mentioned in Wayne Dyer's book bearing that name. I read books on nutrition, women's rights, health, and various pop philosophies, yet I still reached for food as a pacifier for my frustrations."

Echoing her former sharply divided split-screen reasoning, she commented to me, "Part of me wants to get well and part of me doesn't." Bulimic behaviors disrupted her life yet, at the same time, seemed to make it easier to endure.

I know how terribly discouraging it can be — after a period of apparent progress toward recovery — to find that a loved one has backslid into self-destructive eating habits. But since many girls and women have recovered and are leading fulfilling, satisfying lives, there is hope. The saw-tooth progression-regression pattern of these illnesses must be seen in the perspective of the overall trend. Is that trend toward personal integrity and health? If not, it's time to question why and actively pursue courses of action to better understand the problems and alter the individual's path from chronic illness.

Eating Diary

One day when we were chatting, it occurred to me to suggest she begin writing down situations that had affected her eating so that she might gain more control over her food intake.

Later, in one such diary section, Barbara recorded the following:

MARCH 25 – My dancing partner continually comments on how thin I am, and I take this to be admiration. I will diet for the next few days.

MARCH 28 – I have a date with a man I like very much. He likes thin women. I plan to eat practically nothing for the next three days so I will be thin for him.

MARCH 31 – A good male friend tells me I'm too thin and that I need to gain some weight. We go to dinner. I eat a large meal. I feel good inside. Now I'll be healthy for awhile. On the way home I see a thin woman. I look at my stomach, and fear takes hold. I find a bathroom and vomit my dinner. I feel unhappy with myself.

APRIL 1 – I wake up and am very dizzy. There is no food in my apartment. I want and need something to eat. I will go to work at 5 P.M., and know I can get a free meal there. I force myself not to eat until then, when I select a hamburger I plan to digest. While I'm eating, a fellow employee comments on how lucky I am to be thin. I put the hamburger down and don't finish it.

APRIL 2 – I step on the scale with clothes and shoes. It says 113. I experience some fear that I'm too light. Later I tell a friend my weight and he compares me to a fashion model. I know my weight is good.

APRIL 3 – Mom comments on how thin I am, so I buy vegetables and a sandwich, fearing something bad might happen if I don't eat.

Looking at her entries over succeeding days, it was possible for Barbara to recognize that her decisions not to eat or to purge were *seemingly* based on the desire to be thin, but that in reality they stemmed from her *not feeling good about herself.* With this, she became more aware that she was substituting anxiety about her body for anxiety related to feelings of overall inadequacy and un-worthiness.

To get beyond this defense she found it helped to ask herself, "Why am I feeling inadequate and insecure? What do I really *want* to have happen? How can I effectively deal with this situation? Who am I trying to please anyway?"

Using this approach, she worked on deciding what actions seemed appropriate. The affirmation, *"I don't need to prove anything to anyone; I am fine as I am,"* helped remind her of the belief in herself that she wanted to attain.

Barbara also found that keeping an "eating diary" revealed factors that increase the risk of a bulimic episode.

Recent research indicates the benefits of bulimics recording such things as when, where, and what food was eaten, whether it was eaten alone or with others, plus whether it was digested, and the mood and degree of hunger prior to eating.[1] By learning to recognize circumstances, when problem eating is most likely to occur, the individual can plan alternative ways of reacting and avoid, or at least reduce, the likelihood of these situations occurring.

"Unpleasant events" and snacking are associated with binge-purge episodes,[2] as is eating alone or being in a down mood prior to eating.[3] Normal eating tends to be associated with times when bulimics are genuinely hungry, feel upbeat, and are not alone.[4] An "eating diary" recorded daily, or even sporadically, can indicate whether progress is being made.

For though an anorexic maintains a normal weight for weeks, or even months, danger still exists. Similarly, bulimics who for several months squelch the desire to gorge or purge, starve or compulsively exercise, are not necessarily recovered. Until healthy patterns have been established over an *extended* period, and the individual has made a good life-adjustment in addition to maintaining a normal body weight, vulnerability to relapse remains.

Recovery must be thought of as *persistent wellness* — sustained physical and psychological well-being over a prolonged passage of time.

Cohealing Becomes a Way of Life

Three years after her midnight phone call, Barbara visited me at one of the renovation projects that I was managing for my parents. The properties were out of state, and for me, this was a time of separation from my husband. For her, it was an interim period between jobs. She'd intended to spend only a few days there, but chose instead to help out at the site for three months and make money in the process.

During quiet hours after the noise of the carpenters, roofers, and others had ceased, we'd sit with our feet propped up, enjoying the panoramic view below. We were two people working at sorting out our lives and found in each other a supportive, cohealing friend. We talked for hours about what being female meant to us, where men fit into our lives, what directions we wanted to take, what personal changes we wanted to make.

I was working on figuring out what I needed to do in order to make my own life feel better. A big question was whether or not to stay in my marriage. As it turned out, Barbara and I were each at a point where we were searching for ways to heal our own emotional pain and find new directions. The interactive process of *"cohealing"* was becoming apparent. During this time, Barbara and her siblings, and I too, were each paying close attention to what would improve our own lives, and it helped that we were there for each other with emotional support and to share insights.

How Is This Serving Me?

After years of bending over toilet bowls, Barbara was searching for a more relaxed, freer self. She was afraid she might not be able to quit vomiting the day she married. Although she had no one in mind for a groom, she continued to worry, "What would a husband think if he found out — and would he dump me?" Like her old bingeing buddies, she felt that marriage would signal the point of no return: she would have to *completely* give up her "habit." In the past she had reasoned that, once she was married, she would not feel the need to binge or purge anymore, but now doubts were creeping in.

She didn't *want* to be phobic every time she ate, and after working so hard to earn money for food, vomiting seemed irrational. Yet neither did she want to give up this reliable method of maintaining her slender build.

Her bulimic habits were both salvation and curse. She seemed committed to being uncommitted. Since it was apparent that she was caught between opposing options, our discussions took a new tack. The question became, *"How is this behavior serving me?"* With this approach, she began concentrating on weighing the "benefits" of bulimic eating behavior against what she considered the detriments.

She experienced food as comforting when she felt unloved, unappreciated, insecure, overworked, frustrated, fearful, powerless, lonely, anxious, bored, or just generally unhappy. Food was an anesthetic that blocked out the disappointments in life, a tranquilizer that eased the pain. Recovery would involve loss of this "protection" and of having to address emotions that had so long been suppressed. She'd have to learn how to deal with emptiness and anger, anguish and despair, and for a long time wasn't sure she could face this.

In its own way, vomiting was also a solution since it not only remedied her overconsumption of calories but also provided her with a symbolic way to purge herself of unexpressed angry, upset feelings. Barbara had written, "When I'm furious and frustrations immobilize me, if I eat and vomit it's as though the anxiety flows out of me, and temporarily I feel calm. It helps me when I'm climbing the walls of my mind."

Though I thought of her binge eating and vomiting as problems, at that time she actually viewed them as solutions, because along with her obsessions about her body, they were defenses that distracted her from underlying worries. She had been focusing on controlling her body, allowing this to camouflage emotional issues that needed resolution.

During the period Barbara was vacillating between wanting and not wanting to recover, one of the things that proved beneficial was for her to recognize that however destructive her means of coping had been, she had been struggling to survive what had seemed to her like unbearable pain, and she was not a failure or shameful because of the defense mechanisms she had chosen to numb the hurt.

As it turned out, it was also helpful for her to share thoughts about how her current "bulimic life-style" wasn't making her happy; helpful too to think through how all the effort, time, and suffering she'd put into being skinny, hadn't accomplished *anything of real value*. She had been taking pride in something that hadn't helped her feel worthwhile, contented, or connected with others in supportive, meaningful ways. Further, being skinny had not resulted in a lasting male relationship as she had hoped.

She saw that if she was ever going to have an intimate relationship with anyone else, she first had to have one with *herself.* This would mean getting fully in touch with her buried feelings and sharing them with others. She had to know herself before others could intimately know her.

Others could listen and be a sounding board, sharing information and encouragement, but only Barbara could weigh continued reliance on bulimic habits against her opposing desire to feel normal and in control of her life.

Literature Search

While we worked on the renovation project, Barbara and I began gathering research material as background for a book on her experiences with anorexia and bulimia that could be of help to others experiencing serious eating disorders.

As we talked over the possibilities, I found myself getting more and more interested. This project was begun by making scores of tape recordings about the stockpile of experiences tied to her illness. After the construction project was completed, *we conducted computer searches through tens of thousands of medical, psychological, and sociological abstracts on eating disorders written over the previous decade, concentrating on the time span when Barbara and Brenda had become ill.*

For weeks, we read through computer printouts and tracked down professional journal articles. For the most part they'd been written in this country, but many came from Canada, Sweden, Norway, Great Britain, and Australia.

I was struck by the fact that the authors dealt almost exclusively with medical and psychological aspects of eating disorders. At the time, almost nothing had been researched on the *cultural* influences that foster and sustain these illnesses.

The most logical of questions had not been addressed: why are females so much more vulnerable than males? As I read through the literature, I also became aware *that there was virtually no information on what parents could do to be supportive of a daughter who starves or purges. Also lacking were ways to cope with their own distress or any suggestions as to what parents could do while raising a daughter to reduce her susceptibility. Other family members and loved ones were also rarely mentioned in the literature, such as husbands who have wives with these disorders and are wondering how best to handle the situation.*

Self-Fulfilling Prophecies

It was clear that, according to most research reports, Barbara's symptoms were indicative of a poor prognosis. Typical reports stated that among female anorexic patients, "poor outcome" was "associated with . . . longer duration of illness, older age of onset at presentation, lower weight during illness and at presentation, presence of symptoms such as bulimia, vomiting and anxiety when eating with others."[5]

I can still see Barbara running upstairs to my bedroom in tears. She had just read a particularly pessimistic report stating the dismal prognosis expected among older binge-purgers. "I'm never going to get well, that's basically what they're saying!" She was devastated.

Trying to give a more optimistic outlook, I talked about self-fulfilling prophecies and how *we tend to actualize our expectations.* Researchers who authored the material she had been reading had predicted poorer outcomes for these patients, and their results were consistent with their predictions. It was apparent in many case studies that therapist expectations had affected the outcome.[6]

It takes a combination of desire and expectation to get what is wanted. Since it's easier to have positive self-expectations and to work on fulfilling them when those around us *believe* in us, it's important for those with eating disorders to surround themselves with people who believe they can and will recover.

Physicians, nurses, therapists, family and friends, and others, need to be aware that their *unstated expectations* can influence what the anorexic or bulimic prophesies for herself. This in turn can have a profound impact on her. If the self-starver or binge-purger anticipates a continued reliance on self-destructive behaviors, she will likely bring those expectations to pass. Her visualizing these destructive habits as falling away, as slipping into the past, facilitates her overcoming them.

Visualization can transform pessimism into goal-oriented thinking. By repeatedly visualizing what we want to have come to pass as already having occurred, the mind begins to *accept these images as possible.* We must believe there's a chance of success before we'll be motivated to put the all-out effort into a project that will make it a reality. No one learns mountain climbing in a day, but with training and practice, mountains can be climbed.

To me it was significant that Barbara began keeping track of the things she most wanted to have happen in her life. She also took concrete action to bring them to pass. She was developing a more self-reliant attitude, looking for and creating opportunities to achieve her desires. When she talked of being a failure, I reminded her of her past accomplishments.

Barbara realized she needed to release herself from rehashing past problems and especially from projecting them into the future. What helped most was approaching each day as a fresh start. We mulled over the concept that if, in life, you give yourself low marks for the past (say F, D, D –, C –, and another F), you need not think in terms of averaging those scores with the present. If life is good now — that's all that matters. With this attitude, Barbara's baggage of the past was seen as a learning experience.

Finding Satisfaction

Much of her old dissatisfaction with herself had been based on mental pictures of changes she would have to make in order to really be "somebody." Her life was based on *becoming* rather than on *being*. Like a mirage, happiness seemed forever beyond her.

We had many discussions concerning attitudes and actions that fostered our being satisfied today, right now — things that I needed to work on too. We each looked for ways to make ourselves more satisfied with our lives *now* rather than waiting for some future time when we hope things will be better. This was an on-going process, and the changes took place slowly over several years. For me, decisions concerning my marriage were intertwined with dissatisfaction and the need to make significant changes to make my own life feel more satisfying.

Barbara was able to get a clearer perspective on her dieting and weight problems when I asked, one evening while we were watching the fading light of a sunset, "What if you knew there were only 24 hours before the world's end; how would you spend your time?"

As she thought this over, she realized that from this point of view shoulds and oughts that she had considered so important lost their power to victimize. The current fashion dictate, "You should be thin," would be totally meaningless. There would be no reason for pretenses or to "show" anybody. Most important would be making the most out of the precious moments of life. Certainly there'd no longer be any reason to wait.

Incidentally, such present-oriented thinking can help us gradually accept such attitudes as the following: *"Life is okay now; I am okay right now. I am accepting and making the most of being alive in the only time I will ever have, the fleeting moment between past and future: the present."*

Choosing a Name

Barbara wanted a new image and a new name. For years she hadn't liked her given name. Now she talked of wanting to change it to one that would give her a new start. I thought the name we had selected for her was beautiful but wasn't attached to her remaining "Barbara." I felt that what she was called should be her choice.

For several days she wrote down her favorite names as they came to mind, asking for my reactions. This led to our discussing their sounds, along with characters in literature and famous people as well as acquaintances with those names and the mental pictures they conveyed. The process in itself was instructive, as she considered how she wanted to feel about herself and the image she wanted to project.

Finally she whittled her list to three, and then to her final choice — Jacqueline.* She liked the sound it had and its powerful initial consonant. She associated it with a variety of positive qualities and decided to try it out. So after 23 years of being called Barbara, she requested I call her by her new name. For some reason I found it easier to make the change by calling her Jacque, a nickname she liked, and she preferred this spelling, thinking it distinctive.

This name-change decision helped release her from a self-image and a past she didn't want to remember. It also helped her toward building a new image of herself.

---

* To protect their privacy, the names of my children have been changed and "Jacqueline" is therefore a pseudonym to represent the name change made by my daughter during her recovery.

CHAPTER 10

Bulimic Dreams

Jacque's illness was reflected in her dreams. One morning she described three dreams she had experienced the night before. She writes about them, along with some other "bulimic dreams," in her following comments:

"In my first dream of the night I found myself with my sister Lisa, in an empty white room. We were waiting for an evaluation by a physician. Lisa stepped on the scale. It read 124 pounds, perfect for her height and body build. I dreaded stepping on the scale because, if I were too thin, I felt Mother would be upset.

"The scale balanced at 102 pounds. I was horrified that I weighed more than I wanted to! I wasn't thin enough to satisfy myself, but I didn't want to be the weight that would please Mother or the doctor. By sheer force of will I struggled, trying to make the scale drop to a lower weight. Just then Mom entered the room, and instantly I grew a foot taller. My weight remained the same, but now I was six-feet-nine inches tall! I knew they didn't want me to lose any weight, so I satisfied my desire to be thinner by growing taller.

"After waking, I drifted back to sleep and found myself with Mother and Lisa in an upper story of an apartment building somewhere in New York City. It was 112 stories high, and the building was old and dark, built of wood and concrete. We wandered through the hallways looking for some way to reach ground level but could find no stairs or elevators. Everything seemed deserted. There was no sign of life.

"Finally, we discovered one method of escape, which was to drop through a narrow, vertical, dark chute. One by one we slipped downward and began falling. The walls were smooth and straight, so we braced our hands and feet against them, struggling to control our speed. Between floors we could feel tiny ledges that slowed our fall, so we dropped from one landing to the next, ten feet at a time, over and over again.

"I began wondering to myself, 'Is this ever going to end? Are we trapped here forever? Perhaps we should never have tried to get out of the building in the first place.' I called out to Mother and Lisa, who were above me, 'Is this really necessary?'

"Just then an old man in ragged clothing with graying hair, wrinkles, and decaying teeth shot down by me. As he passed, his low hollow voice rang out, 'Of course, it's necessary!' and disappeared out of sight into the darkness below.

"At last I could see light and finally touched bottom. I pushed myself out of the chute to find I was standing on the sidewalk. It was Christmas, and clean snow covered the ground. A small group of carolers approached us and drifted off into the evening. I felt both joyous and relieved. We'd all come through our downward plunge safely; everything was fine after all.

"Suddenly I cried out, 'My God! My teeth are falling out!' The roots had separated from my gums, and I opened my mouth, spitting teeth into my mittens. I stared helplessly at the clasped handful of teeth, thinking, 'Bulimia has finally caught up with me. It's just one more thing I have to accept. Now I'll have false teeth.'

"In the morning, I discussed this dream with Mom because I found it upsetting. To me it seemed that dropping down from one level to the next in the building represented my drop in weight.

"Every time I'd set a lower weight goal and reached it, I dropped further still, from 150, to 130, to 110, and so on downward. The small footholds between floors couldn't prevent me from falling. I asked, 'Is this really necessary?' because this is a question that preys on my mind.

"The derelict telling me, 'Of course, it's necessary!' represents the controlling voice in my mind, and the teeth dropping out must be related to my fears of permanently damaging my body.

"My third dream that night was set in a dimly lit cocktail lounge where I was serving drinks from an enclosed bar. I was nearly through taking a customer's order when I came to an expressionless man. I asked him if he wanted a cocktail, and his single response was, 'I want YOU!'

"Shyly and politely I said, 'I'm sorry, but you can't have me.' I moved to the next customer, a man who said nothing and motioned me to the woman next to him.

"Turning to her, I inquired if she cared for a drink. In a harsh tone she bluntly stated, 'Don't be so sure.' I knew exactly what she meant, but it took me by surprise. 'Don't be so sure' referred to the first man, and that he was going to get me. She pulled a revolver and shot me.

"The moment I realized I was dying, my dream ran back to the point when the first man had demanded, 'I want YOU!' It was like a rerun, only this time when I heard the woman's voice, I was prepared to deflect the bullet. I felt one shot sear through my wrist and another through my leg, but I was still alive. Suddenly another woman appeared behind me with a machine gun and riddled my body with bullets.

"I couldn't win, even with a second chance. I had felt helpless to protect my body from the insidious devastation of bulimia, and in my dream I couldn't protect my body from the attack. I'd been trapped inside the enclosed counter with no protection, completely vulnerable to the commanding male figure. He intended to have me done in, and there was no escape.

"Mother encouraged me to continue analyzing my dreams, and it became clear that most of them reflected fear that I was destroying myself but felt helpless to do anything about it. There was a lot of mutilation, decapitation, and bloodshed in them. Hardly any happy endings. Sometimes I was so scared I felt the need to keep my bedroom light on all night. At other times I'd pace in my room for a half- hour until the fright subsided.

"I remember one dream in which my sister Brenda and I are on an ocean liner with no captain, only crew and passengers. I am unaware of the destination but feel everything is under control. As the dream continues, I sense something is wrong and realize that the ship is turning, headed toward death. I must rescue myself. As I step into the pilot room, I see it's empty. I have complete control over the ship's destiny and reverse its course.

"My interpretation of this dream is that initially the ship was actually sailing toward wellness, and though Brenda seemed to accept this course, I balked, because that course seemed like mental death to me. Since no one aboard attempted to stop me, I turned the ship around and steered it toward bulimia. As I took control, I felt powerful because, at least in bulimia, I knew the rules. Moving toward wellness disrupted my security. It was a threatening unknown.

"Turmoil surfaced during sleep again and again, and it became commonplace to wake up and realize I'd just had a bulimic dream. My most common nightmare was that I'd eaten enormous amounts of food and then fallen asleep before vomiting. Hours later in the dream, I'd awaken, remembering I hadn't purged, furious with myself for allowing sleep to overtake me.

"At this point, I would truly awaken from the dream, frightened and perspiring. Throwing the covers off, I'd quickly run my hands over my empty stomach and sigh with relief that I'd only experienced another nightmare. Each repetition of this dream brought the same jolting fear that obesity had gotten the best of me.

"A dream that remains vivid even today, seemed terrifying at the time. I am sitting alone in my parents' living room. In a corner of the room I see the shadowy figure of a young woman. Ominous, calculating, treacherous, powerful, she watches me. I see that she is after me. I'm terrified, helpless to escape. This time I hope the course of my dream will spare me from bulimia's grasp. She approaches me, lunging forward in quick steps. I try to brace myself and hide from her reach. When suddenly she is before me, I feel I am facing the ultimate horror.

"Later, I experienced a continuation of this dream after making progress toward recovery, and this time I dreamed Mother and I are sitting next to each other in the living room. Father sits across the room. I look to my left toward the hallway, and in the shadows is a figure of a girl, her eyes intensely focused on me.

"I tell Mother my fear that the girl is out to do me harm, but she sees nothing lurking in the hall. Although Mother tries to reassure me, I still see the female figure stalking me, coming closer and closer, ominously taking shape. She looks menacing, despite her small childlike body, and when the figure lunges toward me, I grab for her neck, wrenching it wildly like a killer dog attacking a burglar. I throw the girl across the room, and as she hits the wall, books and knickknacks tumble and splinter to the floor. The figure lies motionless, slumped against the baseboards.

"For the first time, I'd overcome the danger and realized that she was only two dimensional, flat like a shadow. It is clear to me that the small child-like figure represented bulimia and was determined to overtake me as it had done before. Mother and Father seemed unaware that bulimia was still something I was fighting, but I could see the danger. When the girl lunged at me, I was afraid she would enter my body and possess me. In defense I strangled her, rendering her powerless. *This time I won.*"

Jacque's own analysis of her dreams were revealing, relevant, and useful to her.

In dreams, the unconscious mind reviews and "processes a vast jumble of material — new facts, situations, past experiences, unsolved worries, fears, desires and much more,"[1] according to Frances Kennett, an authority on dream interpretation. For anorexics and bulimics, dreams can be used as another way to understand thoughts that lie essentially hidden during waking hours.

I'd kept a "dream journal" for awhile a few years before and had found doing this interesting and useful. Now, being reminded of the benefits to be gained from dream analysis, I again considered this aspect of my own life, something I'll touch on later.

CHAPTER 11

Food Rules
and the Internal Voice

"Vomiting is like a magic charm to keep me thin. It worked once to protect me from fat and every time since, so I'm afraid to stop." Jacque was convinced she'd become hooked on vomiting from the first time she gagged up a binge and lost four pounds. When she first returned home, Jacque had mentioned having food rules but hadn't discussed them, remarking, "You'd think I'm crazy." Now she openly talked about them.

With our new openness to sharing with each other, she began talking about her mental rules on what, when, and how much she could allow herself to digest.

"I have hundreds of rules, and I'm constantly giving myself merits and demerits, making it a struggle just to keep up with how many points I've accumulated or lost in a day. Even when I *want* to keep food down, sometimes the rules conflict, so I can't." Jacque could no longer remember why particular rules had been formed but was sure she dare not break them lest some dreadful fate overtake her.

Compulsive-Addictive Behavior

From our reading, we learned that such obsessive-compulsive rumination is typical among anorexics.[1] Obsessions have to do with unwanted thoughts and fears that are persistent and repetitive, while compulsions are powerful urges to carry out repetitive irrational actions to subdue these obsessive fears.[2]

Once an anorexic or bulimic establishes obsessive-compulsive patterns of eating, purging, or exercising, it's frightening for her to think of breaking these rituals since she feels they protect her against unnameable, terrifying fears.

Obsessive thoughts and compulsive actions are a means of denying and avoiding painful feelings. For the person caught in this pattern, it seems more comfortable to rerun the peculiar notions and carry out the ritualistic behavior than to deal directly with the underlying storehouse of upset emotions. Such compulsive behavior often has sporadic, relatively innocuous beginnings but progresses to full-fledged addictions that occupy and control the individual's entire life. Later we would learn that, like Jacqueline, many bulimics "are desperate in their overwhelming obsession."[3]

Writing about compulsive/addictive behavior, John Bradshaw, an authority on codependent behavior, speaks of "total control (compulsivity)" by the individual or "no control (addiction)," pointing out that they are connected and a setup for each other.[4] He defines compulsive/addictive behavior as "a pathological relationship to any mood altering experience that has life damaging consequences."[5] Jacque recognized that for her, binge-purging was just such a mood-altering experience.

Jacque craved sweets . . . one doughnut was never enough, nor were two or three. Even a *dozen* left her wanting to reach for another. Cookies, fudge, ice cream, frosting, and other sweets fed her snacking-purging cycles. At times when she was trying to refrain from vomiting, she denied herself anything sweet, knowing that she wouldn't stop at a moderate serving. After reading about addiction in *Sugar Blues*,[6] Jacqueline associated her craving for sweets with addiction.

Compulsive Eating

Addiction involves "pathological habit, dependence, or compulsion," according to recent psychological thinking, and "compulsive eating exhibits all the signs of ritual; instantaneous gratification, cultural variation, and destruction of self-respect that characterize drug addiction."[7]

Discussing the "invisible threshold" over which she'd passed into the realm of compulsive/addictive behavior, she was able to identify this as the point at which she had moved from free choice to loss of control. For her, like other bulimics, gorging was not a means of satisfying hunger, but a desperate all-consuming compulsion.

Food provides release from daily stress. Increased tension can increase food cravings until they have become a compelling need that must be satisfied again and again, "not for that first early feeling of happiness but simply to maintain a bearable level of everyday existence,"[8] notes Catherine Houck, in her writings on women and food. At this point, the individual has "joined the ranks of the addicted," who share in common the attempt to flee from their problems rather than working on solving them.[9]

She characterizes the food addict as someone who is lonely. Craving affection, she gives herself "love" by bingeing and relates addiction to feelings of inadequacy and fear, as well as being out of control and helpless. "Eating can be among the most devastating of addictions, bringing on highs and lows as powerful as those induced by alcohol and drugs,"[10] according to this source. Sugar is the substance most commonly used to excess, but "some foodaholics get a high from bingeing on just about anything."[11]

Jacque felt that those addicted to drugs, gambling, alcohol, or cigarettes may have an advantage in that they can stop "cold turkey," but obviously, she and others like her who are addicted to bingeing must find ways of coming to terms with the daily necessity of eating.

There were no local groups to help bulimics and others with related addictive behavior, so we continued our search for understanding on our own. Here are some of the things we found relevant.

For more than two years, Jacque had not relied on laxatives to blunt her fear of weight gain. Now I was learning that in this age of food abundance, we have unfortunately reached a point where "laxative abuse and vomiting are not uncommon" among the general population.[12] Vomiting obviously provides an effective way to eliminate huge quantities of food and prevent weight gain, but it promotes more bingeing "and creates a spiraling of symptoms."[13] Although research indicates that even large doses of laxatives have "little impact on intestinal absorption" and weight maintenance, bulimics persist in downing them in large quantities.[14]

I'm reminded of a slightly chubby older woman who confided in me that she takes up to 60 laxatives a week in an attempt to control her weight — and of the checkout man in our local convenience store who told me that "Twinkies and other sweets, plus a box of laxatives, have become a standard choice of young girls," often buying in groups. Abuse of laxatives tends to cause dehydration, among other problems, and this water depletion gives a false "feeling of weight control . . . which can become habit forming."[15]

Bulimics often obsess about a number of things besides food and weight. Obsessions may include irrational fears that one might injure or kill parents, self, or others, or damage cherished objects. Repressed anger and anxiety often lie behind these fantasies and need to be resolved so that the upsetting thoughts can be laid to rest.

It may seem scary to disclose such disturbing fears, but counselors have heard them all before. Relief and recovery come through understanding the painful self-doubts, apprehensions, and memories behind these obsessions. So, threatening though it may seem, appropriate therapy holds out the promise of making the bulimic's life easier and more comfortable.

Getting Needs Met Directly

It was our experience that justifications for continuing bulimic behaviors are easy to come by. Asking "why" questions, such as, "Why do you vomit?" or "Why do you overeat?" were sure to elicit them. When she looked at how the entrenched behaviors were serving her, Jacqueline uncovered a different set of responses.

Compulsive-addictive eating behavior provides a superficial bandage for emotional hunger rather than healing. *Healing comes through getting needs met directly.*

By asking before an intended binge, "How would ingesting this serve me?" Jacqueline was able to target in on the *need*. This made it possible for her to look at what alternatives might more directly satisfy her, such as calling a friend, taking a nap, going to a movie, handling a job assignment, or taking whatever action would deal head-on with loneliness, exhaustion, tension, apprehension, and other problematic emotional stress.

From this perspective, compulsive eating could be viewed as one of many options. The question became not, "What am I going to eat?" but "What else could I be doing with my money, time, intelligence, creativity, energy? What else could I be doing to nurture and take care of myself?"

As the prospect of spending the rest of her life caught in bulimic behavior weighed more and more heavily on her, this eventually seemed more distressing to her than facing the prospect of change and recovery.

The Commanding Voice

It's common for anorexics and bulimics to feel that an overpowering force *tells* them how to behave. Describing her patients, Hilde Bruch noted that anorexics believe they are directed "by some mysterious force." They'll remark on a split self, saying that "'it is a dictator who dominates me,' or 'a ghost who surrounds me,' or 'the little man who objects when I eat.'"[16]

This therapist spoke of girls wanting to "keep 'the little man,' 'evil spirit,' or some other magic force from tormenting them with guilt and shame."[17] For example, one patient heard voices that instructed her to eat while others commanded her not to.[18]

Jacqueline spoke of a voice in her head that controlled her and enforced her mental rules, ordering her to obey. She told me she felt totally helpless to countermand this voice.

The shift from normal dieting to pre-anorexic dieting to anorexia often takes months or years. In Jacqueline's case, it took about a year and a half. Weeks of food restriction had followed a monotonous course while she tried to cut out enough food to lose weight. No more butter — no more gravy — no more cream sauce. Lower the calorie intake. Drink more tea, coffee, and diet cola. At first the changes were minor and relatively sensible, but from such initial dieting, Jacque had begun dividing foods into categories (as do many dieters and weight-loss diet plans).

These categories included caloric versus low-cal, forbidden versus permissible, unsafe versus safe. The antecedents to her food rules lay in such reasoning. Periodically the deprivation of dieting had become unbearable, and she would splurge on graham crackers and peanut butter, ice cream and cake, pretzels and cookies. Then to make restitution, she would fast the next day or two. The pattern of bingeing and abstinence was being established. Like most anorexics, Jacque thought of carbohydrates as sinful since they were the most tempting when she broke down and ate what she really wanted. Vomiting on a dare had demonstrated that it brought almost instant emotional relief.

Foods she had categorized as too fattening were now no longer off limits; they could be eaten in quantity and then purged. In time they actually were no longer associated with digestion or nourishment. Jacque relates, "When I didn't have to worry about calories anymore, I began separating foods according to those I'd digest and those I had to purge."

As her consumption had increased, vomiting became a way of life and digesting became less important than losing weight. Like every untreated anorexic I have met, she had progressively restricted her food choices and was subsisting on a limited variety of foods. Among the anorexics I have known, one ate only meager portions of lettuce and tuna fish, another only allowed herself eggs, and still another was subsisting on applesauce and fresh oranges. Another lived solely on baby food. Each had devised bizarre mental rules as to what she considered safe and unsafe to digest.

Merits and Demerits

Jacque spoke of giving herself "merit points" based on factors like her weight that day and what she'd eaten. Points were added or subtracted, based on such assorted input as whether she had a date that night and what she wanted to wear. But no matter how many points she had accumulated, she only permitted herself to digest if she had exercised vigorously. Although four years had passed since she had returned home ill, and she was now eating healthful foods, she rarely felt she'd earned the right to eat more than 100 calories at any one time.

"Many of my rules contradict each other, and there are all sorts of exceptions, so I'm constantly trying to calculate whether I can eat," Jacque explained. Some foods required more points. For instance, it was easy to "earn" a carrot but more difficult to "earn" a hard boiled egg.

When she talked about how the voice told her what she could and couldn't digest, trying to understand what she was experiencing, I asked her to describe it. "Well, it's like a powerful force in my mind which knows the answers. I hear it chanting, 'You have to get rid of those calories. Quick! Don't let them digest!'"

Jacque did not feel that she was the originator of the commanding voice in her mind. She believed that it spoke to her independently. When I inquired what would happen if she were to go against the voice, she responded, hesitantly, "Just thinking about it feels like overwhelming blackness and a terror I can't describe."

Food Categories

It was clear that Jacque felt helpless to simply eat what and when she wanted, though she might be hungry. *It seemed that if the voice she referred to could be demystified, she might regain a sense of control over her eating and lessen her fear.* As a first step, I asked whether she might want to write down some of her basic food rules. She didn't hesitate, quickly typing out her "food lists" on one sheet of paper. Handing it to me, she commented, "Actually my junk food list could go on forever. I only listed a few. However my *safe* food list is very limited, so I put down all of them."

Jacque explained that she could digest nothing she currently considered junk food. Foods she considered healthy and low calorie could not be digested if she was over her desired weight, or hadn't exercised that day. Proteins and grains could only be eaten sparingly. As it turned out, this listing of mental food rules was another breakthrough and became the starting point for demystifying the voice she felt spoke to her.

MY FOOD RULES:

Rules say I cannot eat these foods, just because.	Junk foods I cannot digest!
Bread	Candy
Boxed foods	Cakes and pies
Milk	Cookies
Turkey	Ice cream
Ham	Salad dressing (non diet)
Red meat	Soups
Mustard	Soda pop (with calories)
Grapefruit	Pastries
Dates	Granola
Pizza	Nuts and Lifesavers
Hamburgers	Crackers
Hot dogs	Canned foods
Noodles	Frozen foods
Rice (white)	Yogurt
Fried eggs	Marshmallows
Potatoes	All sauces
Yams	Buttered foods
Most fruit	All foods containing sugar
Raisins	Anything that tastes sweet

MY FOOD RULES (cont.):

Safe foods.

High calorie foods that
I can eat in small portions
when necessary or when
I'm thin enough.

Fresh vegetables	Fish
Broccoli	Chicken
Cabbage	Cheese
Carrots	Brown natural rice
Onions	Whole grain oats & wheat
Zucchini	Eggs — hard- or soft-boiled,
Sprouts	not scrambled
Celery	
Calorie-free soda	
Spices	
Lettuce	
Sometimes . . .	
Apples	
Bananas	
Oranges	
Pears	
Strawberries	

Safe food can become junk food if too much is eaten at a time.

The Voice Demystified

To demystify the internal voice that Jacque heard, we explored what it "said" and her responses. When she'd tell me, "My mind says I can't eat that because it's been frozen," I'd ask, "How do you feel about that?" To which she might reply, "Well, I like frozen strawberries. I picked them myself and I'd like to eat them, but the voice in my head says if I eat them I'll have to THROW UP."

She experienced the voice as a domineering overseer issuing orders she must obey. It "spoke" much as a controlling, dictatorial parent would, and her responses were those of a pleading or manipulative child. We struck on the idea of buying several books on "structural analysis," based on Transactional Analysis (T.A.) theory, and began applying this approach to the conflict between her desires and the voice that she felt controlled her.

T.A. was originated by Eric Berne,[19] who gave us the concept that each of us has three separate ego states, that of *Parent*, *Adult*, and *Child*.

The *Parent* ego state reflects the attitudes and behaviors absorbed during childhood from authority figures, particularly our parents. The Parent component transmits cultural scripts. It involves two parts, one that's nurturing, loving, and sympathetic, and another that's opinionated, critical, and controlling. This latter part, referred to as the Controlling Parent, gives orders and defines things. It's the basis of identity: "I am this; I am not this."

The *Adult* ego state gathers and organizes information based on our education and experience. It tests reality by looking at options, predicting consequences, and making decisions.

The *Child* ego state contains our natural responses: our innermost feelings and impulses. It has three distinct parts: the Natural or Free Child, who is spontaneous, expressive, inquisitive, and pleasure-seeking; Little Professor, or Tricky Child, who displays natural wisdom, intuition, and cleverness at manipulating situations; and Adapted Child, who contains the adaptations of our natural inclinations, usually in response to demands in childhood made by parents and other authority figures. The Adapted Child compromises and adjusts to cultural norms.

Reflecting on the commanding voice in her head, Jacqueline could see that it was a Controlling-Parent–type voice issuing orders, making rules, and saying that she must fast or purge or limit herself to particular foods, and put herself through designated exercise rituals. These were Crazy Parent messages that disintegrate the personality and which her Child felt helpless to disobey.

Now, when she heard herself saying, "Boy, I love jello salad," she was able to relate that to the Free Child ego state; the part of her that felt happy and sad. When she gave in to Controlling Parent messages, "If you eat that you'll have to vomit it!," she realized she was being her Adapted Child; compliantly adapting and obeying the rules.

She found that when she was overeating she could hear her mind saying, "Wow, I can eat all this delicious stuff and not absorb any of the calories! Tricky me — lucky me! I've outwitted the system!" This was Tricky Child.

After a meal, she would run through the various mental conversations aloud that had taken place while eating, with our identifying which ego state was speaking. In this way it was possible for her to consistently identify the commanding voice of black fear that she felt coerced her, as her own *Controlling-Parent* voice saying such things as, "If you don't do as I say, you'll be sorry!"

Injunctions from the Controlling-Parent ego state had not seemed to Jacque like her own mind. Her Child ego states had been what she had associated with herself — her own feelings of helplessness and submission to the rules, or of trickily maneuvering around them.

Conversations that took place between her ego states during a trip to the grocery store, Jacque later analyzed as follows:

Standing in the dairy section:
"Boy, that cheese looks so good, soft, creamy, and yummy." (Free Child)
"But you know you can't eat it." (Controlling Parent)
"Yes, I know. It's too bad it has all those calories and food dyes. I could never digest it." (Adapted Child)
"Let's move on." (Controlling Parent)

Pushing her cart past the luncheon meat department:
"Don't even consider buying it. You absolutely can't allow that in your body." (Controlling Parent)
"I'm sure you're right." (Adapted Child)

Entering the fruit and vegetable section:
"Yum, oranges, apples, peaches, and grapes. Sweet and tasty! I love grapes!" (Free Child)
"Yes, it does look delicious but there's a rule about not eating grapes, remember?" (Controlling Parent)
"That's a stupid rule!" (Tricky Child)
"But it is the rule, nonetheless, and must be obeyed." (Controlling Parent)
"But I'd like to have some grapes." (Free Child)
"What's more important, grapes or being thin? Being thin, of course, and don't you forget it!" (Controlling Parent)
"Well, I know I have to follow the rule, but I sure don't like it." (Adapted Child)

In the vegetable section: She selects broccoli, lettuce, carrots, and scallions.

"I'll buy green peppers to put on my salad." (Adapted Child)

"Fine, that's a good idea, but remember, only diet salad-dressing and no croutons or little extras. You wouldn't want to get fat, would you?" (Controlling Parent)

Leaving the checkout stand:

"So much food, and I can't eat it." (Adapted Child)

"Don't think about it that way. Think of all the people who are getting fat because they're eating. And think of all the unhealthy ingredients in that food." (Controlling Parent)

Jacque said she never knew when she might eat one bite too much and her Controlling Parent would insist she regurgitate it. Typically, the Parent voice and her reactions, she said, went as follows: "What have you done? You've eaten way too much! How could you have let such a thing happen? Quick, it's beginning to digest! *Do* something!"

Continuing to describe the process, she said, "My Parent voice tells me I'm going to get fat, and my Adapted Child panics. I feel my heartbeat increase, and fear takes over. Then Tricky Child appears: 'Hey, I know a way we can get out of this mess. Find a bathroom so you can get rid of it.' This done, my Controlling Parent voice is satisfied and quieted. Adapted Child once again feels safe because Tricky Child found a way to resolve the situation."

"I'm Only Okay If . . . "

Having analyzed her mental conversations, the voice no longer seemed mysterious to Jacque. She could identify her ego states and how they were interacting. From this we went on to consider the conditional premise that set up the course of events.

"Hey, you want to know how to feel good about yourself? I'll tell you how. Make yourself pleasing to people by being thin, beautiful, and feminine." Adapted Child, being sensitive to who holds the power, looked at the feminine-role expectations and adapted by being compliant. The driving force was the belief, *"I am not intrinsically okay as I am. I'm only okay if* I measure up to some external standard of beauty that will make me pleasing to others."

Her feelings of inadequacy fed into a repeated internal sequence, starting with her enjoying eating. Then her Controlling Parent voice demanded that she get rid of the food before it digested. From panic, she moved to the next stage in which Tricky Child saved the day. The final step in the sequence was disappointment. "If I'm so thin, why am I so miserable?" From delight, to panic, to relief, to meaninglessness.

"Things seem so useless. Even being thin seems useless. It hasn't gotten me anywhere. I'm still dissatisfied." These were feelings that led back to her immersing herself in the pleasure of eating. The basis for this sequence was the conditional *"I'm only okay if,"* which again emphasized the need for Jacqueline to accept and feel good about herself.

It was easy to see how Jacque's food rules reflected our current "social mind-set" that reads all sorts of judgments into what foods are considered beneficial or detrimental based on such things as calorie content, cholesterol, fiber, and all sorts of other measures. She had become obsessive about what she would digest, carrying this common form of mental juggling to an extreme and cementing it into rules from which she dared not vary.

Egograms

It also proved useful for Jacque to look at her internal conversations in terms of an egogram.[20] This model uses a bar graph, the egogram, to indicate the amount of "psychological energy" a person spends in each ego state.

By paying attention to her internal dialogues, she could identify the relative amount of energy and time she was spending in each of her ego states. In relation to food, she found most of her time was spent in a continuing battle between her Controlling Parent and Adapted or Tricky Child, with less time spent in Nurturing Parent, Free Child, or Adult. (This kind of egogram is associated with alcoholism and drug addiction.)

In a healthy egogram, most of the activity and energy is spent in Adult functioning, Nurturing Parent, and Free Child, with the least activity in Controlling Parent and Adapted Child. It's a distortion of personality when an excess of energy gets directed into Controlling Parent.

Jacque had been channeling much of her energy into nonproductive thoughts and activities. She needed to be able to envision

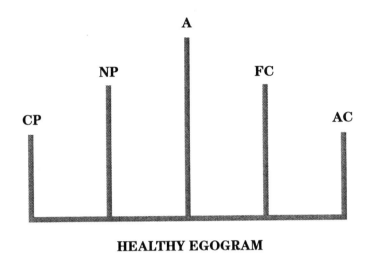

HEALTHY EGOGRAM

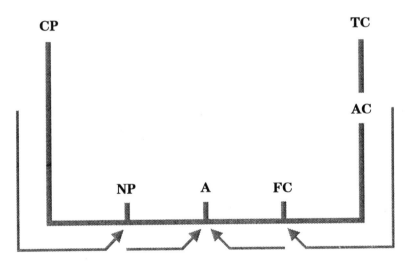

JACQUE'S EGOGRAM

(Arrows indicate the transfer of time
and energy needed for recovery.)

CP — Controlling Parent   FC — Free Child

NP — Nurturing Parent   AC — Adapted Child

A — Adult   TC — Tricky Child

how this *same time and energy* could be shifted so that the healing process could move forward.

By recognizing the interplay between her ego states, Jacque could make sense out of what had formerly been nonsense. She no longer felt helpless to disobey "the rules," for as she later put it, "When I understood that the voice was one of my own ego states, it became within my control."

However, before she could recover, she needed to go through a process of strengthening her own Nurturing Parent so it could provide her with permission to act in ways that were in her own best interest, and develop a healthy Adult that could provide security nothing frightening would happen if she discarded her bulimic patterns.

Jacque's earlier anorexic reaction, that she did not need to eat and that I was trying to make her fat, were the result of a crossed transaction in which my comments on human nutritional needs (information aimed at building her Adult) were, at times, interpreted by her as threatening to her Child; over time, however, they provided a basis for her to update her assessments about herself and objective reality so that she could recover.

On this she subsequently wrote, "Adult logic was misread as persecution by my contaminated Parent-Child team, since health-promoting information threatened the system. The new data indicated that old beliefs were incorrect, inappropriate, and even harmful. It was like having your belief system pulled out from under you."

From this it became apparent that loved ones need to consistently address the Adult in the anorexic (or bulimic), and avoid Critical-Parent–Child standoffs, in order to foster the cohealing process.

CHAPTER 12

Expanding Food Choices

Historically, our diets consisted of natural foods. Our nomadic ancestors ate what was available and, if they were lucky, what they liked. With the move from an agrarian society to an industrialized one of giant food conglomerates, we have entered an era of highly processed, mass-produced convenience foods.

In recent years there's been widespread concern about the safety and nutritional value of what we ingest. Publications have been fanning anxiety with such statements as . . . "the lunch you eat today may help cause a disease that kills you 20 years from now,"[1] made in an exercise and diet article entitled "The Risks of Eating." The author goes on to say . . . "the food industry has created . . . supermarkets dominated by foods which are both nutritionally inferior and, in the long run, harmful to health."[2]

While Jacqueline was working to overcome her fears of eating, we came across numerous articles that stressed the presence of hidden dangers in the food we eat. Fear was being fostered by announcements such as . . . "the American diet is a prime contributor to serious health problems," in the *Nutrition Action Newsletter*.[3] This source speaks of the "national outrage" of the food industry's foisting on the public, "over-salted, over-sugared, over-processed junk," and concludes that we must battle "the very real menace of today's confusing 'supermarket jungle.'"[4]

"Health" Foods

After her self-starvation phase, Jacqueline's fear of calories had become complicated by her exaggerated response to such food warnings. At the time she arrived at the renovation project to visit me, she believed that most supermarket and restaurant foods were unhealthy, and limited herself accordingly.

She avoided foods in metal, plastic, paper, or other types of "unnatural" containers, believing the packaging substances would contaminate the food. She was afraid to eat anything frozen, dehydrated, canned, pickled, spiced, or dried, and this list went on. Her grocery shopping was based not on price or on a balanced diet, but on how safe she imagined foods to be, and she considered few of them safe enough to eat.

So that she could assess these fears realistically, we collected a large pile of articles denouncing particular foods as harmful. Comparing these articles, Jacque found over and over again that they contradicted one another. What one considered beneficial, another considered objectionable. The only points of agreement among them seemed to be to eat a varied diet that was nutritionally adequate, while reducing cholesterol, sugar, and saturated fats as well as sodium, and increasing fiber and complex carbohydrates.

At the time, I had returned home and Jacque was living with her stepfather and me, working to improve her financial situation. To circumvent her fear of supermarkets, she and I began shopping at the small local cooperative grocery store and eating lunch, almost daily, at one of the pocket-sized eateries that served "natural" foods. Jacque felt safe eating at these establishments because, in effect, she was entrusting them to make healthy choices for her.

At the grocery co-op, Jacqueline selected an expanding variety of foods: tofu, tamari, agar-agar, bamboo shoots, water chestnuts, mung beans — foods for which she had no long-established phobias. Her new eating patterns included many vegetarian dishes plus some of Oriental and Mexican origins. New flavors, textures, and aromas from foods she'd never considered taboo helped reduce her anxiety about eating.

She began turning her gourmet talents (expressed previously in fabulous pastries) to experimenting with "health food" recipes. On this, she remembers, "I soon realized that I was hearing my Adult suggesting rational alternatives to my Controlling Parent's insistence, 'You can't digest that.' I could recognize my Free Child expressing, 'I'm hungry,' and my Nurturing Parent responding, 'Then you need nourishment,' supported by my Adult, suggesting foods I could select."

Certain foods held more "trauma" for her than others. "I remember the idea of eating fat had seemed absurd, and since meat has a good deal of fat, I'd avoided it. It had made much more sense to digest a carrot since it didn't have a layer of fat around it. Because of this it was an ordeal learning to eat red meat again — calories, fat, gristle, hormones, dead flesh — so many rules and so much fear to overcome. Eventually I did learn to savor meats again, though the change was gradual, beginning with small amounts of lean cuts."

I seldom commented on Jacque's food choices, but from time to time ate meals she'd prepared and complimented her experimentation with health-food recipes, interesting exotic foods, and menu planning, so she'd know I was aware of her progress in digesting a wider variety of foods (though she continued to restrict her calorie intake so as to retain her thin figure).

For both Brenda and Jacqueline, an interim period of emphasis on "health foods" and foreign foods proved a practical way to dissipate encumbering mental food rules and rituals. New habits and beliefs were established. For example, since canned goods, frozen foods, and dehydrated products that Jacque had formerly considered unsafe were among her purchases from the co-op, in time these became acceptable when purchased at supermarkets and restaurants.

Progress came in many small steps such as the first week that she digested breakfast every morning. It showed in the first day in more than four-and-a-half years that she ate three meals and digested them all. It was also apparent in the first time she was again able to eat a sweet dessert and feel comfortable keeping it down.

For some, however, the health-food scene becomes a trap in itself, because all sorts of new phobias and taboos regarding food are established. Therefore a judgment must be made as to whether existing eating patterns are promoting health or disease.

There are no simple solutions to overcoming food phobias — no easy answers that will work for everyone. A wide variety of methods have been tried by physicians and therapists in treating anorexics and bulimics. There's considerable controversy as to what techniques work best. The essence of the problem is how to maintain a comfortable attitude toward eating while consuming a nourishing diet in response to the body's needs.

Body Fat

During the starvation stage of her illness, Jacque had equated any fat on her body with being fat, insisting that fat was useless. Since body fat was what dieters tried to shed, then its absence was the objective, was it not? Back then, she would pinch the skin on her thighs and abdomen to test the thickness of the fatty layer beneath her skin, always being disappointed that it was thicker than she felt it should be.

Jacqueline had been trying to maintain an adolescently thin body, pretty much free of the curves that come with maturation. Like other anorexics and some bulimics, she had reverted to a preadolescent state in which child-bearing wasn't possible. (A minimum amount of stored fat is directly related to ovulation.)

She had continued to think of fat as her enemy, so I suggested we take a look at some material I'd located on the need for fat in the human body. By now, she was evidently ready to consider this, and based on this reading, she came around to accepting that fat provides us with stored energy and is essential insulation for the maintenance of body temperature, besides cushioning and protecting body organs and other tissues.

By looking at a chart for *"minimal weight for particular height necessary for the onset or restoration of menstrual cycles,"*[5] Jacque discovered that she would need to weigh a minimum of 120 to 122 pounds in order to achieve the equivalent of 22 percent body-fat–to–body-weight ratio necessary to restore menstruation. This was a revelation to Jacqueline and was one of the factors that contributed to her eventually returning to an appropriate weight.

Based on the same weight-height chart, we checked out some of the vital statistics Brenda had collected on well-known fashion models and movie actresses. We found a number of these symbols of sensuality and femininity were *substantially below* listed weights in the chart.

Jacque was amazed to learn that though prior to adolescence, girls have only slightly more fat than boys (10 to 15 percent), when they reach maturity, "they have *twice as much* fat as boys."[6] She also noticed that because fat weighs less (per equal volume), than lean tissue, if a woman gains the *same amount* as a man, she will most likely look as though she has put on *more* weight.[7] It may not have seemed fair to her in this age that idolizes leanness, but reality was setting in.

Little by little, Jacque was slowly accepting the idea that her concern about being fat was unreasonable, and that concentrating on being afraid of weight gain had become more comfortable to her than facing her more basic fears of coping with life in general — particularly making it in the world on her own.

CHAPTER 13

New Awareness — New Choices

I remember that early in recovery, Jacqueline dreamed that she was walking through a thick, dark forest and couldn't find her way. The next morning, when she was telling me about the dream, I could see how frightening and ominous it had been and how lost she'd felt. The atmosphere, she said, was of dreary dankness, with no light, no direction, no hope of anything better. She remarked, "I wandered around, trying to find my way out, but no matter which direction I took, everything still looked the same. I was trapped and couldn't escape." I could associate with her feelings in that dream, because the same metaphor had occurred to me. I sometimes felt as though we were in an unfamiliar wilderness and were trying to find our way through it. Yet, in spite of the stresses and changes in my own life, as well as the problems the girls were having, I thought somehow we would make it to the other side.

During "year five" of her struggle with bulimia, Jacque was still purging. Nothing had freed her from this habit. Because of this, I tried to become more aware of social as well as ongoing family influences that might be related to her having become ill — particularly ones she continued to face every day.

With this motivation, while on my out-of-state trips to work on renovating my parent's property, I took advantage of being in a large metropolitan area. There I was able to locate some excellent, short "interactive courses" on parent-child relationships, body-image and health, power and success, and male-female relationships as well as anorexia and bulimia. In these sessions I was able to ask questions and get responses that I found helpful, along with an abundance of material for the girls and me to consider.

"Body Hate"

When Jacque and I discussed the current epidemic of eating and weight phobias women are experiencing, we were frequently reminded that a sign of our times is how critical most women are of their bodies. We're perpetually wishing our shape was somehow different — either reduced, or firmer, or something else, believing *it's never all right as it is.*

Many young females "react to their bodies as if they were at best alien territory, at worst enemy land, often treating their bodies as *unacceptable objects that have to be manipulated, starved, disguised to become more acceptable* to others in an attempt to make this body conform more closely to the painfully narrow stereotypes of female beauty in our culture,"[1] according to *The American Journal of Psychoanalysis*. It emphasizes that "most young females want their bodies to be smaller, *miniaturized*, with the possible exception of the breasts."[2] This type of information helped us see how the girls' experiences related to the overall culture.

Jacque had certainly felt unacceptable, had starved herself, had tried to disguise her "unacceptable" body with a girdle and by other means, and attempted to miniaturize herself, all in an attempt to be beautiful. Apparently she had lots of company in these attitudes and efforts, a thought, she said, that was comforting.

We knew that such disgust with the *body* carries over into lack of acceptance of the *total self*. Clearly, self-love is weakened by such negativity. It was disturbing to realize that so many young females think, "You'd better be thinner, or you won't fit in."

In our society, what is considered beautiful in women is undeniably limited. While watching television, Jacque and I couldn't help noticing far greater latitude in what we find acceptable in men's appearance (including showing their age). In some of our reading, we noticed that *unlike women,* men tend to give themselves the benefit of the doubt regarding their weight, generally considering themselves to be lighter and thinner than they actually are. We knew that the desire of young females to diet and "slim (down) contrasts with the prevalent male lack of concern with his shape or else his wish to be bigger and stronger."[3]

Both Brenda and Jacque keyed in on the fact there is no contradiction between what is regarded as an attractive male physique and what is healthy. Both eventually decided that it is not the masses who are out of step but rather the young female models and actresses who are unusual in their slight builds.

On the subject of self-disparagement, psychologist Marsha Hutchinson, who studies women's attitudes about their bodies, pointed out that there is currently "an epidemic of self-hatred, an incessant 'inner jabber' of women telling themselves 'I'm disgusting, I'm fat, I'm grotesque.'"[4]

She states that these "voices of self-hatred reverberating in their own heads," dwell on cruel and "savage self-criticisms for the parts of their bodies that are the most feminine; breasts, hips, and thighs."[5] Since women generally judge their bodies critically and consider their most feminine parts ugly and unacceptable, we questioned, "What is our basic unacceptability? Is it really not our bodies but instead our move, in recent decades, toward greater equality of the genders that we fear is still unacceptable?"

I was struck by Hutchinsons' statement that today's females are psychological cripples "hobbling around in bodies they detest."[6] According to this source, the "majority of women in America come close to that level of pathology" found in bulimia and anorexia.[7]

Since Jacque was still so self-conscious about her weight, it was reassuring to her when I happened on the statistic that nearly nine out of ten women in this country are trying to lose weight or at least not gain.[8] Again she found she had lots of company in her concerns.

Diet Advertisements

Because dieting, weight loss, and being thin had absorbed so much of Jacqueline's attention, at one point I started collecting all sorts of diet ads and soon had a pile of them on an end table. (I wished I'd done this years before!)

I remember one evening, after a quiet dinner of steamed veggies, I spread these ads out on the living room floor. Many of them were full page and in color, with bold headlines. Looking at the ads objectively and in quantity, the pressures toward "bulimic thinking" were obvious. Jacque and I sat cross-legged on the floor together as she began commenting on their absurdity.

Sketches of women showed them becoming progressively more slender until they were smiling bean poles *mysteriously taller and decades younger*. In the magic of advertising, the diet product had not only removed flesh but had also increased height and reduced age! Women were shown in all sorts of childlike or peculiar positions, such as crawling on all fours or gleefully hugging the balance mechanism on a physician's scale.

One caption, which read "Eat All You Want and Lose Weight,"[9] Jacque quickly pegged as *typical bulimic reasoning.*

In diet ads, simple elimination of fat was the way to a happier life and improved self-esteem. "You must have a healthy slim, shapely figure to attract the most satisfying love and romance with the opposite sex. (Remember, fat girls finish last!)"[10] according to a diet product ad. Typical headlines included "Are You Too Fat to Love?,"[11] "The Ultimate Cure For Fat,"[12] and "Lifetime Freedom From Fat."[13]

There were tablets that supposedly "Can Make You Skinny in 45 Days."[14] Diet products and services were pitching the idea that we could lose weight rapidly without abstinence (just like the bulimic).

Judging from diet advertisements, no one would ever guess that body fat is essential to life! For the first time, we both noticed that most diet ads don't tell us to lose weight if we're stout; they simply tell us to *lose* no matter what weight we are!

Jacque was still living with us at the time, so for several weeks, each time she and I were at the grocery checkout stand, we paid attention to the headline captions on tabloids touting quick weight-loss plans *aimed at women.*

Women's magazines on the rack by the checker also headlined powerful unrelenting messages that female bodies need to be reduced. Here we were, buying a cart full of food while reading the usual media blurbs that our bodies are too large and need to be reduced. The candy racks were directly opposite these weight-loss headlines! It was obvious why guilt about eating a simple meal is so easy to come by.

With our examining pressures on females to diet, it became apparent that we're deluged with messages that full female figures are undesirable, a sign of self-indulgence, a lack of personal pride and self-control. "Hulky" football players can have big bellies and be admired, but not females in *any* occupation.

Somewhere along the line, we decided that the real issue is not whether women should be thinner or fatter. The core of the problem was how they can lead satisfying lives and become full partners in the scheme of things. (It struck me that much of the time and energy women direct toward altering their bodies, could be better spent on altering *society* to make it more conducive to everyone's overall well-being.)

Male-Female Calorie Differential

About this time, during one of my visits with my son Roger at his fraternity, he had offhandedly commented on having enjoyed seven fresh-baked cinnamon rolls for breakfast that morning. When I'd asked whether he was worried about weight gain, he'd replied, "No, just concerned about not being late to my first class." It was obvious he lived in a different world from his sister Jacqueline, who still considered even one cinnamon roll far too caloric to digest.

We were well aware that, because men have greater muscle mass and are often bigger, they burn more calories and can consume more without gaining weight. For instance, in some checking we did on this, we found that the average male can eat about 2,800 calories a day, to a female's 2,000, in the 23 to 34 age group.[15] That is, men can consume 800 more calories than women without weight gain, unless these women alternately diet, exercise more vigorously, or resort to purging. Jacque's rueful comment was, "At 140 calories per chocolate covered doughnut, that's more than *five* a day! More and more men are weight conscious and counting calories, but they sure have an advantage."

Obsessive Role Models

Actresses and models are held out to us as examples for our own lives. With this in mind, during one of our get-togethers, Brenda shared a collection of magazine articles she'd saved in which actresses and models had been interviewed regarding how they stay so thin. She selected a typical story about a television personality and read it aloud.

This woman was quoted as saying she eats no breakfast but allows herself a few dried apricots and walnuts before lunch, half an avocado with lemon juice at noon, and a dinner consisting of the remaining half avocado, some fish or lean meat plus fruit and a salad. She indulges in a glass of water flavored with lemon and a half teaspoon of honey before bed. Along with this meager diet regimen, she disclosed that to maintain her slight build she runs 14 miles a week plus doing strenuous daily exercises.

I remember Brenda's comment. "There's so much of this type of stuff in the media. We're continually being invited to copy these stars and become as obsessive as they are." We were benefiting by the give and take of each other's exploration and new insights, and having fun in the process.

Magazine Comparisons

One time when Jacqueline and I were out shopping together, we spent some time browsing through a massive magazine rack. We ended up picking out 20 magazines, half of them women's, half men's, which I bought so we could study them later at our leisure. Over succeeding days, as we compared them, we were struck by how remarkably different they were! Jacque noticed, for instance, that even though men make up half the wedding pair, there are no magazines or articles for grooms, only for brides.

Men's general interest and hobby sections of the magazine rack had included issues about electronics, mechanics, fishing, audio equipment, cars and trucks, sports of all kinds, science, boating, stereos, and other topics related to equipment and self-entertainment. The latter category included several "girlie" magazines in which female nudity and sexuality were featured, but this was the nearest any of the men's magazines came to dealing with relationships with women.

Women's sections had dealt with beauty, brides, style and dieting, cooking, glamour, hairdos, home care, and there were a surprising number of movie and daytime television monthlies and "sensationalist" romantic-confession–type publications. It was apparent that our media directs its marketing to men and women in entirely different ways. At the time, Jacqueline wrote, "The emphasis in women's publications is clearly based on *self-improvement and handling relationships with men. In fact, everywhere we look, billboards, television, books, magazines, and newspapers are consistently telling females how to be pleasing to men while telling men how to please themselves.*"

In many of the women's magazines, slim fashions and diet articles alternated with rich gourmet recipes, entertainment menus, and luscious full-color food advertisements. Successful meal preparation and gourmet cooking were ways to "win and hold" a man, as was having a thin, firm body. A typical woman's magazine headline was "'How I Stay Slim,' Eight wafer-thin women tell the secrets of their success,"[16] a perspective which *equates thinness with success.*

Indulge-But-Be-Thin

For the first time, I really paid attention to the many double-bind (conflicting) messages in most women's magazines, which say, in effect, "indulge-gloriously-but-be-thin!" (See: Reclaiming

Our Rights — Our Right to Good Health.) After counting, I mentioned to Jacque that one of the women's fashion issues featuring *pencil slim* spring styles, had more than 34 ads for food, plus articles on gourmet cooking and a "special" titled "A Grand Tour of Spectacular Desserts."[17]

The pressures were clear. As females, we were expected to cook and enjoy fabulous meals but be fashionably *wafer-thin* at the same time. Women, as the main food purchasers and preparers, are caught in the cross fire between sophisticated motivational researchers coaxing them into craving food products and other professional marketing experts striving to lure them into buying diet products and thin fashions. The media reflects this conflict, constantly intermingling diet ads and skinny high-fashion models, with ads for all manner of food products and scrumptious recipes.

Caress-your-taste-buds-but-be-skinny messages, so common in women's publications, were completely absent in men's. Men weren't being hounded by *crazy contradictions* typified by a thin model in an advertisement for a highly caloric food product. They weren't challenged, page after page, to be gourmet cooks but also try the newest weight-loss diet schemes in order to wear the slender styles also being shown in the same magazines.

Purchase food! Prepare it! Serve it! Relish it! If at the same time we're being told to diet, trim down, lose fat, and wear thin fashions, *a way to "survive" the conflict is by becoming bulimic.* Then it's possible to indulge gloriously and (by purging) remain thin at the same time. It seemed to us that paradoxically, under our economic system, *the bulimic has become the perfect consumer.*

Negating Messages Abound

We all live under the shadow of the mass communications network that now has a pervasive impact on our lives. It *reflects* our current values and opinions and also *creates* trends. For women, many of the messages are highly contradictory as well as detrimental.

We found that the extent to which women are talked down to in the media and elsewhere was difficult for us to assess because we are so *used* to it. Some examples, however, were blatant, like an article in a popular women's magazine I shared with the girls when they both happened to be at home. It was headlined "Up and Out of the House in 45 Minutes Flat."

It detailed how to get "to work on time looking (and feeling) all-pulled together."[18] Assuming we couldn't manage this on our own, in step-by-step photos covering four pages, a blond model shows us: how to sit up in bed when the alarm goes off, wash our face (with a reminder to brush our teeth), stand on the scale and weigh ourself, towel dry after showering, dry our hair, do some stretching exercises, boil water for coffee (only one cup to save time), and takes us through how to pull on our clothes and leave for work on time, confident that we look "sensational."

Similar material is insultingly common. In a book for preschoolers, an essay on how to get up in the morning might make sense, but for adults, it's absurd. As you can imagine, a lively discussion developed around this one. We couldn't imagine this story line in a magazine for men. What editor would write such offensive material for a male audience, since men's competency in such basics is taken for granted?

Jacque did her own "reviews" of magazines and newspapers plus some movies, but her disenchantment was greatest with certain women's magazines because she had looked to them as gospel for so long. As this uncritical acceptance gave way to a more analytical attitude, she kept coming back to the theme we found in many of them — self-improvement: here's how you can improve yourself. Here's how to have just-right glossy lips, painted eyes, lacquered fingernails, bouncy hair, body perfume, silken skin, stylish clothing — so that you can be more attractive. This presumes we're not okay as we are but need all sorts of products, effort, and expense to make us appealing. The underlying message was that we should spend considerable time and expense, suffer discomfort, and even have surgery, to appear sensual and sexually appealing to men, again underscoring our need to alter ourselves to match an "ideal."

Add-Fat, Lose-Fat

Jacque had been overly suggestible to self-improvement pitches for a long time, but this was changing. Now she saw that these "shortcomings" had only been marketing schemes to sell products having little or nothing to do with health, practicality, or even aesthetics.

We had particularly noticed ads in the back of some women's magazines for products to build firmer, larger bust lines. Here advertisers were letting us know that *cleavage* is essential to feminine beauty and self-worth. We read, "The size and shape of the female breasts have a great psychosexual significance. In our society, breasts have become not only sexual objects but a yard-stick used in the *evaluation* of a woman."[19]

As if we don't have enough to worry about with pressures to diet while being gourmet cooks, we're also supposed to have an "ample" bust line. Instant transformations were being promoted — like a product headlined *"instant inches on the bust line,"*[20] which claimed to *increase* the bust by four inches in less than a week! Turning several pages, another product was being pitched to *decrease* our body from a size 12 down to size 9, "all in one day without dieting."[21] We noticed that enlarged fat cells needed to be created, according to bust development ads. In contrast, "large fat cell chambers" needed to be *dissolved*,[22] according to anti-cellulite and size-reduction promotions. The paradox was that there must be women buying products, hoping to increase "fat globules" in their breasts, while at the same time buying other products, hoping to rid themselves of cellulite and other fatty tissue "problems."

It registered that these add-fat/lose-fat messages, though op-posing, were actually saying the same thing. They are showing us how to fit the cultural *Cinderella slipper*. "You need to be skinny and have a full bust and cook satisfying meals so you too can wear the 'princess slipper.'"

Makeovers were definitely the big thing in many women's mag-azines, an approach that stresses the need for a revamped self, generally through the correction of *"defects"* or hiding of *"flaws."* Again, this was reinforcing personal dissatisfaction.

For us, the dangerous extent of this dissatisfaction was high-lighted in newspaper advertisements by surgeons whose practices were devoted solely to "instant body sculpting." These commonly feature young, overly thin women, suggesting surgical fat removal and contouring of face, midriff, stomach, hips, buttocks, thighs, and knees, plus augmentation of breasts. (If you can't diet it off, *cut* it off!) The number of these ads has expanded alarmingly, making it all the more obvious that products and services aimed at a largely female market, often have little or nothing to do with what's *healthy or even safe*.

How are we to deal with the reality that no matter what part of our body comes under scrutiny, it never matches the perfection held before us as the goal? By putting women's publications under a magnifying glass, Jacque gradually took a more critical attitude, noting that, "The carefully air-brushed and retouched perfection of models in magazines is unreal and unattainable. No one really *looks* like that in person."

A magazine rack I happened by recently had a shelf with *Gourmet — the Magazine of Good Living* next to two successive issues of *Bon Appétit* along with *Bon Appétit — Barbecue!* Sandwiched in between these and *Chocolatier — A Taste of the Good Life* was the *Weight Watchers Magazine.* Ironic, isn't it? Eat and diet. And on the shelf just above these stood five swimsuit magazines (*Swimsuit, Bikini, Swimsuit Posters, Swimwear U.S.A., Swimwear Illustrated*), each featuring skinny young females. On the shelves below were several magazines for men, including *Male, For Him, Esquire, M — The Civilized Man.* As one might expect, none of *them* featured almost naked male bodies.

Jacqueline had become keenly aware that many media messages are detrimental and not to be taken to heart. She knew too that many of the models have had breast implants and other surgery to achieve their unnatural physique. Along with this, she'd come to recognize that as long as we, the buying public, continue to purchase products and services that diminish our well-being, we make it profitable for advertisers to continue in their current vein.

Overcoming Perfectionism

Though we're deluged with messages that foster female desire to be thinner than they currently are, fortunately in recent years a new genre of women's magazines is appearing on the market. These magazines are more sophisticated in terms of gender stereotypes and invite intelligent women to feel better about themselves than the standard media do.

Some editors have been making an effort to inform their readers about eating addictions. They have regularly carried informative articles about anorexia, bulimia, and related issues. Additionally, many of them feature articles specifically aimed at promoting self-esteem, personal satisfaction, and general well-being. Jacqueline began paying attention to this positive input, reading with interest articles on such topics as "Nobody's Perfect — So Start Enjoying Who You Are, Warts and All";[23] "Wasting Away: Why You Can Be Too Thin";[24] "The Most Important Love Affair of Your Life — With Yourself! How Are You Handling It?"[25]

It's regrettable that while editors and writers have attempted to be more helpful in feature stories in recent years, advertisers, in their quest for financial security, have not kept up with this conceptual advance.

Perfectionism is a common problem among anorexics and bulimics, and we had noticed that the media continually carry suggestions about what women *should* do to be more perfect. Certainly men's publications were not into detailing what was wrong with their readers' facial features or into severing the male body into small segments as women's magazines regularly did, showing close-ups of waists, lips, eyelashes, thighs, hands, and other parts, focusing on how we were to perfect each of them.

Jacque had wanted the "perfect body." After recognizing that preferences in body styles are inconsistent and transient, she no longer held that as her goal. How could there be any "perfect" shape? Being perfect would assume having total control, yet her addictive behavior was clearly out of control — another incongruity that helped her put perfectionism into clearer perspective.

In the past, Jacque had considered that being perfect meant having no flaws, no hidden imperfections. She felt this would bring satisfaction and confidence. However, even at times when a dozen fashion models, a well-known movie photographer, and others had admired her, saying she had a perfect body for modeling (such as during an extended vacation she'd made to Los Angeles a few months before), she still felt dissatisfied.

Perfectionism, Jacque concluded, "means setting impossible standards for yourself and then feeling angry and self-critical for not reaching them." Because this drive had fueled her agonizing struggle for thinness, she now perceived that the goal itself was imperfect.

On one occasion when Jacque and I were each trying on clothes at a department store and analyzing our figures in the large mirrors, we were sharing our mental pictures of how we pictured our perfect self. We were talking about specific things we'd like to change about our bodies, when we jointly concluded that since *perfect* refers to something that's *whole and complete* (with all of its parts), then as whole human beings, by our very nature we must in some sense be perfect! We repeatedly told each other, "You look fine to me," which I think also probably helped us be more gentle with ourselves.

Television's Thought Environment

During childhood, Jacque had been an avid TV viewer, and she continued to watch several hours a week. Research conducted during the years when Jacque had been a teenager revealed that television commercials seldom indicated women were moving into the business world or that they were "capable of performing responsible tasks other than those associated with the family and home."[26]

It's been estimated that children each watch about 22,000 television commercials every year.[27] Reviewing the period when our daughters were forming their world view, we can see the impact these messages had on their psyches. A study written during Jacque's teen years reports that television portrayed males in prime-time viewing as "more mature, more serious . . . than females" and that leading men "are more powerful, smart, rational, tall and stable"[28] than women.

We figure Jacque, like the average young person in this country, had watched approximately 15,000 hours of television by high school graduation, as opposed to 11,000 or so spent in school. It's estimated that 45 percent of all households have their TV tuned in during their dinner hour.[29] Thus our daughters eat the main meal of the day while being exposed to a medium that, despite advances in recent years, still associates female attractiveness with slenderness and sensuality with youthfulness.

Jacque put together a checklist for judging TV programming according to those elements that seemed relevant to bulimia. On a pad of paper kept near the set, she'd analyze shows by asking herself: were female characters central to the plot? Were they self-sufficient or dependent? Did they possess a level of knowledge and skill equal to that of male characters, or was their intelligence and competence largely ignored or downgraded? Were the female characters assertive? Rational? Courageous? Powerful? Silly? Bitchy? Helpless? Flirtatious? Were they *slender?*

Looking at commercials, she noted that there was still the usual authoritative male voice-over instructing thin females in domestic chores including buying and preparing food. After several weeks of analyzing the programs she regularly watched, Jacque's former sponge-like absorption gave way to awareness of the brain-washing effect these media messages produced.

The 1980's brought a new and significant trend toward showing more females in contemporary roles. With this, we gradually became accustomed to females being newscasters and sports announcers on prime time, as well as portraying strong, successful characters, many of whom work outside the home. These new messages were particularly noticeable when contrasted with TV reruns of old movies having stereotypical gender roles.

But just how far have we actually come in "upgrading" the presentation of women on television? Now that we've entered the nineties, the last decade of the twentieth century, TV continues to cast "women as inferiors, harpies, and obstacles to male domination,"[30] as television critic John Carman has noted.

Recently he pointed out in his newspaper column that in prime time, the traditional male "holds sway in TV," routinely sending messages "that establish, confirm, and reinforce standards of gender roles. It's not surprising that they'd reflect the make up of the people (usually male) who create, write, produce and schedule the shows that reach the air."[31] Along this line he commented that typical programing portrays wives in family sit-coms as being "a threat . . . to male autonomy."[32]

Another television critic, Joyce Millman, calls attention to the fact few new sitcoms feature women but instead, feature "male-headed single-parent families."[33] Almost exclusively, in current TV series, women are shown in the roles of "wives, mothers, and daughters," even when they're portraying "single working mothers,"[34] Millman reports.

She notes "another disturbing trend," that of "the widespread use of female authority figures as TV's new bad guys" who are "exaggeratedly domineering."[35] Women are being portrayed in prime-time television series as "sour, suffocating, sexually repressed" — and so flagrant is this recent sexist stereotyping that Millman speaks of it as a depressing "backlash against strong and successful women" and of a new mood of "woman-bashing" in the media.[36]

It's troubling that despite some previous advances, some recent shows fall back on the presumption of women as inferior and an impediment to masculine endeavors, a view that continues to be presented as though this were a mirror of life as it actually is.

Magazines, movies, television, billboards, newspapers — stimulate body dissatisfaction and a mindset that are related to female eating disorders. With this media backdrop to our lives — and the value system on which it is based — it's little wonder that informal survey results indicate that as many as three out of four women in this country consider themselves *"positively ugly."*[37] Since self-presentation is important to most women, think how this affects their confidence and the choices they make in other areas of their lives.

Compulsive Exercise

During the early stages of her recovery, Jacque had exercised obsessively on a daily basis with runs of seven miles or more through the hills, 500 sit ups plus 500 repeats of various other exercises, along with vigorous jazzercise routines. So, at some point we began paying some attention to, and reading about, how women in our society relate to exercise.

We found that for a great many women, the guilt and remorse of food "overindulgences" touch off bursts of rigorous exercise. As in Jacqueline's case at that time, worry about weight and supposedly ugly body parts leads to compulsive exercise. We read about "aerobic nervosa" and the "exercise bulimic" (referring to individuals who binge and then overdo exercise to work off unwanted calories). Unlike vomiting, which often brings feelings of disgust and shame, workouts burn calories and restore a sense of relief and virtue. But overexercising can become a life-distorting obsession that can do physical harm.

Some anorexics who engage in exhausting physical exercise report getting a high from their exertion, though it can seem amazing that anyone so scrawny has so much energy. Gymnasts and others who must maintain an artificially lean build, including those who compete in athletic events with weight categories, are particularly vulnerable to bulimia. I recall the gymnast who reported that she and her teammates celebrated victories with high-calorie treats after which they'd all adjourn to the rest room to take turns vomiting.

Females can reduce their body fat through exercise to the point that they become amenorrheic — their menstruation is suppressed (this is particularly true of marathon runners). Women who overexercise also risk loss of bone minerals, a condition called osteoporosis, in which bones become less dense.[38] This, we discovered, can even happen with excessive "jazzercize."

As Jacque tried to understand her own feelings toward working out, she began to see that there is no clearly defined line between exercise that is *beneficial* versus that related to unresolved conflicts. It comes down to the matter of the motivations behind the exercise and how it's carried out.

For Jacque, exercise proved beneficial because she could eat more without feeling guilty and overall felt healthier physically and mentally. In time, as she felt better about herself, she became less compulsive about her exercise. Eventually she developed a well-rounded, moderate exercise routine based on the logic that being healthily *"in shape" included all aspects of physical well-being*. It included cardiovascular and respiratory endurance, flexibility, strength, and appropriate body composition.

I mentioned to Jacque that how much we weigh and how fat distributes itself on our bodies is determined in large part *by our genes*,[39] adding that exercise and diet can *modify* our genetic makeup, but we all have tendencies to certain contours based on our ancestry. When she had accepted having regained some curviness, it was an indication that she realized nature *intended* this rather than feeling it was due to "lack of will power" on her part.

Throughout this five-year period, we were essentially looking for insights that might promote recovery. Instead of getting hung up on thinking, "Why can't you just get well?" I held onto the perspective that we were only one household among countless others struggling with life-distorting eating problems. There had to be background social and familial causes, and if we could get to the heart of some of them, we might find answers. I never gave up hope, repeatedly visualizing to myself that, like Brenda, Jacqueline would be among those with a successful outcome.

During this period, Jacqueline worked on developing new ways of dealing with irrational social situations that were gender related. For instance, she could make better choices when she asked herself such things as: "What am I feeling? Why am I reacting this way? Am I acting or just reacting? What would serve my own highest good? How would I like this to turn out? What's the most effective way to deal with this?" Such thinking placed the emphasis on *increased awareness* and *self-responsibility*, important steps toward recovery.

Counseling Again

For four months Jacque met with a counselor named Denise who invited her to discuss her goals and fears. When she asked Denise why she felt fearful in certain situations, the therapist would respond, "That's a good question. Why do you think that's so?" Jacque said she never gave advice, instead working on helping Jacque figure things out for herself. This seemed to help her examine her options and act more assertively.

She enjoyed Denise but expressed frustration because she refused to provide any assistance on how to reduce her food phobias and other bulimic symptoms. Writing of her reactions to this she subsequently noted, "In a way this made me feel secure because I didn't have to disclose that secret part of me. Yet somehow, it made me feel weird. I had been in therapy to recover, but my counselor refused to deal with any of my food-related problems and she wouldn't tell me why."

Perhaps Denise reasoned that since Jacque still clung to bulimic behaviors, discussion of them would be premature. In any case, when Jacque left this counseling she mentioned that "I seem normal to others, but on the inside I still have the same old crazies running around in my head."

A year or so later, Jacque located a psychiatrist who'd had several anorexic patients and began weekly sessions with him. She said he was puzzled about her craving for sweets and thought it strange she showed up at his office on her own. "Anorexics and bulimics don't want to get cured. Why are you here?" he'd asked her.

He listened at length to her problems but had made no suggestions for dealing with them, instead responding, "How can we get you to love and feel good about yourself?" She told him she didn't know the answer and guessed that must be why she was there.

Eventually she became distressed over her lack of progress and discouraged that fully a quarter of her income went each week for an hour's therapy. This psychiatrist had told her that he anticipated she would need a minimum of three years counseling, probably four, on a weekly basis and admitted that he didn't really know if he would be able to help her. Although his honesty was admirable, Jacque didn't want to invest her hard-earned wages on four years of uncertainty as to whether she'd feel better or not. In time she decided she was wasting her money and quit seeing him.

After approximately five years of struggling with eating problems, Jacque eventually decided to visit a counselor who Brenda had seen a few times. Brenda had found him to be practical, insightful, and most important of all, helpful. Over a period of a couple of months, Jacqueline went to a dozen or so counseling sessions with him, most of which dealt with family background. Unlike the other therapists she'd visited, this one was able to help her gain insights into why her life had taken the twists and turns of the previous years.

"Don't Be — You"

The following is Jacqueline's description of this counseling:

"To the therapist's question about early childhood with my natural father, I found myself explaining, 'I felt I was a disappointment and that he didn't want another daughter. I remember his singling me out for teasing, purposely speaking to me in a foreign language I couldn't understand to frustrate me. When I'd break into tears, he'd laugh. He did things to purposely upset other family members too, and seemed to get some sort of perverse satisfaction from this. I've wondered many times whether this was related to his having been violently physically abused when he was a child.'

"The counselor simply listened, without comment.

"'It's confusing to remember the visits after my parents' divorce and the sense of emptiness in his words. It was always my sisters who rode with him in the front seat of his car and I who rode alone in the back. I would trail along behind as the three of them walked abreast on the sidewalk. My sisters received expensive mementos of visits with him while I would get only token gifts. I couldn't understand his favoritism. Why wasn't I as deserving as my sisters?'

"'Through non-verbal cues, a daughter may sense the disappointment of a parent who wanted a boy,' the counselor remarked. 'A parent seldom states openly, "I wish you weren't a girl," but the child translates nonverbal impressions into injunctions which are don'ts: "don't be female, don't be you, don't think, don't grow up." The opposite of injunctions are permissions, like "be assertive, be *competent* — be you."'

"I told the counselor that I remembered my father wanting superior children. I was afraid of being ordinary and of going through the process of being female. If I stayed malnourished I wouldn't have to face being an old wrinkled woman, because I'd die first.

"To this distressing memory the counselor responded, '"Don't *be*" is the ultimate rejection. Slowly disappearing through anorexia was a way of complying with your father's injunctions.'

"'In elementary school I began believing I wasn't smart or good enough. When I got eye glasses in fourth grade, my father told me I couldn't be beautiful with glasses and that I shouldn't wear them if I wanted to be pretty. However, I couldn't see without them. I became convinced that I was ugly, and all through school never got over feeling stupid and ugly, even later when I got good grades and contact lenses. I felt my high marks must have been due to luck, easy classes, or teachers who liked me. I dreamed of becoming beautiful and smart when I grew up, and convinced myself that someday I'd prove to everyone how terrific I really was.'

"'You decided that you were not good enough, and in order to survive you needed to be what?' the counselor asked.

"'Beautiful! I had to become beautiful.'

"Patiently he explained, 'A person's primal script comes from the interrelationship between parent and child, and the most potent shaper of children is the parent of the *opposite sex*.'

"Looking back, I can see how much I wanted protection and compassion from my natural father. Instead, I was left dangling, feeling inferior and useless as his daughter.

"After I explained this, the counselor commented: 'Those feelings are fuel for, "I'll show you." There are four steps in a counter-script: the *driver* (which is "be perfect"), the *stopper* (which stops basic needs from being met), the *vengeance* (wanting to *show* somebody), and the *payoff* (which, in the case of anorexia, is despair). The person cycles through these four stages. You were trying to be the perfect female.'

"'Some of my fondest memories are of the period after my mother and natural father divorced. Then my mother returned with us to live with her parents in their large English Tudor home with spacious rooms, fireplaces, crystal chandeliers, formal gardens with brick pathways, and fish-pond. Fortunately our grandparents were far less strict with us than they'd been with their own children.

"'For that year and a half when my mother was completing her college work, we lived surrounded by beautiful antiques and our neighbors were all well off. Money never seemed to be a constraint. I recognized this as how I wanted to live. Two years later, when my mother remarried and we moved into a small crowded rental unit, I recall envying other kids who had their own bedrooms and closets full of clothes.

"'As I watched my mother and new stepfather sacrificing for us children and scrimping to make ends meet, I thought, "I'll never sacrifice for anyone, and I'm never going to settle for less than affluence." Since I felt incapable of ever providing myself with wealth, I developed fantasies of marrying into money.

"'I remember how for years I wanted to show my former classmates that I'd become someone "special." In reality, back then, I was naive and shy and didn't know how to be part of the "in" group. I always felt sort of out of it and vowed that one day I'd impress them all by doing something outstanding and becoming famous.'"

Submissive Example

"'While I was growing up, I saw my mother as being dependent and a homebody. I didn't want to be like her. She was self-sacrificing and willing to put herself out on others' account. That had seemed okay when I was a child, but as I approached adulthood, I was critical of her.

"'I wanted more for myself — more time, money, and energy to pursue my own desires and goals. I was also critical of my mother's decision to abandon her career plans and university education when she remarried. She stayed at home, adapting her life to my stepfather's wishes and devoting herself to her children.

"'In my teens, I also hated seeing so much of my mother in myself. I wanted to be a dependent homemaker like her but also feared following her example. Because of the way she'd been raised, she gave in to my stepfather's domineering ways. I knew she frequently disagreed with his approach to raising us, yet I'm sure she was afraid that if she broke with him, she might be unable to support us.

"'I found myself being submissive to my step-dad, just like my mother, detesting my inability to stand up to his unreasonable demands and his insistence that I obey him unquestioningly. His premise was that he'd taken on the responsibility of being my parent and, since he was older and wiser, I should obey without complaint. Although I tried to give him little cause for thinking that I was not a reflection of his value system, I bitterly resented his rigid, moralistic beliefs.'"

Appeasing and Pacifying

"'Since Dad squelched his children's anger with his own anger and punishments, I could never express resentful feelings. To his question, "What's going on inside that head of yours? Tell me what you're thinking!" I'd mumble, "Honest, I'm not thinking anything."

"'I knew if what I said didn't coincide with his beliefs, he'd lecture me. I couldn't accept his belief system and felt he'd reject me if he knew what I really thought. My stepfather adopted and helped raise me. From his point of view, I'm sure he tried to be a loving parent, and at times we enjoyed activities together, laughing at old movies on television and playing basketball in the driveway, or going on family hikes in the woods.

"'Yet when I recall the past, I tend to remember those times when I'd be sitting in the bedroom I shared with Brenda and hear his footsteps stop outside the door. My mind would race . . . was I in trouble? Had I forgotten a household duty? Had I neglected hanging up my coat? I was always relieved when his face was smiling; scared if he was upset.

"'Individually many of the house rules were reasonable, but they seemed endless, and I hated them . . . close your bedroom door, turn off lights you're not using, make your bed, put your shoes away, put the telephone cord under the table, complete your duties early. Even when I thought I'd met them all, I was often sharply scolded for having forgotten one.

"'At times my sisters rebelled and antagonized him. I could see how angry and frustrated he got with them, sending them to their bedroom and punishing them. I chose instead to obey without questioning, making a point of pleasing and pacifying him, apologizing even when I felt I was in the right. My sisters resisted his authoritarian stance and were punished, while I repressed my reactions in an effort to avoid disagreeable scenes. I don't know who was better off.

"'Growing up, Dad's warnings never to trust guys because "they only want to get into your pants" filled me with fear. Would men overpower and control me just like my stepfather?'"

Heart-Hungers

"After this long explanation, the counselor remarked, 'So anorexia may have been the ultimate attempt to rebalance the power. Since you didn't want to be like your mother and stepfather, what did you decide?'

"'The image of women I decided to adopt was based more on the media female than my own mother. I wanted to look, act, and talk like the females I saw on television and in the movies — long legs, thin, sexy. I felt they were the epitome of feminine success and decided to copy them.

"'In high school, though I was well liked and was earning all A's, I still kept feeling dissatisfied with myself. I wanted to recreate my face and body, escape mediocrity and having a humdrum life. I remember in college, when people told me I was pretty, I didn't believe them because I felt the true me was that child my biological father had described as ugly when I first got glasses.'

"'You held on to both fathers' put-downs in your early childhood. Early emotional convictions are hard to change,' the counselor remarked. 'The emotionally abusive influence of your natural father and stepfather undoubtedly had as much or more to do with your having become ill than anything else.'

"'Vomiting was a way of releasing resentment when my stepfather criticized me. It was something *over which he had no control.*

"'Just before my first vomiting, from day to day I was *living* my fear of being a powerless nobody with no change in sight. I ate treats to make life bearable, and the pounds crept on. In time, I hated myself and every part of my being, wanting a new body. In the beginning, my main reason for vomiting was that as I'd gained weight, my dates had diminished. I ached for a loving relationship with a man and was determined to shed the extra pounds.'

"'So, what I'm hearing is that the basic need was not to be thin, but to be desired by, and have a supportive relationship with, a man. Thinness was a symptom, a means to an end,' he remarked. 'Not digesting, and therefore almost disappearing, was almost like death. Burial was symbolized by getting rid of the former self who had been betrayed, hurt, and rejected. Rebirth would be the new thin, beautiful woman. Was anorexia a way to slowly melt down to nothing?' the counselor asked.

"'Anorexia meant that I was going to start over, thin and beautiful. I'd be in control and attract a really loving male partner.'

"'How did this work for you?' he questioned.

"'Well, I was so depleted from starvation I just wasn't up to meeting men. And because of my peculiar eating rituals, I couldn't be *myself* with other people, so I spent my time with other anorexics because they shared my reality and weren't disgusted by my vomiting.'

"The counselor told me that early in childhood the anorexic experiences emotional deprivation. This made sense to me, considering memories of my natural father.

"'Food became a substitute means of nourishment, but there was danger in that,' the counselor said. 'The more you fed your emotional hungers with food, the less acceptable you felt. Food became the major issue, though it was intimacy you needed but didn't have permission to get.'

"I thought about this before replying. 'In college I'd lost my identity and direction. After two long years of desperation, I'd lost my ability to deal with the world. Depression controlled every waking moment. By moving home there was the possibility of a new beginning. Despite my resentments and irrational thinking at the time, at least I was back with people who loved me and had my best interests at heart. My mother's care was something I could trust. I was getting recognition and okay messages from her and the rest of the family.'

"'Health comes from making *new assumptions about the world,*' the counselor remarked. 'In your case, you were trying to gain love and recognition through your looks. But thinness isn't a solution to any human need, and it didn't reduce your emotional deprivation. *Human needs are involvement, trust, security, belonging, achievement, absorbing interests. Needs have to do with things you can control. Healthy individuals use their energy directly toward satisfying their needs and achieving their objectives with vigor and happiness. You don't need a man or physical beauty for happiness.*

"'You felt your natural father never gave you the things you needed as a child when you were dependent and helpless, but your later substitute was no solution.'

"'Do you think if I'd received the loving acceptance I wanted from both fathers, I wouldn't have felt so desperate to find a man?' I asked. 'As it is, I still feel an emptiness in my life, like part of me is missing.'

"The counselor's response was immediate. 'You're still in *transition.* Part of your cure is getting affection, caring, trust. But if you attach yourself to a man, hoping he'll be your daddy, you'll do yourself in one more time. There is no Mr. Wonderful who has all the answers. On the other hand, if you can find someone you love, yet stay your own person, then you can succeed. When you find a man who is a good companion and supports you in taking good care of yourself, your *real* needs will be met.'"

Over time, Jacqueline talked with me about various aspects of her counseling, including how, when she was small, her natural father had talked to her in German so she couldn't understand him. She recalled how he'd done this because he knew it upset her and had laughed at her when she'd become upset and stuttered, "I, I, I . . . " repeatedly as she tried to talk. She considered how helpless she'd felt as a child when he'd taunted her, and that he would carry on all the more if anyone tried to intervene to help her. (Eventually she stuttered every time she spoke, a problem that lasted until her early teens.)

She asked me questions about her early childhood, trying to fill in "missing information." In answer to her questions, I finally shared with her that as she had guessed, before she was born, her natural father had wanted a son. (He was so disappointed, in fact, that for weeks after she was born, he had hounded me about wanting to give her away. I'd felt distraught and frightened by his insistent outbursts, and had simply stuck to saying that she was my precious daughter and no way was he going to give her away!)

But, although Jacqueline had felt the counseling was direct, on target, and beneficial, she still struggled daily with bulimic problems that had been a way of life for so long.

CHAPTER 14

Living with Male-Female Stereotypes

One weekend morning after having read a boldly printed notice in a woman's fashion publication, I got to thinking about how *the words we use* and the images they convey are intimately tied to how we think about ourselves.

This full-page layout read "Shape — The Fashion Word Today! Lines are Lean & Clean! It's a Body Conscious You! Straight and *Narrow* is Now! Strictly yours, The Editors."[1] I couldn't help thinking about the fashion authority who had stated that women are "competing with each other for male partners or husbands. Fashion lives off the *competitive spirit*."[2] The editors were telling us how to compete by being *lean and narrow* now — plus being self-conscious about our bodies.

Fullness, Not Leanness

I took out my dictionary and thesaurus and started looking up some of fashion's key words. I found that "thin," when used accurately, means lean and gaunt, lacking in "substance, strength, or richness."[3]

Thin implies something that's weak, lacking in fullness; *something that is not broad.* Jacque was home, so I commented on this to her. "What about the old slang for a woman being called 'a broad?'" She laughed, and commented, "Yeah, today we'd have to call her 'a narrow!'"

We turned to "female" and were not too surprised to see it defined as *"a broad."*[4] We found that "broad" was defined as *"woman"*[5] (in recognition of a natural tendency toward breadth).

Broad indicates being *unrestrained*. Does "narrow," we speculated, indicate the opposite — that of being *restrained?* Having some fun with this, we found "narrow" indicates being limited, cramped, rigid, barely sufficient. What were our current social values trying to "tell" us?

Because "slender" refers to something that's *"inadequate"* and meager,[6] we considered how this relates to the current belief that it's *normal* for women to be slender and therefore inadequate.

Why is telling a woman she's thin considered a compliment these days, since "thinness" actually means something that's underweight, *undernourished*, and *inadequate?*[7] Thinness denotes a skeletal, starved, scrawny, even haggard appearance. It was this paradox that had led me to comment, "What healthy adult male would want to be described as being fragile, weak, gaunt, or scrawny" (all synonyms for "lean")?[8] In contrast, words used to describe the idealized male physique were ones related to strength, energy, and power, indicating the ability to act commandingly.

Admiring dates had often praised Jacque's overly slim figure. Being unsure of herself to begin with made it all the more difficult for her to choose health. Looking up "healthy," a word that should certainly be just as applicable to women's bodies as to men's, we found it defined in terms of "full strength and vigor,"[9] robust, sound in mind and body. Since health is defined by *fullness*, not leanness, why are we currently conditioned to think that women should be lean and spare?

Entrenched Gender Stereotypes

Earlier, when I'd asked Jacqueline about her "ideal man," she'd told me, "Well, he'd be large, muscular, powerful, and also protective — sort of a hunk." As for herself, she had felt she needed the *opposite* characteristics to attract such a man. Back then she'd bought into the male-female polarities, both as to physical and character traits.

At Jacque's university it had seemed to us as though there was a *presumed equality* between the genders. But was there really? Campus life had been the social setting in which she'd become ill, and in which so many millions of other young women are currently succumbing to eating disorders. I began wondering — how did her peers feel in their heart of hearts about what it means to be male or female?

We located some sociological surveys conducted among her fellow students during her college years, and these revealed a campus life laden with gender bias. Results *characterized females* as: submissive, modest, yielding, innocent, shy, inexperienced, squeamish, vulnerable, helpless, and worried. They were also referred to as dependent, passive, gentle, pretty, coy, slim, subservient, compassionate, self-sacrificing, weak, cute, and self-conscious. Women were described by her classmates as people who "follow men" and "want to get married." Many of these were characteristics that might very well apply to people who are inferior and could therefore logically be considered subordinate in the social order.

Jacque's fellow students had listed *masculine characteristics* as: logical, practical, ambitious, bold, adventurous, successful, competitive, decisive, prepared, aggressive, strong, commanding, intelligent, aspiring, confident, virile, demanding, independent, and clear-headed (traits we associate with dominance and success).

Obviously *Jacqueline's classmates had held staunchly traditional gender-role expectations. Both men and women interviewed had viewed women as lacking power, initiative, competence, effectiveness, and self-direction — all problem areas in her own life.* Before she looked at these and other similar studies, neither of us had realized how entrenched the male-dominant–female-submissive stereotypes have remained despite the feminist movement.

"Crazy-Making Messages"

It's well for us to remind ourselves that "The larger share of those traits that are taken by men of any given era to be timeless components of femininity are, actually, only passing customs and manners," a situation noted by medical chronicler, Morton M. Hunt.[10]

Contemporary philosopher Alan Watts is among those who has called attention "to the unsoundness of hard and fast distinctions between male and female, masculine and feminine,"[11] yet in today's paradigm, we consider ourselves a divided species, with one set of traits associated with males and another with females.

We're living in a transitional time in which both genders discount female capabilities while giving lip service to "equality." Based on this realization, the girls and I each began paying closer attention to this illogical and confusing situation and how it was being reflected in our daily lives.

Jacqueline noted that we continue to encourage aggression in boys and reward them for displaying their intellect and leadership, but double-bind messages, both *encourage* and *discourage* these same qualities in girls. "That's a crazy-making situation if I ever saw one," she remarked.

Trying to adapt to New-Age pressures on females to use all of their capabilities, along with opposing social messages not to, is a prescription for emotional distress. In college, Jacque and Brenda had been living this female agenda when they had become ill.

"Feminine Characteristics . . . Devalued"

From infancy, each of us internalizes cultural messages related to gender. Girls who adopt supposedly "feminine characteristics" generally have lower self-esteem and a limited, rather than expansive, approach to life. Once, while talking about this, the conversation got around to how in the past, when male domination was admittedly the accepted norm, a woman could blame many of her culturally-based problems on obvious legal and other limitations related to being female. (She couldn't vote, she couldn't own property, etc.)

Jacqueline's reaction was, "Now women tend to blame *themselves* when they bump up against frustrating gender-related situations in what's still largely 'a man's world,' as far as the power structure is concerned. Like me, they feel it must somehow be *their fault.*"

A research report that caught our attention pointed out that "'Feminine' characteristics, like the women who tend to express them, are *devalued*" in our culture, "while 'masculine' characteristics, like the men who tend to express them, are *valued.*"[12] It's clear that what are currently viewed as "masculine" traits usually predominate, and are rewarded, in the business world.

How much clearer could it be that characteristics we associate with masculinity are pretty much those considered indicative of a *mature well-adjusted adult, but that many of those associated with femininity aren't?* Most bulimics stress supposedly "feminine characteristics," and Jacqueline had gone overboard in this direction.

Gradually, over time, Jacque moved toward becoming a "whole" human being, as she thought of it, with a balance of traits — willing to act strong and powerful, directional and with confidence. She was no longer striving to be the femme-fatale but was accepting a full range of attributes in herself. This process benefited from spending some time, with her brother and her sister Lisa, in Alaska. They worked as deck hands in the fishing industry, a setting just about as far removed as you could get from Madison Avenue and Hollywood influences. Because of the almost frontier atmosphere and the newness of the surroundings, she felt that breaking old patterns became much easier.

Anger and Power

Since childhood, Jacque had found it difficult to express anger. For that matter, so had I. As a child I hadn't been able to escape my father's raging temper which triggered derision and painful beatings. I'd carried my childhood fear of anger into my adult life, and rarely showed this emotion, doing so only guardedly, since it seemed unsafe and even frightening to express it.

In particular, I experienced feelings of insecurity, sadness, frustration, and anger in reaction to my husband's controlling ways, but seldom revealed my anger, fearing his threatening outbursts of temper. He believed that, as "head of the household," it was his prerogative to get angry at anyone in the family he thought was "out of line," though he didn't feel other family members had a right to express their anger.

As Jacque and I searched for reasons aggression and anger are considered unfeminine we found in our reading that the answers all came back to one thing — power.

There are many ways to define power. Geneen Roth, in *Breaking Free from Compulsive Eating*, describes it this way: "Being powerful is giving yourself permission to feel good . . . . allowing yourself to be as creative, outrageous, honest, sensual, and demanding as you are . . . . (and) realizing that you don't have to hide."[13]

We reviewed research by psychologists, only to read that "Warm, sensitive, dependent, passive . . . the old string of adjectives describing women, is not so much a description of femininity as it is of a social and psychological state of powerlessness."[14] In contrast, "the opposite adjectives generally applied to men — aggressive, active, cold, task-oriented, competitive, intellectual, objective, independent — do not represent masculinity per se, but more accurately describe the attributes of a person in possession of *power*."[15]

Problems of gender stereotyping were recently highlighted by a New York consulting group called Catalyst that works with employers to integrate family and work issues. Their study, "Women in Corporate Management," found that gender preconceptions are still barriers to advancement for women in the workplace, despite chief executives' statements that women should be encouraged to shoot for top positions. "There's been very little change in attitudes and perceptions of women," according to Catalyst research director, Mary Matis, who notes that attributes of the ideal manager still "tend to be male."[16]

Around this time in her recovery, Jacque and I worked together to become more aware of the inner rage we'd been suppressing for years. We both associated this "museum" of collected anger with having behaved in powerless ways. As for Jacque, like other bulimics, she'd swallowed her emotions, then forcefully tried to purge herself of them.

Anger and *hunger*, we learned, are closely allied. Self-starvation, guilt, and depression are all associated with extreme anger. For years Jacqueline had denied this internal fury, having prided herself on never getting mad. As a child as well as a teenager, she used to say, "I never feel angry." Now she saw that defensive attitude as a cover-up for feelings she hadn't wanted to face, and worked on identifying the origins of her feelings and dealing with them more appropriately.

When we read about anger, it called our attention to factors like poverty, low status, and rape. All these tend to generate depression. Anger comes from frustrated needs and hurt feelings. Classically, depression is described as anger turned inward. Apparently depression, helplessness, and self-absorption were all descriptive of anorexia and bulimia.

Jacque found *The Angry Book*, by Theodore Rubin, particularly helpful. From it she saw how anxiety breeds a variety of symptoms. These include irrational thoughts (obsessions), irrational repeated actions (compulsions), irrational fears (phobias), and depression. These are themselves anxiety-producing, which feeds into continuance of the symptoms.[17]

Depression is associated with feelings of *sadness, isolation, fear, ineffectiveness, despair, and self-depreciation*. Problems that Jacque had considered private and personal to herself, were themes that kept resurfacing throughout the literature on powerlessness, anger, and depression. In a news article I'd clipped and saved when Jacqueline was an adolescent, a noted psychologist reported that the "usual reaction by a woman beset with the problems of adjusting to women's role in our society today is depression, a sense of futility, and narcissistic attention to self."[18]

Jacque and I had a favorite local eatery where we liked to have lunch together at a large curved table in a sunny corner, away from the noise of the usual luncheon crowd. We'd eat slowly to prolong these pleasant interludes. It was reassuring sitting there together. Since we'd both had difficulties dealing with anger (her stepfather's as well as that of others), we talked about this. One of our conclusions was that when someone is raging at us and is obviously out of control, the best thing to do is find a way to absent ourselves from the situation rather than accept verbal abuse.

Theoretically we both knew that anger, when expressed constructively, releases hurt feelings and gives a sense of control. It can resolve conflicts, foster closeness, and, in caring relationships, actually reaffirm them. But how could we begin using this attitude and approach in our own daily lives? Neither of us wanted to continue squelching our angry feelings, but we were both basically afraid of discussing them. In time, we agreed that if either of us had a "beef," we'd share it by first saying something *positive* about the other, and then stating our gripe. This would be followed by a suggestion for working things out and a discussion (affirmation, consideration, negotiation, compromise). This supportive approach proved to be a good choice and helped us get started on expressing dissatisfaction and anger, though in time the set sequence became flexible and more relaxed.

"Archaeological Anger"

Most of us harbor some feelings of disappointment, and often resentment, toward our parents. Jacqueline was certainly no exception. She had a storehouse of pent-up anger at her natural father whom she hadn't seen or heard from in many years. Lisa had managed to locate him, and together they arranged to meet with him. To Jacque's delight, he commented on what a lovely young woman she'd turned out to be, so bright and well-informed. This seemed to be somewhat of a release from past messages from him which she'd felt were hurtful and disparaging. He had a new family and hadn't told them about Jacque or her siblings, so when they parted that day, she accepted his request that they not contact him again.

She felt that expressing past anger to her stepfather would only hurt and disappoint him. She chose not to confront him, believing it wouldn't lead to any resolution of her hurt, only to hard feelings. Now, for the most part, she and her stepfather avoid discussions of the past and "stay in the present," which seems to work well for both of them.

Quite naturally, she also felt angry and resentful toward me for a variety of past "omissions and transgressions," and she had done things that had angered me, but which I had avoided discussing. This "archaeological anger" presented a whole new area for us to explore. As a result, we spent hours, comparing our different perceptions of the same incidents from the past, surprised at times to realize how differently we'd viewed them. Brenda became involved, as did Lisa, in this process, with the four of us sharing past anger, disappointments, and regrets as well as current resentments.

These exchanges got quite emotional at times, but there was no doubting that they proved constructive, resulting in a catharsis of hurts and disappointments we had each experienced in relation to one another.

When discussing present disagreements, we concentrated on "I feel" messages rather than blame. We realized that each of us chooses our own feelings; no one *makes* us feel one way or another. For this reason, we stuck with "I feel angry when you . . . ," as opposed to "You make me feel so angry . . . . " This approach helped immeasurably in our ironing out all sorts of past and current differences.

During these times, as you can imagine, there were tears, regrets, apologies, and, of course, hugs. Anger from the past seeped out gradually. We simply let our hair down, so to speak, thereby gaining a much better understanding of our shared past. It took time, but gradually having learned to be comfortable with this openness, the girls and I were able to defuse old misunderstandings and resentments.

Obsessive Control

My husband and I were unable to resolve the conflicts we continually experienced. Having grown up submissive and fearful of anger, going back to when we were first married, I'd felt apprehensive and unable to effectively deal with the orders my new husband had begun issuing to me and the children, now that he felt "in charge" of the family. From my standpoint, I had felt as though we'd entered military training, and told him so. He saw my point, but said we needed to be "shaped up."

He felt that, as his wife, I should "stand behind" him — which meant always agreeing with him, especially on disciplining the children. If I disagreed with his approach, thinking it too harsh and restrictive, he felt angry because, according to him, I was "undermining" his authority. However, when I was disciplining the children, if he disagreed, he felt it was his responsibility as "head of the household" to intervene. If I resisted his intervention (a situation he found inexcusable), he was then angry not only at the child, but also at me.

He had expected and demanded that if he and I disagreed, his opinions would prevail. He'd been adamant about this, refusing to negotiate any alternatives. His justifications had been based on his "duty," as a husband and father, to take charge of the family, and on his "rights" as the breadwinner, both of which he felt were indisputable. We were playing out, in our own lives, the current social dominator ethos.[19] (The "dominator model" has been discussed in-depth in writings, by futurist Riane Eisler, on the dire need in today's world for replacing it with an egalitarian, partnership ethos.)

Reviewing our family past, Jacqueline could better understand how the excessive control and rages of her stepfather had affected her. Obviously, the criticism, shaming, and moralizing she'd experienced had contributed to her feeling unsure and inadequate, and I had not provided her with an example of someone who insists on healthy, mutually supportive co-independent relationships.

Her stepfather had frequently described himself as being "very good when I'm good, but when I'm bad, I'm horrid," from the old nursery rhyme. It was confusing to all of us that, when the children were young, on the one hand, he made substantial efforts to be caring, helped with the children's homework, played games with them, took them on bike rides, did all sorts of kind and caring things for them, but on the other hand, his approach at home was authoritarian and his temper frequently lay close to the surface.

Over the years, his angry moods had increased in frequency and duration. He'd been let go from two jobs and fired from another, eventually starting a business which thrived, then later failed. He'd had a falling out with his sister, was angry at his mother, was upset with co-workers. These and other aggravations — situations he felt were beyond his control — had resulted in his control at home becoming more and more oppressive. This was in marked contrast to how he reacted *outside* the home, for with his parents, bosses, co-workers, friends, and others, he was overly humble and solicitous. The resentment he built up by deferring to them was released on the only people over whom he felt he had authority, those at home.

I understood his frustration and was sorry that no matter what was actually going on at home, he was frequently angry and dissatisfied. Just as it takes "two to tango," it takes two to continue such a situation, and I had perpetuated these exchanges by tolerating them and not leaving. I found it confusing that he'd flip-flop between threatening to divorce me if I didn't obey him and his saying he'd "feel lost" if I ever left him; between chastising me and saying how much I meant to him. Life had an uneasy, unpredictable quality to it, with my never knowing what to expect — and feeling on guard much of the time.

Co-independence takes a willingness on the part of those concerned to negotiate, compromise, resolve conflicts, and work on resolving anger. But it takes cooperation between the parties involved; where this doesn't exist, dissension remains.

After 20 years of marriage, almost every evening my husband launched into chastising me for an hour or more, as well as telling me what I *must do as his wife.* Since many of his demands were contradictory, there was no way to avoid criticism or his unrelenting need to control. It was apparent that this was his way of venting his pent-up rage at life's disappointments, but that made it none the easier.

The simplest situations were reason for continual conflict. For instance, he was angry if I fixed him an early morning breakfast ("I want to be *alone* and fix it myself!"). He was also mad if I didn't prepare it ("As my wife you should get up and fix my breakfast!"). Whether or not I made his breakfast, he was angry and similar scenes were repeated over and over. There seemed to be no way to negotiate solutions that he found satisfactory. Yet many days he'd apologize for previous outbursts, saying he was sorry, promising to work on "getting control" of his temper. But promises are not the same as action and the truth was, his rages were getting worse.

I had looked to marriage for companionship, but it had actually turned out to be a *trap.* Because I was financially dependent, I feared challenging my husband's "authority." During angry outbursts, when he knew I was distressed, he'd say, "You can't divorce me. You couldn't survive on your own!" I'd never lived on my own or supported myself, so in years past, any time I'd considered getting away from the marriage, I couldn't see how I could adequately support the four children and myself. Now that the children had left home, I was older, with an adult lifetime of being a "homemaker" — not the best background for a resume.

Wondering how I might build some sort of career outside the home, I checked with the local employment agency. They said my best opportunity lay in such jobs as carving meat at a cafeteria or waiting banquet tables at minimum wage. My university degree and experience writing a free-lance column for a large metropolitan newspaper, I was told, counted for nothing in the local job market. Enduring my husband's anger was agony, but how could I make it on my own?

Later, remarking on her stepfather's anger, Brenda noted, "Looking back, I think he did the best he knew how. His intentions were okay, but his actions weren't, and I'd have to say his parenting wasn't conducive to our building confidence or feeling good about ourselves."

The children's stepfather had been well-meaning; he had wanted to be thoughtful and helpful, but he simply hadn't known how to deal with his storehouse of rage in a more constructive way, though he recognized the problem and made periodic resolves to change.

As I thought about the years of frustration and resentment, anxiety and anger, worry and concern that I had felt over the girls' problems, their suffering, and my increasing concern over the female "eating-disorder phenomenon" currently in progress — I felt that this book, which was underway at this time, seemed the best way to turn our experiences into something that could help others.

I began writing this book during the period described at the beginning of this section on bulimia, and it was continued as we moved through dealing with those problems. We didn't know what the outcome would be and progressed through the stages as they have unfolded in these pages. The section on anorexia is taken from early notes I made during that time. There was a drawer in a built-in cabinet in a guest bedroom that no one ever used. Into it, I slipped comments to myself about the situation. This was my "secret drawer," which served as a basis for sorting out the jumble of confusing events and emotions surrounding that difficult period when Jacqueline was starving herself.

CHAPTER 15

Problems with Low Self-Esteem

No one watching Jacque at work or while socializing could have guessed that this lovely young woman (who certainly seemed calm and cheerful) had months when she experienced herself as having trouble holding her life together. Problems of purging, and the guilt and secrecy this created, as well as coping with life in general, would really get her down. For this reason, among others, many of our conversations during the first five years of her recovery had to do with situations we felt might be *related to difficulties she was having in feeling good about herself. They broadened the issue from Jacqueline to women in general.*

Questions, Questions, Questions

How did her insecurities and lack of confidence fit into the overall social picture?

Most of Jacque's negative feelings came out of times when she was under stress and expressing a sense of malaise in which she felt that life seemed like an endless struggle. During such periods, her *fear* level would rise. Apprehension and anxiety seemed to combine to increase her bingeing and purging. This then added to her feeling downcast.

In an effort to break this pattern, we asked ourselves many questions. For instance, what was the significance of her many dreams as a young child in which she'd been "a boy" involved in all sorts of bold and exciting adventures? We looked at studies showing that many little girls wish they were boys, but that boys rarely wish they were girls.

She thought a lot about why her natural father had been so disappointed that she was a girl. Along this line, we both wondered why many expectant parents want a son more than a daughter. What does this say about how we value girls?

As a small child, Jacque had enjoyed being a tomboy and loved climbing trees as well as all sorts of active sports. Why, we tried to understand, is it that a girl being a tomboy (behaving like a boy) is considered okay but the reverse is not acceptable? Women wear loafers and slacks (even if similar to a man's), but men shun dresses and high heels (the attire of women). Is this because such dress is symbolic of the "weaker sex?"

We read that certain types of preferential treatment were routinely given to male students. Why was it, for example, that, in blind testing, an essay signed with male name would, on average, receive a higher grade than the exact same essay with a female name? Why, in class, are boys called on more frequently and given more leeway in their behavior?[1] Why are teachers more likely to remember boys' names?[2] Why are they more likely to call on boys and "listen attentively to their answers?"[3] Why are "male students and their contributions" taken "more seriously" than females' contributions?[4]

All along, marriage was very much on Jacqueline's mind. She felt that the longer she went without getting married, the more it might seem to others as though no one had asked her. She wondered, "Why are bachelors envied but spinsters not?" Beyond this was the question "How does men's general preference for women younger than *they* are affect the situation?" It's recognized that men tend to be more sought after as marriage partners as they become older, more mature, and more financially secure and as there are progressively more single women to single men in their age group. We could guess how this relates to women's fears of getting older!

Jacque wondered whether men have an easier time valuing and accepting themselves. Greater power and influence (more likely to be their inherent lot) are attributes associated with esteem. The reverse situation seemed to apply to being a woman. The dilemma was that self-esteem is basic to emotional well-being. Bulimics typically have developed the habit of underrating themselves, feeling they are less worthy, less smart, less attractive, and less capable of controlling their lives than others would perceive them to be. Jacque had been no exception.

Career Guidance

Since identity and feelings of personal worth can be influenced by the kind of work we do, as well as by our financial situation and social status, I wondered about all the girls who must have had similar experiences to Jacqueline's, when she took a high school aptitude test along with her graduating class. She ranked highest in forestry, a field in which she'd developed a good deal of interest.

Boys who scored as she did were, *without exception*, advised to attend college in order to pursue careers in forest management. Ours was a relatively small university town, and yet even with this major influence in the community, the guidance counselor had advised Jacque that her best option was "flower arranging."

Here was a straight-A student with an aptitude and interest in forestry, but because she was female, she had been guided in a direction that had left her feeling devalued and dejected.

"What's the use; why even try?" Jacque had told me when she got home from school that day. Now, years later, she considered how different her life might have been had she been supported and steered toward a challenging career as her young male classmates had been. How had this and similar input from her environment over the years affected on her self-worth, her confidence?

It was as if history had been repeating itself. Twenty-five years before, I too had scored highest in forestry, in senior high school aptitude testing, yet I was told I should consider "truck gardening." I remember feeling perplexed and wondering how growing vegetables related to my interest in forestry. I'd felt angered by the counselor's suggestion and totally uninterested in her recommendation. It seemed as though career counseling hadn't changed all that much in the previous quarter century.

Asking girls about their *ideal* career choices can start a wide range of responses. Yet, based on how they view their alternatives, many later change their aspirations to occupations conventionally held by females. The result is an adverse self-perpetuating situation that limits the number of role models for women in less traditional fields.

Individual Potential

Somewhere along the line, I picked up some materials on admission to an elite college, and in them "students' potential" was discussed. The administrators obviously considered such potential the basis of success.[5] Jacqueline and I, along with Brenda, talked at length about this.

"Potential" refers to something that has power or is potent.[6] Certainly, power and potency are vital to actualizing our potential, yet many research reports confirmed our perception that males and females alike consider these attributes as more in the *masculine domain.*

Much of our reading had to do with women consciously or unconsciously limiting their efforts toward achievement, afraid of the negative payoffs that success might bring. Yet achievement is intimately related to self-confidence and pride. Jacque and I looked at studies indicating that in school, girls tend to hold back so as not to appear "too brainy."[7] Social acceptability takes precedence over learning, because this restraint seems necessary for popularity with the opposite gender (rather like applying one's brakes while trying to move forward).

Jacque had bumped up against situations in which a man she was dating had actually told her he couldn't tolerate her being as capable as he was. At such times, she struggled between wanting to be competent and act confidently, and not wanting to "bruise the man's ego" and be rejected.

Vulnerability

It seemed to Jacque that her nebulous feelings of fear and uncertainty, were all very much interrelated. Hoping to shed some light on this, we considered various concrete reasons that she and other women have to feel vulnerable and apprehensive. Were her fears and insecurities rational or irrational — reality-based or not? Common or unusual?

Jacque had experienced sexual pressures and threats that had provoked a sense of helplessness and powerlessness that she hadn't been able to put aside. For example, in her freshman year, before she had ever binged and purged, she'd maintained an A average up until the final weeks of the semester in an English class. Her professor had asked her to stay after the lecture one day. Then, when the other students had left, he suggested their having a sexual encounter. He said she looked sort of "naive" to him and that this would broaden her education and be a "good experience" for her. He had even told her he hoped that when his own two daughters reached college age, a man of his maturity and experience would be willing to give them the type of learning experience he was offering her.

She listened in amazement, and when he pressed her against the wall, fondling her breasts, she dropped her notebooks and struggled to free herself. Distressed and humiliated, she begged him to please let go of her. He argued his point, and when she stood by her refusal to have a sexual affair, he became alarmingly hostile. Belittling her, he had said she was immature and "stupid," announcing that anyone that dumb didn't deserve a passing grade in his course. He interrupted his derisive tirade with the ultimatum, either she have an affair with him for the remainder of the semester or "receive an F in the course!" She felt powerless and demeaned but argued, even pleaded, that this incident should not determine her grades. He made no recognition of her remarks.

Although Jacque continued to attend his class and study diligently as before, and completed the course, turning in an extensive term paper and taking the essay final, she received the failing grade. Jacque had been denied a passing grade in the course because she wouldn't provide her professor with free sex, a situation that had left her feeling degraded. We had talked, at the time, about whether she might want to report this sexual harassment to the head of his department, but she was so sure that her word would count for nothing against his, she decided against this, figuring it might even have negative repercussions in the department against her. (Interestingly enough, she later met another coed who'd had a similar experience with this same professor. We couldn't help speculating on how many others there might have been.)

Agony of Rape

Before becoming ill, Jacque had been at her assigned campus work-study job at the library one evening, about 10 P.M., filling index cards after hours. The floor she was working on was almost deserted, and she was alone in a small office doing her work. She had looked up when a professor she'd never met (but recognized because she'd seen him checking out books) came in and closed the door quietly behind him. She thought this strange, but turned to ask him how she might be of help. Instead of answering her, or making any comment at all, he grabbed her neck and shook her so violently that her head bobbed helplessly back and forth.

In the panicked minutes that followed, despite her pleading and the physical struggle she put up, he brutally raped her and left her hurt, aching, bruised, and terrified. When done, he left as silently as he'd come, with no explanation as to why he had picked her as his victim or why he had attacked her. When she called me, she was so distraught, she could hardly get across to me what had happened, but I got the picture and brought her home. I felt she should report the rape, but she resisted, saying that she was afraid the man might retaliate, and she couldn't stand the thought that he might brutalize her again.

For an extended period after that, Jacqueline had been haunted by fear every waking hour. She could make no sense of this attack, by a presumably responsible male, nor could the rest of us. She worried constantly. When might someone else suddenly and unexpectedly attack and rape her? Her world felt shattered and dirty. She kept reliving those moments and, as she spoke of them, we shared her trauma. She was afraid to turn him in because he might retaliate by brutalizing her again, and since it would be her word against his, a *professor's*, she felt she didn't stand a chance of being believed. The trauma shortly preceded her illness, leaving us to wonder at its impact on her becoming obsessed with controlling and remaking her body.

At the time, when Jacque and I had begun dealing with her storehouse of submerged anger, she tried to come to grips with the rage she felt at this man and at a society in which rape has become so common that every town of any size has rape crisis centers. Other young women she knew had narrowly missed sexual assault, under different circumstances, but also related to campus life.

Sexual Harassment

My heart went out to Jacque as she puzzled her way through various events that may have contributed to her feeling insecure and devalued. At a campus job in the administration building (prior to the library job), an admissions manager had repeatedly pressured Jacqueline for sex. She had hated the tedious job and hated even more that he kept threatening to fire her if she didn't eventually give in. Looking back, she recalled how financially strapped she'd been as a freshman, and how frightened of losing her job. The situation had compounded her feelings of vulnerability and anger and of being treated as an inferior, not worthy. His harassment had been based not on attraction, but on dominance and sexual bigotry.

Now, as she reconsidered this and similar incidents her sisters had experienced, I began keeping an eye out for news articles on the subject. She expressed feeling much "less alone" when she read reports that 45 percent of working women suffer sexual harassment as compared to only about 2 percent of working men.[8] It helped to realize that such harassment is based less on sexuality than on gender and on creating an atmosphere in which the subject feels inferior, belittled, unworthy, and as though she does not belong.

One physician's comment hit home. He stated that at work women "must cope with unequal treatment and uninvited and unwelcome sexual overtures or even harassment."[9] No matter how harassment is defined or what leeway is given for unreported cases, women are far more at risk than men. Jacque's experiences fit like a puzzle piece into the overall picture of gender inequality.

We learned that sexual harassment is related to *binge eating* as well as to dramatic loss of weight and appetite.[10] "Anger, fear, depression, anxiety, irritability, loss of self-esteem, feelings of humiliation and alienation, and a sense of helplessness and vulnerability" are all associated with sexual harassment in the workplace.[11] The symptoms sounded disquietingly familiar.

All three girls had been subjected to derisive, deliberate sexual harassment of one kind or another. I recall the time Brenda was asked to report to her superior's office, supposedly regarding some urgent business matter. With no foreshadowing, after she sat in the chair across from his desk, he told Brenda that he'd had his eye on her for "a couple of months" and wanted to have an affair with her. Apparently he'd expected she would feel delighted by his suggestion and was obviously miffed when she turned him down. She tried to placate his ruffled feelings, but he became nasty, telling her she had a choice — of either making herself "available" to him or being fired.

She had been caught off guard but remained seated, responding calmly, "What about your wife and two children?" She spoke of how she devoted herself to the job, saying that to be fired for such a reason would be not only unfair but also illegal. He simply scoffed. The discussion had only lasted about five minutes, but when Brenda phoned to tell me about it, she said he seemed furious at her "rejection" and that the problem wasn't over.

Brenda had been with the firm for several years and loved her work. She had planned to be with the company for a long while. But she had refused to have a sexual affair, and the next day, as soon as she arrived at work, he fired her. It had been a shock to have been one of the top people in the company on Tuesday, with an exemplary record, and suddenly out of work on Wednesday morning, packing her things to leave. What had brought on this sudden change of events? She never found out. He was relatively new with the firm and had been ambitiously climbing the power ladder. He stayed with the firm; she didn't.

Just as with Jacqueline and her English professor, Brenda had been punished for not providing sex when it had been demanded. Their sister, Lisa, and I had also been through intimidating experiences of a related nature. It was important to be able to talk about distressing events — about residual feelings of fear, shame, sadness, and anger, so that they are no longer buried or repressed and perhaps still having a negative impact. So, in the process of opening up and expressing our feelings, we began discussing these experiences, finding that we each were helped by the compassionate feedback we received from each other.

I remember saying that once I had kept an office appointment with an attorney who was old enough to be my father. He had done business with my parents for years, and I was there handling some legal work for my father. As I got up to leave, the lawyer commented, "I *like* you." The *way* he'd said it made me feel something was definitely wrong, so I had hurriedly gathered·my things.

My intuition proved correct; he shoved me against his desk to prevent my exit, while telling me of his fantasies about having an "affair" with me. He was talking about how good we'd be in bed together as he grabbed my arms and tried to French kiss me. When I resisted, he began mauling me. I struggled to pull his hands off me, while pleading with him to let me go. Eventually, I managed to get to the door and ran down the stairs to the parking lot with him following right along behind me. He wedged me against my car door, holding my arms and grabbing me to prevent me from unlocking it, while I tried to do just that.

I kept thinking, "Why is this happening?" and for days afterward felt distressed and particularly vulnerable, along with revulsion and disgust for this man.

It was impossible to forget this and similar incidents such as the time when a male stylist, who had just cut my hair, suddenly reached down inside my blouse to fondle me. There was even a physician who, after having treated my back problem, unexpectedly pulled my gown down, attempting to stroke my chest. Such memorics helped me relate to the girls' traumatic experiences and to all those women who have had similar humiliations.

Cohealing regarding the sexual transgressions we'd each experienced had also led to my finally disclosing the until-then hidden distress I had experienced from having been repeatedly sexually assaulted by my grandfather during a vacation stay with him when I was nine years old. He had threatened that this must be "our secret," but when the vacation was finally over and I returned home, I had mustered enough courage to tell my mother what he'd been doing. I remember emphasizing that I never wanted to be left alone with him again.

It was obvious that my mother was very uncomfortable discussing the matter and wanted to somehow color the situation in a way that I wouldn't feel critical of *her* father. I remember her explanation was that in "the old country" (he was an immigrant) "this was probably the way older male relatives *helped teach* young girls about the 'facts of life.'" She indicated that though he should not have "done that," he'd undoubtedly had my best interests at heart.

I knew what had happened seemed wrong, and for months I worried that I might be pregnant, unaware of how to detect this or that I was too young. Yet, even as young and naive as I was at the time, I recognized that what he had been doing had been for his benefit and had nothing to do with trying to help, or teach, me anything. But this reality, my reality, had been denied in an attempt to protect my grandfather. I remember my mother indicating that no one else was to know what had happened, so while growing up, I never again mentioned my distressed feelings about this matter to anyone, not even her.

Now, years later, I realized how important it was to finally work through the buried anguish this experience had engendered. It seemed appropriate to share my recollections of how I'd felt badly about myself at the time for not having been able to somehow prevent my grandfather's sexual transgressions. It was a relief to talk of this hidden past, and as I worked at releasing and resolving this emotional trauma, the girls couldn't have been more sympathetic or supportive. It also helped to discuss this abuse with other women who'd been incest victims.

I was fortunate that the molestation by my grandfather had been of relatively short duration. It did, however, give me some understanding of the distress that children experience due to sexual abuse experienced at the hands of relatives.

Brutality Glorified

After discussing such personal incidents, we paid more attention to how male heroism is equated with violence in movies, on television, in video games and explicit music recordings, plus in innumerable other sources in our everyday environment. This, of course, reflects the values of a culture that glorifies males overcoming, subduing, and brutalizing others. The problem of male violence is amplified by women often being physically weaker and afraid to act on their own behalf, along with their tendency to define themselves through connections with significant others. That is, women generally look for *satisfaction within a relationship*, and many battered women blame themselves when they can't make this happen.

It seemed, to Jacque, that part of what's considered "being a man" in this society is "having authority" over women.[12] We knew from various news reports that each year in this country about six million wives are physically abused by their mates and that more females die from battering than from car accidents, rapes, and muggings.[13] We questioned how the tradition of male dominance relates to male aggression and violence, and how this perpetuates and reflects inequality and injustice in all sectors of society.

When we consider the pervasiveness of physical brutality against women in our society today, we need to heighten our awareness of the input in our environment that stresses force and conquest as a way of demonstrating strength and dominance. The message of the desireability of brute force comes through in such popular entertainments as professional wrestling and other physical contact sports, as well as all sorts of other everyday input that portrays men's power and aggression as *admirable*. We wondered what could be done about this insidious, continual emphasis on male aggression in a world that so badly needs to promote harmony and cooperation.

So where is justice and fair treatment to be found? Certainly not in the judicial system. Sexual bias runs so deep that equal justice, in our courts, is essentially a myth. Women are discriminated against throughout the legal system. Significantly, domestic violence against women has been given far less attention than is appropriate. What's more, female lawyers, expert witnesses, and victims are all routinely given less credibility than males.[14]

We discussed such matters as rape, sexual harassment of women, and the like, with various men we knew and found that they were deeply concerned about all aspects of women's vulnerability to gender-based mistreatment, particularly as this related to their own daughters, wives, mothers. It was reassuring to Jacque that these men held views so similar to her own. We each perpetuate the status quo by accepting it, or we work to change it. Like us, these men were trying to be aware of gender-based stereotypes and limitations and to think beyond them.

Fear of Poverty

From the time she returned home so ill, Jacqueline had expressed an almost desperate fear that she might end up living alone as "a poor old woman in some forgotten town." Eventually we realized that a great many women, me included, even those who are working, "are afraid of ending up *destitute*."[15] The more we looked at the financial inequities women face, the more they seemed related to difficulties in developing a strong sense of personal power and *worth*. Money provides a basis for self-reliance and, thus, self-assurance.

News reports on television and in the press inform us that full-time female workers receive little more than *two-thirds* of men's pay[16] and often have to accept lower-echelon jobs. After having worked five difficult years to put herself through college, it was disheartening to read in a report titled "Women haven't made it" that, on average, female college graduates who work "full-time, year-round" make about the same as "male high school drop-outs."[17]

Headlines telling us such things as "Women in top management (are) still scarce" or that "Job Gains Still Slight for Women," in spite of a phenomenal increase in the number of working women in recent years,[18] are a clue to how firmly established traditional approaches are in the work place and how difficult it is to make substantive changes in them.

In spite of this, strong resentment in recent years has come from men who believe women have not only already achieved equality in the work force, but have also been favored over men. There has been considerable backlash, so women must now deal not only with the inequities, but also the fallout from this powerful, insidious backlash that would push women back into traditional self-limiting roles. This new counter-assault against treating women as *equally human*, this resistance to accepting them as deserving equal opportunity and justice, equal representation and recognition, has become more hidden in recent years and more diffuse, which makes it all the more difficult to recognize.

Many women report having worked longer with a better work record than their male counterparts, yet continuing to receive less pay and recognition. All three daughters had experienced this in their jobs. For years, Jacque had been underpaid, and on occasion she had to borrow from family members to keep afloat financially. Her fear of poverty had not just been idle musing but drawn from her own daily existence.

We paid attention to statistics on poverty. Jacque came across figures taken from "The Feminization of Poverty," which reported that fully half the families headed by a female live in poverty.[19] Divorce, death, illness, separation, and other circumstances can lead to female-headed households; clearly the vine-covered cottage, celebrated as a symbol of marriage, is not a panacea for happiness and financial security.

Recent census figures show that more than 10 million female heads of households live below the poverty line — five times the number of men in this situation.[20] It's dismaying that anyone lives in poverty, and it was unsettling to read the statistics, but Jacque did gain insight into her own fears of becoming destitute, particularly when she read that of adults living below the poverty line in this country, fully 90 percent are women.[21] Jacque was also interested to read that "Among older women, the poverty rate is about twice that of older men."[22] Examining these statistics helped her understand that her fears had a basis in reality; yet, in facing this, she came to realize that she could take positive steps to bring about a different future for herself.

Double Binds

How was Jacque's earlier pursuit of thinness related to her fear of financially fending for herself? Her own assessment had been, "I'd felt that the more physically appealing I could make myself, the more successful man I could attract. If I looked good, I thought I'd feel good about myself."

It was interesting to discover that during her illness, researchers were reporting on studies which confirmed her perception that physical attractiveness is *not only a significant factor in the evaluation of females by males, but that it's the prime predictor "of a woman's marriage to a high-status man."*[23] Because of the value men place on a woman's appearance, it wasn't difficult to understand why women worry about their looks and why physical attractiveness is correlated with their self-esteem. Yet enduring self-esteem needs to come from accepting and liking our essential self, not our "packaging."

Many of our after-dinner conversations were about double binds. Jacque noted, "It seems like there's lots of antagonism and resentment toward the so-called 'liberated woman,' but there are also jabs at those who are considered 'unliberated.' Women are expected to be sexually passionate, but also pure and virginal. They're supposed to be assertive, but not pushy; glamorous, but also natural and earthy; to do their best, but not outdo men. They're to be worldly and independent, yet domestic and dependent. They're to put the needs of others first, but look out for themselves as well. Have opinions, but not be opinionated. Be determined, but not aggressive." She was trying to make sense of these and other related conflicts.

As she mentioned one double bind after another, I had to agree with her that "damned if you do and damned if you don't" situations are a given, and that girls in our culture learn early in life that they can't go wrong by being *thin.*

Jacque had not been alone in thinking that if losing five pounds is good, perhaps ten would be better.

In considering the double binds women face, it's helpful to remember that men also have their share of gender-based double binds, though these are certainly different from the ones we were examining. For instance, current male-role definitions demand that men be strong and assertive, even unemotional, yet have the capacity to be sensitive and gentle. Jacque's conclusion was, "Being born female isn't easy, but then neither is being born male!"

Self-Responsibility

After all our discussions about family and social influences that might have inhibited her in the past from having strong positive self-identity, self-esteem, and self-confidence, the problem came down to this: what was Jacqueline going to do about it? The issue for her then became "How am I going to deal with the reality of the world in which we live? How can I feel a sense of security — power — purpose — well-being?"

We agreed that no matter what society's attitudes are, the best each of us can do is to define ourself as *valuable and worthwhile*, choosing to exert our efforts in directions that we feel are most likely to prove satisfying. For this reason, Jacqueline wrote out numerous affirmations for herself, as well as some wonderful ones for me. A positive expectation was created, she found, with such simple decisions as "I will make the best choices I can. I will live to the fullest extent possible. I will take charge of my life and pursue the things I want most. I will use my talents and energies as appropriately and effectively as I can."

An affirmation we particularly liked went like this:

Dear (Self),

I love you and forgive your imperfections. I accept you as a total person with feelings of joy and unhappiness, confidence and uncertainty, courage and fear, love and hate, satisfaction and dissatisfaction, hope and discouragement — and accept that this is part of the human condition. I do not expect perfection.

I will do today what I can toward achieving my goals, having faith that I can accomplish what is important to me as long as I set reasonable objectives. I trust myself and act in my own highest good.

I am a powerful, capable human being who assumes my personal rights and responsibilities. I recognize those matters that I can change and the ones that I can't, and avoid wasting energy on the latter. I have a right to pursue personal fulfillment and explore my potential — no less than anyone else.

Love, (Self)

Eventually Jacque was helped by deciding that she could choose to feel good about herself and by realizing that no matter what the social or family setting, life can be viewed as an adventure.

Jacque and her sisters, as well as I, had asked ourselves so many questions over the years Jacqueline had struggled with eating problems. Asking these questions helped all of us immeasurably. They hadn't all needed answers. *Just asking had given us direction* because we became more acutely aware of the detrimental influences around us and our reactions to them. Individually, we might not be able to change society to any large degree, but over time, we did change our own attitudes and actions substantially.

Thus, through the questioning that sprang from our urgent need to understand Jacqueline's, as well as Brenda's, self-starvation and purging and by taking a problem-solving approach to their problems, we had set a pattern of questioning our personal lives and family patterns, in addition to the general social setting of our times. In so doing, we gained insights that had eluded us before. Cohealing included our sharing these insights and supporting each other in gradually making personal changes that would make our lives more satisfying. In terms of Jacque's problems, the first step in recovery was *heightened awareness*. (See: Reclaiming Our Rights — Awareness) That lead to her forming new attitudes about what is real and healthy, as well as what possibilities were available to her. From this had come a willingness to change old patterns.

This openness to experimentation and change, along with the progress it generated, increased our confidence and the momentum of this change. We'd set a pattern of exploring, searching — of restructuring our world view.

Jacque and I had a good time giving ourselves new "permissions." We looked on this as giving ourselves permission to more freely choose between alternatives, more readily take calculated risks toward our goals, and more easily assess our options, deciding what we wanted to do about them.

We talked a good deal about inhibitions and how they lead to ineffective behavior. "Permissions," as we chose to think of them, are the opposite of inhibitions and provide release from them. We could, we decided, work on freeing ourselves of shoulds and oughts, limited thinking and fears, replacing them with decisions based on what would be satisfying and expansive in the long run. (See: Reclaiming Our Rights — Personal Rights)

During this long period, increased awareness of external gender-related social problems helped Jacque put internal ones into clearer focus so that she could deal with them in a more defined way. For instance, poor career guidance and planning, plus inadequate practical training, had reduced her options and income. To overcome this, she gradually took on more challenging job assignments. A couple of years ago, she went into business for herself as a way to more fully take charge of her life. Because she makes her own choices about who she'll work with and on what specific projects, she now has much more control over her work situation.

Expressiveness, naturalness, excellence, worldliness, independence, healthy self-care, determination — these were all things that Jacque was striving to acquire. Happily, all this began to be a reality for her.

As for problems Jacque had previously had valuing herself, she concluded that though our culture may have reinforced her feelings of powerlessness and self-devaluation, this evaluation is *not the truth*. The truth is simple. Like everyone else, she is special and valuable. In time, she learned to believe in herself. Anyone meeting her now can tell that she's confident and astute as well as creative and practical — a strong combination. These days Jacque feels good about herself, and this comes across in her dealings with people. She's spontaneous and, at last, feels "whole."

Life Is Fragile and Precious

Understanding some of the current social forces that foster the emotional outlook associated with eating problems had shifted our attention from Jacqueline alone to a much larger context. With this approach, she was not limited by thinking in terms of "my phobias, my shortcomings, my inabilities." She had expanded her thinking *beyond* that.

Remembering her past fears and uncertainties, she learned that she had lots of company, knowledge that provided reassurance that she was basically okay. She saw also that it isn't just individual men or women who cause social injustice but that all of us interact to form the social mores of our time. It is therefore up to each of us to participate in the process of change toward greater well-being for all humanity.

Recovering from a long-term malaise, Jacqueline came to see life as both fragile and precious. Along with this, she found a sense of purpose and direction that makes her life feel worthwhile. Today she looks at herself quite differently from the way she did in the past.

PART III

Recovery — Growth and Transformation

CHAPTER 16

Recovery

For Jacqueline, recovery was a search for understanding herself and the influences that had precipitated her eating problems. I'm thankful that she now finds contentment in her life and feels good about herself. She radiates a sense of purpose and is a delightful, positive young woman. The following is Jacque's own commentary on her recovery and commitment to health:

Inner Direction

"Wellness comes through a continual but nonlinear process of growth. Though my family stood by me with loving assistance and hope, the changes in my life had to come from within me. Improvement took place in stages.

"Before and during my illness, I'd been wrapped up in trying to impress and be pleasing to others. Progress toward more sensible attitudes was gradual, but I particularly remember a day when I was running at the neighborhood track. In the past, I'd compared myself with the other joggers, wanting to *look good* to them and feeling pleased or disappointed with my performance depending on how I measured up against them.

"On this day, I got caught up in running, enjoying the cool wind against my face. The sun and exertion built up a healthy sweat, and I moved comfortably. No one else on the track mattered because I wasn't comparing my pace with theirs. They could just as well have vanished, and my experience wouldn't have been more or less satisfying.

"That was the day I first realized I'd begun to have that wonderful feeling of *inner direction* in many areas of my life. I'd finally accepted that there'll always be others who are better than me at certain skills. Instead of feeling defeated by this, I started concentrating on enjoying what I was doing. Now I do what's meaningful to *me* instead of trying to match what I think *others* would want me to be.

"I decided that the 120 pounds I weighed in high school was inadequate and that 128 was the most comfortable weight for my height and build. My friends and people who meet me tell me I look good, and I can tell they're expressing their honest feelings. At last, I *believe* compliments when I receive them."

Sharing the Cohealing Process

"Over a period of several years, Mother and I shared thoughts on all sorts of social issues that seemed relevant to us, but most of all, we considered family patterns and how they had affected our lives. Brenda and Lisa were involved in this also, with each of us reevaluating what we wanted for ourselves. In this interactive process, each of us was lending motivation, encouragement, and ideas that helped the others. Together, we talked and laughed, cried and listened. We shared our hurts and our hopes, and in the process we each built a new worldview.

"As a child and teenager, I'd seen my mother doing for others and rarely for herself. Since she seemed to put everyone else first, I saw her as being overly self-sacrificing, something I definitely did not want to be. During the time I was recovering, Mother was making major changes in her own life, including finally looking after her *own* needs.

"At some point, I realized that she was doing exactly what I'd been wanting her to do for as long as I could remember. She was setting limits, considering what was appropriate and best for her *own* well-being. In so doing, she was setting a new example; in essence, giving me permission to start looking out for myself. With this, I began disregarding prohibitions that had haunted me since childhood and began deciding how I could best take care of myself.

"It wasn't until after my mother and stepfather separated that I was able to look more objectively at how I'd changed. Before that I'd sort of thought of myself as an extension of my parents. Now mother had become a new role model, and this gave me courage.

"After Mother had been on her own for awhile, I began noticing that her decisions and changes were rubbing off on me, helping me see how safe and acceptable it is to be independent. She was finally doing the things she'd always wanted to do, making up for lost time. It was surprising at first to see her acting carefree, brave, unrestrained, spontaneous — did mothers act that way? From this, I decided that as I become older, I must never let youthful attitudes in me die. I could see by watching her that we are as free as we allow ourselves to be. We can become spontaneous, co-independent, adventurous, and build a satisfying life for ourselves by making appropriate choices. I learned I could get well when I chose to.

"In the past, I'd thought of my mother as dominated by my stepfather and dependent on him. Later, after my college graduation, when she began seeking new directions, I could see how competent she actually had become. She was proving to me that life doesn't have to be scary or burdensome. I recognized power in her that I hadn't seen before and found, by watching her grow, that I don't have to choose to live in fear. As a child, much of my life had been based on fear — fear of growing up, fear of responsibility for myself, fear of making others unhappy with me, fear of being wrong, fear of not being acceptable.

"When in the pits of anorexia, I feared life itself.

"During the years of my recovery, after I had returned home depressed and suicidal, I came to respect Mother for her intelligence, resourcefulness, and compassion. She was there for me when darkness fell and gave me back my life."

Self-Expression and Competencies

"As Mother worked to establish a career path, I drew courage from her example and began focusing on building a career of my own. Realizing that I wanted to get into sales, I took a job in an outlet of a chain of men's clothing stores. Since I had no experience, I started as a part-time employee. Within six weeks I was consistently selling more from our outlet than any of the full time salespersons, becoming one of the top sellers in the entire chain. I'd spent so much time in the past, psyching out what other people wanted and expected, that fitting suits to people's personalities and tastes came easily.

"Within a year, I moved from selling merchandise to directing a local business. My responsibilities included purchasing inventory, handling invoicing, correspondence, bookkeeping, and taxes. I also managed staff and business promotion. In time, I worked into a position of authority and liked it.

"Beyond gaining job competencies, I also needed to better deal with my anger. Since my previous pattern had been to withdraw or placate, I practiced first with Mother (it was safer), and then gradually with others, mustering up the nerve to express upset feelings. It was harder to express anger to men, so at first I would write out what I wanted to say to them.

"Speaking up became easier with repetition. These days I don't let myself forget that I have a right to my feelings and expressing them. I know that things work out better when I own up to my anger and ask for changes. Being competent and creative in my work and thought well of in the business community has definitely helped me stand up for myself.

"I expect and figure out ways to get my objectives met. In the past these included promotions, pay raises, deletion of undesirable job duties, more job benefits, longer vacation time. If the answer to something was 'No,' I didn't back down, I just came at it from a different angle. It's been my experience that when you know what you want and feel confident, eventually you find ways to make your objectives happen. It's a matter of choices and how much time and effort we're willing to expend on them.

"As recovery progressed, life improved in many ways. I had a successful career and many friends. I exercised moderately but regularly, and my food intake was relatively healthful. Despite all these positives, I sometimes reverted to relieving stress with mini-binges and a trip to the bathroom to disgorge. After more than eight years of bulimia, I wanted to give up vomiting entirely, but it wasn't until I really faced my own mortality that I finally made this commitment to myself."

Releasing Destructive Habits

"Mother and I had often discussed the bottom line that, in order to overcome eating disorders, the desire for change is necessary. I remember turning on the radio, and Karen Carpenter was singing about how she was never going to fall in love again. I remarked to Mother, 'That's one lady who didn't make it. She was a vomiter and self-starver, and she'll never be able to do *anything* again.' This was some time after I had read that she'd died of complications from anorexia.

"When I was anorexic, I'd shared with Mother that I had looked on death as a release from present problems but hadn't faced the finality of it. Back while I was still in college, Mother said she was going to take an evening course at the local college about people's approaches to living, based on their personal concepts of death. She asked Brenda and me whether we'd like to take the course with her. Since we could get college credit, we all decided to attend this 'death and dying' weekly course for a semester.

"The class discussed mortality in some depth, which led to the three of us talking about how our views of death affect how we choose to live our lives and what we consider important. This, too, was part of the healing process, since it focused on how precious life is, something to be treasured and lived to the fullest. After a few sessions, I'd sensed in a more profound way that life could be cut short suddenly and unexpectedly at any moment.

"Later one night, I had a prolonged 'dream state' that repeated the refrain, 'Release yourself; why don't you just let go and die?' In it I was pleading, 'Please, no, I don't want to die!' When I woke up, I was terrified that life might slip away. I lay in darkness for four or five hours after that dream experience, when the first rays of daylight came through the curtains. It was beautiful to watch, and I kept thinking how lucky I was to be alive and have a new day and a fresh chance.

"I remember sharing with Mother the next day, my realization of how fragile the body is. How wonderful it would be to eat well and stop taking stupid chances, maybe rupturing my esophagus, having my heart stop, or causing hemorrhaging in an eye because of vomiting. After talking this over, I considered the possibility that this experience might have been conveying a message to stop doing unhealthy things like binge-purging, a message that said, 'Let that part of you go.' I thought about the things I wanted to do and things I didn't want to do anymore, realizing how much I wanted to live.

"Facing my mortality was the last little push that helped me see that there is nothing more precious than being alive and healthy. I reminded myself that I had sight, the use of my limbs, my sense of touch and taste, and could hear! Finally I appreciated how dear family and friends were to me and realized how much I wanted to live a long, productive, happy life.

"I allowed myself to awaken to how great existence could be. That love of life, plus a new sense of purpose, gave me the incentive to give up the old self-destructive behavior. Lots of things had improved, and at last I resolved not to binge or purge ever again — never!"

Fully Living, Not Just Existing

"These days, I seldom think about calories, nor do I have any foods I consider off-limits. I eat sensibly and maintain a healthy weight without dieting. Several times a week I lift weights and often take long walks or jog. I have endurance and strength and like how my body looks.

"I don't want to be dependent anymore on habits that are destructive and dangerous. I keep this inner commitment to health by recognizing how lucky I am to be alive. I believe we can ask for and receive strength, wisdom, and guidance through prayer, so I pray to reinforce my resolve to lead the best life I know how. 'Help me be good to myself,' is a typical prayer. 'Help me to do good in the world and see myself as significant.'

"I feel blessed that I have a future and enjoy each day as fully as possible. I make a point of noticing the meaningful events, remembering that every day is precious and trying not to waste time on petty matters. Mother encourages me not to become jaded or cynical no matter how discouraged I get, but to keep looking at life from fresh perspectives and with a sense of wonder.

"In time, I discovered that I could be happy even if I didn't have a man in my life. I had my own interests and goals. Having a successful career helped me learn that I didn't need to rely on anyone else, and that was very reassuring. I also developed hobbies, such as traveling, collecting art, and playing tennis. These added to my overall pleasure, and I found I could be content just taking a walk or going to a movie with friends.

"I had reached the point where I felt productive and relaxed and didn't constantly run shoulds and shouldn'ts in my mind. I dated now and then, and in the process learned a lot about myself along with what I'd want in a long-term relationship. It was interesting that I didn't form a satisfying relationship with a man until I had a sense of purpose and direction and felt self-sufficient. The last counselor I saw had told me, 'The secret of a good relationship is a good choice.' When I wasn't feeling needy, I could do this.

"I also took another major step when I decided I'd be much happier being in business for myself. It's gratifying to see that my business is growing and doing better than I'd anticipated. There is a sadness and sense of loss for the childhood I wish I'd had, but I seldom think about it and instead focus on the present.

"I have no contact with my biological father and accept that this is for the best. When I was ill, my stepfather never asked, 'What can I do to help you get well?' and never became involved in my recovery. At the time, it was hard to understand why he didn't want any part in this, but now I accept that maybe this was for the best. After he and my mother divorced, he went for extended counseling, this being the direct result of their breakup. He says this changed many of his attitudes and that he feels better for it, again an impact of the extended healing process in which we'd all become involved.

"When I was growing up, I resented and feared him. But that was a long time ago. Now we've become friends, and when we talk, he's careful to stick to non-controversial subjects and makes it a point not to give me advice or tell me how I should run my life.

"Sharing the cohealing process prompted each of us to change our lives in significant ways. I know that the personal changes Mother made in her own life were so much a part of my recovery that they really can't be separated. Her example helped me immeasurably.

"It's been about ten years since I first returned home after having lost a third of my body weight through self-starvation and vomiting. In many ways, I regret wasting nine years of my life. They were wasted in the sense that I felt physically unhealthy much of the time, wasted because I was afraid, wasted because I worried so much about what others were thinking of me.

"On the other hand, I learned a lot from the perceptions gained during the long, slow recovery process. Now, when I look in the mirror I like the person I see. I feel worthwhile, caring, whole, and fully alive.

"These days I see that there is no greater gift than being alive. Having been to the depths and been miserable for so long, I know that if I could get well, so can *others*."

In college, Brenda had succumbed to bulimia following her sister's lead. Fortunately, the period during which she purged much of what she ate lasted only a few months, after which she worked to normalize her eating. Though she reestablished a more normal food intake, the bulimic pattern of mini-binges followed by purging persisted in times of stress, disappointment, and boredom. Brenda was never as thin or ill as her sister, and she fully recovered in less than two years. In contrast, Jacque had severe to moderate eating-disorder symptoms for more than nine years.

This book is based primarily on Jacqueline's story, but I include a brief synopsis of Brenda's recovery because it shows how, in the same family, daughters can have significantly different patterns. Also, her experiences were part of the overall cohealing process. Brenda writes about her recovery:

Commitment to Health

"When I read that stomach acid could burn holes in a carpet, I couldn't stop wondering what the acid was doing to my teeth and throat each time I vomited. I worried about the possibility of damage to my esophagus, an electrolyte imbalance that might result in heart failure, or some other harm that might result. I knew my frequent sore throats were related to vomiting and couldn't kid myself that my eating habits weren't damaging my body.

"Looking back, if I had continued chaotic dieting and purging, I might have died. I remember wondering back then, if they did an autopsy on my body now, what would it look like?

"I adopted an emaciated kitten and pampered and nourished her because I knew she would die if she didn't get some flesh on her bones. As I nursed her back to health, my worry over my cat helped me understand the worry my parents were feeling for *me*. Sometime before finding the kitten, Mom had pointed out that if I had a pet it would seem cruel to starve it, watching it sicken day by day as I was doing to myself. Having this kitten helped me comprehend and act on what she'd been saying.

"During and after the months of my recovery, Mom was a constant in my life, someone who continually shared practical insights that progressively helped me feel better about myself, resolve conflicts, be assertive, and deal effectively with detrimental social situations. It was as though she were giving me the 'tools' I needed to build myself a more satisfying life.

"After she and my stepfather divorced, I was fortunate to be her 'roommate' for awhile and later to live nearby. This meant I could tap into this resource of love that I had so undervalued during my early bulimic days.

"Recovery was slow and gradual; one step forward, one back, then forward again. In time, because I wanted to be healthy again and live a long life, I finally made the commitment to myself not to vomit anymore. At that point it was no longer a tentative 'I'm going to *try* to stop vomiting.' It had become, 'From now on, I'm *not* going to do that anymore.' When I made that decision, it became a concrete fact in my life.

"Committed to recovery, I developed new strategies to replace old habits, ones that would better serve me. If I was hungry, I generally steamed some vegetables; if I wasn't really hungry but just wanted to ingest something, I reached for tea or mineral water. Each day, I made sure I had eaten adequately from all the major food groups. If I ate a piece of apple pie and felt guilty, I knew I would be doing more damage by throwing it up than keeping those calories down, so instead I counted it as part of my bread and fruit for the day.

"My new resolve was bolstered by information from medical journals that indicated if I didn't change, I might not be able to have children. Because having a child one day was very important to me, vomiting a piece of pie couldn't compare to this life goal.

"At first, I was afraid of gaining weight, but I had made the decision to be healthy, so I stuck with digesting a carefully balanced diet. Being a vegetarian in the beginning helped heighten my awareness of eating healthfully. In time, I found a balance between too little concern and overconcern about what I ate.

"My weight reestablished itself around 126 pounds, which at five-feet-seven, is a healthy weight and what I'd been in high school. In my starved state, I recall that my stomach had protruded while the rest of my body was skinny. Now my weight became well distributed, my hair thickened again, my posture improved, and I had more energy. My complexion was clear once more, my sore throats were gone, and (very important to me) I became less tense and high strung. I realize that if I were to revert to vomiting, in time my appearance and health would again deteriorate.

"Since eating and then purging was no longer an option when I was stressed, I gradually developed other ways of handling my finances, relationships, and other problem areas. I noticed that by simply being more assertive, I experienced less stress. In time I made friends who were also into health, which reinforced my commitment to regular exercise and good eating habits."

Cohealing Exchange

"During the recovery process, I took a long hard look at what attitudes and emotional background might have triggered my eating problems, and steadily worked on changing and channeling them so that I could establish a solid basis for a balanced, well-rounded life.

"While growing up, I had both appreciated and resented my mother. I'd appreciated my mother's unconditional love and that she believed in me. We had shared so many good times together. I had always been able to count on her *being* there — encouraging me, helping with school and scouting activities, homework, and all sorts of things. Yet at the same time, I used to be angry at her, feeling that in a number of ways she wasn't being a good role model. She wasn't showing me how to be assertive or have a career outside the home.

"Most of all, I hated that she tolerated situations that weren't in her best interest. She was capable and smart, and in many ways I thought she was great, so her staying in an obviously unsatisfactory marriage simply didn't make sense to me. Why was she staying when it was so degrading to her? Why didn't she just leave and set up her own life with her children? She deserved a good relationship; why didn't she go out and get one?

"It was only after I developed an understanding of our family's generational patterns (no female relative had ever worked outside the home after marriage, and each had been subservient to her husband) and an awareness of my mother's own childhood that I could understand *why* she made the choices she did.

"Significantly, she was the one who proved to be the turning point between the restricted lives of past generations of women in our family and my generation, who were searching for more freedom and opportunity.

"During the years covered in this book, Mom restructured her life in many ways that I could never have imagined. She is involved in activities she loves doing, has a successful career, travels, dresses glamorously, and does all sorts of things she only used to dream about. At some point, I realized that she had become an example I greatly respect and admire. If I were to describe her to someone today, I'd say, 'My mom's self-reliant and creative. She respects herself and sets limits on what she will and won't do. She's happy and contented, and I like seeing that for *her* sake as well as for mine.'

"I had wanted so much to have a mother role-model who could show me how to be successful. When I saw that my mother's life had now become satisfying to her, and that she was content and enjoying herself, I gained confidence that I could do the same. I was strongly influenced by her changes as well as her insights, and she was influenced by mine. I felt good that she frequently told me that my input and observations were helpful to her, and comfortable knowing it wasn't a one-way street. I played a part in her process of change and growth just as she did in mine, and this continues as an ongoing exchange between us."

Recovery

"It's been a number of years since I fully recovered from bulimia. These days, one of the nicest things about being well is feeling and knowing that I'm acceptable *as I am*. I have no desire to overeat, and sweets seldom seem appealing. I eat whatever I want and, without effort, maintain a healthy weight. In good weather, I usually jog a couple of miles after work, two or three times a week. This seems to reduce stress, and I enjoy the exercise. I rarely think about the past when eating and weight were problems.

"My work brings satisfaction, contacts with interesting people, and travel as well, which is a nice bonus. For me, compulsive food-related problems were a stage I went through. Because of them, I was forced to look more closely at my life and the influences around me. It was a painful process, but I'm stronger and better grounded for having gone through it and come out the other side. Now I'm determined to make the most of life. I enjoy what I do, have many dear friends, and feel far more aware than before."

One thing that may have helped Brenda recover much more quickly than Jacqueline was that at no time had she been able to convince herself that bingeing and purging were safe. She had always been aware of their danger and knew that she was playing "Russian roulette" with her health and her life.

She never denied the damage she was doing to her body and never sank as deep into problematic eating behavior as her sister. Brenda had watched the lives of her four "bingeing buddies" become progressively distorted and their health deteriorate, and she realized that this could happen to her if she continued.

From as early as fourth grade, Brenda had been into planning her life, talking about a career, marriage with children, and wanting to live to an old age. From this perspective, temporary skinniness during dating years had seemed desirable, but not nearly as imperative as it had to Jacque who had been counting on a man to save her because she felt she couldn't provide for herself.

Lack of a sense of self-worth, difficulty in being assertive, and the other problems Jacque had experienced had been problems for

Brenda also, but to a far less degree. She had grown up believing in her ability to take care of herself and intending to share financial responsibilities with a husband. Brenda's greater self-respect, as well as her independent spirit, had made her more open to input that encouraged recovery. At present, it is estimated that more than 25 percent of our young females experience bulimic and other eating disorder symptoms at one time or another in their lives. Considering this, Brenda could count herself among those lucky ones who recovered within a relatively short time.

Since her recovery, Brenda has put time and energy into developing a highly successful and challenging business career. She is well known and respected in her field. Her stepfather's preaching that, because she is female, she should plan to be a typist because she couldn't go far in the business world never daunted her spirit of adventure or stopped her from taking on highly responsible positions wherever she has worked.

Both Jacqueline and Brenda are bright, lovely young women, each with an outgoing nature. In spite of busy schedules, they maintain close friendships along with other absorbing interests. Some of their friends have commented to me that they are among the most delightful, empathetic, sincere people they know. Fortunately, at last life feels good to them.

CHAPTER 17

Breaking Free

Starting in childhood, my parents had made it clear that helping others *"above and beyond the call of duty"* was not only admirable but also *expected* of me. Like so many women of my generation, I'd been taught that I should be selfless and self-sacrificing and should take care of *others* before myself. I had been a helpful wife, daughter, and mother, but couldn't shake a gnawing sense of restlessness, an indefinable feeling that life was passing me by.

Most days, and even months, had blended in unmemorable sameness, and I had found myself thinking, as I gazed out the kitchen window doing dishes, of "Some day . . . " when I hoped life would feel more satisfying.

I had been a dependent wife, and having grown up submissive, I had put up with my husband's domineering ways. There had been better times, but always there was his temper and his need to control. Then, after 18 years of marriage, my parents (who were then in their late seventies) had needed me to refurbish and sell their real estate holdings. That had given me the opportunity every few months to spend three months at a time out of state, working on my parents' projects. During those separations, I had switched from household tasks to directing challenging projects and, in the process, had been quite surprised to discover in myself initiative and competencies I had never realized I had.

Eventually I was able to sell my parents' properties for a good deal more than realtors had originally anticipated, which assured my parents a comfortable retirement income. The overall experience with all its many facets had contributed to my developing a greater sense of personal power. And, as mentioned earlier, it gave me a chance for separations from my husband that helped me reassess our marriage.

I recognized that after each time away I had dreaded going home. In a personal journal, several weeks after having returned, I wrote, "At home I'm again retreating — no longer venturing forth but reactive, dependent, and subordinate. I experience doubt and isolation." But over time, primarily through the cohealing process, I had been expanding my concepts of life's possibilities and was no longer willing to continue this way.

Looking back, when Jacqueline had first come home so ill, I had wished I had a counselor to whom I could turn. But we couldn't afford this financial burden, and in our area there had been no self-help group that dealt with eating disorders or related problems. I could have used some guidance and reassurance.

During that period, I was not only trying to help Jacqueline and Brenda but also caring for my mother, who was gravely ill, plus another relative with health problems who was living with us. Each of them is doing well now, but at that time there had been no way to know what the outcome would be. All in all, it had been a particularly rough time.

Now, after nearly 20 years of marriage, the childrens' stepfather and I were better off financially, and I wanted marital counseling, hoping our many differences could somehow be worked out. After considerable urging on my part, my husband consented. However, feeling defensive and resenting the changes the counselor was suggesting he make, after only three brief visits he chose not to continue.

So at this stage (approximately three years before Jacque's recovery), I decided to pursue counseling for eight weeks on my own with a minister-teacher-counselor who knew our family well. He is the counselor who had helped Jacque better understand why she'd been vulnerable to anorexia, and the one Brenda had also consulted. (Lisa had taken classes and seminars from him, so he had acted as a mentor to her also.) It was helpful to work with a counselor who had a depth of understanding of other family members, and who could give me what I thought of as a "tool kit," filled with insightful, practical "tools" for dealing more effectively with problematic interpersonal situations and to better understand my reactions to them.

If we consider a mentor as a wise and trusted friend, as well as a counselor and guide, then he was that indeed for me. With his help, I gained new insights into long-standing problems and how to deal with them.

Childhood Scripting

He discussed my childhood with me, concentrating attention on how, as long as I could remember, my mother had considered herself to be in delicate health and expected special attention and consideration from other family members. I recalled how as a child, I'd hear my father wryly commenting that, at parties, his wife could "dance for hours and be the 'belle of the ball,'" yet at home always be tired, "with one sort of pain or another." On such occasions, he'd imply that she seemed able to horseback ride and swim, and do whatever other things she liked, but somehow wasn't up to doing things she didn't want to do, using spurious health excuses to avoid them.

"And how did you feel about this situation?"

"I felt frightened when my mother indicated I'd failed to please her because she'd act physically distressed, clasping her chest and heaving deep sighs. She acted so frail, and with her groaning and panting, I felt that I had to cater to her needs."

To this the counselor replied, "This scenario is the basis for guilt; 'You're good if you help your mother, bad if you don't; good if you adapt to whatever she wants, bad if you don't. If you upset her, you're endangering her life."

After further discussion, he pointed out that my mother was still using this "stick" and I was still trying to protect her.

Questions regarding my childhood relationship with my father centered in part on his explosive temper and his having repeatedly and unexpectedly hit me violently for supposed "misdeeds." This brought to mind my recollection that, "There seemed to be an understood 'rule' in the family that my father's temper and violent thrashings of me and my sister were not to be discussed or questioned by anyone. It didn't seem possible to question the system or avoid the abuse and I remember feeling very alone with no one to turn to."

The counselor questioned, "Describe a time when you were a child and he beat you; how would you, as an adult, have perceived such a outburst? Go back and recall a particular incident."

I closed my eyes, remembering an incident that took place in our living room when I was about eight. "Well, an adult would see my father walloping me with all his strength, over and over again between mid-back and the knees, and yelling something about teaching the small child a lesson. She is being hit repeatedly with great force. She is crumpled over, submitting silently, not making a sound. He continues flailing away, venting his rage all the while cussing and chastising her.

"He seems to gradually be expending his rage and is finally regaining control of himself," I observed.

"Now he's stopped and is releasing her from his grasp. He is shoving her away. I see her head out the back door. She is standing at the top of the porch stairs, grasping the railing, trying to draw in a breath. She can't inhale and tries desperately to get some air. I can tell her lungs ache and that panic is setting in."

Still concentrating on the scene, I continued, "Finally the first air rushes into her lungs. She is slowly, painfully making her way down the back steps to a quiet secluded corner of the yard. Using her small right index finger she wipes away tiny chips of teeth that she'd broken as she had clenched them against the pain. She touches the margins of her teeth to feel if this will be noticeable. Then, alone in the far reaches of their backyard, she lets herself cry. Sobbing, she waits for the pain to subside. She is afraid to go back into the house."

Pausing, he responded, "As a child, how did you react?"

"While he was hitting me, I knew there was no escape and I felt terribly frightened. I didn't struggle because that only made him madder and the situation worse. He'd be shouting 'I'm only doing this for your own good!' but I never could figure out what I'd supposedly done wrong or what he thought I should be learning. This was very distressing because there seemed no cause and effect between his actions and my behavior, and no way to avoid getting hit."

"*Emotionally* — how did you react?"

I confided, "I felt a lot of anger at my father and this was mixed with a heavy load of guilt. I knew he was providing well for my material needs and thought I should feel appreciative and loving. In some sort of mixed way, I felt justified for being angry at him and also that I was a bad person for feeling this way."

The counselor remarked, "Like all children, you were helpless and dependent. You needed protection but didn't receive it or the feelings of loving acceptance you deserved. These were lessons in being docile and uncomplaining, and in tolerating abusive situations."

"In spite of fearing and even hating my father, I also admired him, especially how he took on life with such verve and confidence. He was well read and worldly, and quite adventurous. I wished I could be that way." I also mentioned, "I had repeated childhood nightmares that were probably related to his beatings."

"Do you recall what they were?" he asked.

"My most frequent ones were of being chased by some horrible beast that wanted to do me in. When I tried to escape, I'd become immobilized and no matter how hard I tried, I couldn't run. I'd wake up in terror, with my heart pounding. For a long time I was afraid to go to sleep at night because I might have another of these dreams."

The counselor commented, "As children, we often have a great deal of insight and can see into conflicted situations with great clarity. Overall, how do you suppose you saw your situation back then?"

Pausing to remember my perceptions as a child, I said, "Well, I knew my parents wouldn't understand my resentments or apprehensions, and I realized they only saw me as their cooperative little daughter and didn't know how angry and frightened I was. I was aware that my father would never physically abuse a friend or even a stranger as he did me, yet I knew he thought of himself as a highly principled and moral individual."

I thought to add, "I recognized my mother enjoyed hobbies that took stamina, yet often acted like she might have a heart attack at any moment and die. I knew she was manipulative and self-serving but still I felt guilty if anything I did upset her."

Recalling how lonely I'd felt, I remarked, "I had no one I could confide in who could confirm these perceptions. There was nobody with whom it was safe to share my distress." I told him that only recently it had occurred to me that my mother had not tried to stop my father from beating me, nor had she comforted me after he did.

"You felt shut down, as a child, with nowhere to turn," he said.

"Yes. My mother used shushing sounds to insist I be quiet and my father's most frequent command was, 'Shut up!' I was expected to pay rapt, silent attention while he monologued. When I did risk sharing a personal thought or feeling, it was insulting being told 'You're *not* that way!' for this denied my reality."

After several sessions the counselor began pointing out some of the confusing, negating messages I had received as a child:

Try hard (but don't expect success).
Don't make mistakes (heaven forbid!).
Don't trust yourself (others know better).
Don't complain (or else no one will like you).
Wait until you're more prepared (you're not ready yet).
Do as I say (don't upset me).
You can't make it on your own (you need a man).
Don't be selfish (take care of others before yourself).
Don't hit anyone (but it's okay for me to hit you).
Don't be angry (nice girls don't get angry).
Don't reveal your inner self (that's not you).
Don't think too well of yourself (be modest).
Don't take risks (they're dangerous).
Life is a struggle (but maybe, if you're patient, things will improve).

With these were other messages that had conveyed positive expectations and attitudes, such as: be capable, creative, dauntless, and be all you can be (as in my father's approach to life). The counselor explained how I could look to such messages to build an expansive, confident attitude about life's possibilities.

Guilt and Suffering

The counselor told me, "You received childhood script messages that, for you, there's *virtue in almost martyred service to others and virtue in guilt and suffering* because they are a way of showing penitence. You're good if you're giving and good if you're guilty."

To my question "Why is guilt a virtue in this script?" he replied, "Because your parents indicated that you're guilty doing for yourself. Yet freedom and autonomy are synonymous with health and having a good life. *The distorted messages given you by your parents are that you should be docile and dependent and that, for you, freedom and autonomy are bad. This was powerful preparation for a similar role in marriage.*"

When I talked about times when things had seemed briefly to be improving in my relationship with my husband as well as that with my parents, he said, "It's clear these have been times when you were choosing and doing for yourself. But your scripting and your parents hold that if you have fun and good times, if you do what is in your best interest, you are 'selfish,' so this is almost immediately followed by pressure on you to 'pay the price' by feeling guilty."

Related to wanting to choose for myself, I commented that "It wasn't until after my husband and I were married that he felt it his duty to guide and control my life, but now he's always trying to change me and is never satisfied with who I actually am."

"Yes, he keeps wanting to fit you into the mold of what he feels you should be as 'a wife.' But you don't fit and will *never* fit his mold."

"My husband tells me what I should believe, do, say, and even *feel*. For example, he's yelled at me so many times, telling me, 'You *should* be angry at Lisa and not be on speaking terms with her!' when *he's* the one who is angry at her. Because I continue to visit and have a loving relationship with her, he curses and condemns me. At times he's threatened to throw me out of the house if I don't 'stand by' him on this and reject her, as *he* has done."

The counselor's response hit home. "What everyone needs is to be an *individual,* which means deciding what he, or she, values and needs, wants, and likes to do. The 'I,' which has to do with identity, is not subject to negotiation. Intimacy satisfies the need to belong, to be needed, to be touched. This involves conflict-resolution skills in order to negotiate compromises on shared interactions. You need a strong sense of self, of who and what you are and are not, before you can have a satisfying intimate relationship."

When I explained that I had never held a full-time job, had no resume, and feared going on my own, I was surprised to hear his reassuring response: "In many ways you've excelled on behalf of *others* — you can do the same for yourself."

During our last meeting, it seemed natural to ask, "As you see it, what sort of changes do I need to make?"

He thought a while, then answered, "Hope, you've been willing to take all sorts of verbal abuse from your parents and your husband. I consider you an abused wife, though the abuse hasn't been physical. You need to take care of *yourself.* Your husband has been critical, controlling, and raging with anger at you. He insists on his own way and does what *he* wants. He plain and simply doesn't listen to you. You have no authentic relationship. You're so far apart that it's astonishing you've let it continue. Your soul wants to sing, to explore, to savor life. He works hard, pays his 'dues,' so to speak, and hopes someday there'll be a payoff when he'll start enjoying life. For you, it's the journey and being here and now that are important."

While I was still considering this thought, speaking slowly for emphasis and choosing his words carefully, he added, "You've suffered tremendous deprivation. As a child you were the victim of violent physical abuse by your father, and all your life your mother has used the implication of fragile health to get you to put her needs before your own. She is a master at creating shame and guilt. You tolerated situations in both of your marriages that no one should have to endure. You're a testament to survival and have come through this as a well-put-together person anyhow. *Now you need to refuse to be influenced by rage and criticism. You need now to cut off the sources of unhealthy script messages wherever they are being reinforced. They demean the human spirit — they squeeze you. Refuse to be influenced by those who would downgrade or constrain you.*"

He followed this by commenting, "You always have your childhood script, but you can choose to make appropriate decisions based on your strength in the present."

I was trying to absorb his comments when, leaning forward to stress his point, he said, "Hope, you need to remember, there is *no morality to human needs*. They just *are*. It's important that you become an expert on your *own* needs. Give yourself permission to explore your potential wherever it leads."

I'll never forget that, as I was leaving, he remarked, "You are lovable and deserve to be treated well. You deserve having your life feel good to you. Find ways to get your needs and wants met fully. No more crumbs!" With a smile, he commented, "Remember, 'hope' is the ability to change; to change your environment, to change who is in it, and to change yourself."

Basic Requests

These few counseling sessions had a major impact on my life. They gave new direction and the conviction that tolerating abusive situations was no longer acceptable and certainly not an example I wanted to be setting for my children.

My husband had repeatedly warned me that I couldn't make it on my own; "You'd starve to death!" he would say. Now, at last, I realized that in a sense I *was* starving. It seemed that even if the only way to start out on my own was to go through some really lean times, I could accept that — almost anything would be better than the life I was living. From all the rethinking I'd been through during the cohealing process, I was no longer willing to accept crumbs.

I remember dreaming that my husband had put my favorite hand-knit wool ski sweater in the washing machine in hot water. It shrank so much that, in my dream, I told him, "But you've made it so tiny I can no longer fit into it!" I could no longer fit into the symbolic sweater or my marriage.

Within the same week, I had a nightmare in which my husband insisted that he had to put me on a ship and send me somewhere. The strange thing was, he insisted that I must be sent in a particular size box that was too small for me. To fit me into his box, he had to cut off my arms, legs, and head. I woke up terrified since it had seemed so real. It didn't take me long to interpret that I didn't fit into my husband's marital limitations.

When my husband had been present at the three counseling sessions, my request had been for him to regard me as *me*, my own person, with a right to my own thoughts and feelings. I wanted to feel safe expressing them and negotiate ways for us both to get our needs met. I couldn't stand his overbearing rules anymore.

I talked of divorce, telling my husband that if I couldn't negotiate for these basics, if I had no chance to be *me, myself, my way*, I couldn't stand being in the marriage any longer. I made my position clear. His reaction was increased anger and the tightening of his grip with more rules, demands, and threats. Since I couldn't be what he wanted ("be strong but compliant, use your own judgment but be obedient, be honest with your feelings but only feel as I tell you is right . . . "), he was further frustrated and resentful.

I felt that if I left him, I'd have a chance for a new start. I hoped that a side benefit might be that some healing could take place for him also. I was no longer willing to live by his commands, "No wife of mine will do . . . " such and such, or "I'm warning you, as my wife, you'd better do as I say!" I'd had more lists of "rules" I must follow than anyone needs in several lifetimes.

The solution was inevitable — I decided to get a divorce.

Breaking Free

I'd had continual headaches for years, some quite severe, plus muscle cramps in my back, which I realized were all reactions to stress and to my having internalized anger and distress that I had been unable to safely express to my husband. I needed to listen to my body's messages. I had hoped that my mother would understand and be somewhat compassionate when I explained to her that I needed to get out of my marriage. This didn't happen.

One fall day I sat with her, sharing the history of my husband's abusive anger and how distressed and unhappy I'd been for such a long time. I told her how I had lived with endless rules set down by him and how, most evenings in recent months, I'd endured an hour or two of his loud angry tirades and criticisms, with threats that "If you don't do as I say, I'll kick you out and you'll have no place to go!" I told her about the continual pain I was experiencing, directly related to stress. I shared my sadness and my longings. Though I tried to keep my composure, as I spoke I broke down and cried.

I ached for her to put her arms around me, hug me, and say she cared. I wanted her to understand. Instead, she sat across the room staring, saying absolutely nothing. Finally, when I talked about divorce as the only way to begin building a good life for myself, she angrily told me, "You *have* to stay married! There's no *way* you could support yourself!"

She came over to where I was sitting, stood right above me and, glaring at me, said that though she had been "miserable" in her marriage, she had put up with it, and I could do the same. If I had to work, I would have less time to devote to helping with her many daily activities. Staring angrily down at me, she continued, "You *have* to stay married for *my* sake. Who else is going to take care of things for me?"

Distressed by her reaction, I tried to reassure her that I'd continue to drive her when needed, do shopping and errands for her, take her on excursions, and help with her hobbies. I would even hire someone to help her on a daily basis, if she wanted. But no matter what I offered, she was unyielding in her insistence that I was to *stay married*.

As to my getting a divorce, she said, "If you do, I'd rather kill myself than live." (If I didn't comply with her wishes, again there was that threat of her death.) Within 15 minutes of this comment, I overheard her in the garage angrily telling Jacqueline, "Your mother *has* to stay married. Otherwise how is she going to have the time to help *me*? I'd rather be dead!" Jacque listened but didn't respond.

Later that evening, when we were by ourselves, Jacque reassured me: "You know she isn't going to do herself in. She's just trying to shame you. You're doing the right thing — don't let her get to you." Still upset by my mother's reaction, I remembered the counselor's previous comment to me that "No matter what you do, or don't do, you won't be the cause of your mother's death."

Though I realized my mother felt threatened by the idea of my working outside the home and changing previous patterns, I was crushed that she had no compassion for my situation. Oddly, as it turned out, her reaction was so blatant, so undisguised, that it helped me see what the counselor had just recently been telling me. He had stressed how important it is to decide for myself what I "value and need." So, at last, I worked on giving myself permission to take care of myself and to do so without feelings of guilt or shame. There was no turning back. As I worked at breaking away from the past, I kept reminding myself of his impartial advice.

At the time I left my husband, my mother was so angry she cut me out of her life. No more get-togethers, no more phone calls, no more correspondence. I've sent cards and letters over the intervening years, thanking her for things she had done in the past that I appreciated and reminiscing about some of the good times we shared, but all went unanswered. Her rejection of me was indicated in many ways, including such things as her offering Jacqueline financial help if she would promise not to see me again.

I felt hurt and angry but also relieved. In a sense, I went through a period in which I mourned the loss of the mother I had wanted her to be. The sadness, anger, and disillusionment were very real. But I had taken a step forward, and that was healing.

Brenda and Jacqueline candidly shared their perceptions about the relationship between my mother and myself. Brenda, for instance, had previously remarked, "Have you noticed that your mother makes a point of refering to you as being on your 'father's side of the family'? Of course, you *do* look more like him than her but its strange that she so completely identifies you with him. It seems as though on some level, she treats you as having come only through your father, and she resents and dislikes him."

Jacqueline had also commented on this peculiar division my mother made regarding my being on my father's "side of the family." Brenda's perception was that my mother had a great deal of antagonism and anger toward my father which she didn't feel safe to aim directly at him. For whatever reason, she thought of me as his daughter, not hers, and it was safer to release some of this hostility at me instead.

On another occasion, Brenda phoned to tell me, "I've been thinking. You inherited your father's looks and athletic build whereas your mother inherited a short, unathletic build and spent years being very overweight. Looking at this from *her* standpoint, you have a strong, healthy body, and she doesn't. You have things she probably always wanted and never had. I think, on some level, she feels terribly envious of you."

Continuing this train of thought, she shared with me the following: "It seems to me that your mother couldn't face your leaving your marriage because this might seem to invalidate *her* decision to stay in an unhappy marriage all those years. We kids all see how over and over again she's tried to sabotage you. I think unconsciously she may have been insecure about her appearance, among other things. People just don't act as superior as she does unless they feel *insecure.*"

This was an entirely new thought to me. My mother being insecure? I had always thought of her as being so emphatic and absolutely sure of herself. But it made some puzzle-pieces fit together.

During this same phone conversation, Brenda observed, "I think your mother could never allow you to think of yourself as deserving because this would have reduced her hold on you that said, 'You *owe* me.' Though I'm sure she herself didn't realize it, she used guilt and shaming you as a means of control."

In the past, I had noticed my mother's comments regarding my being on my "father's side of the family" and had thought them strange. There had been some sort of internalized barrier I couldn't get past that seemed to prevent her from feeling close to me.

New Beginnings

At first, after leaving my husband, I felt terribly alone. I moved into a small, somewhat dingy apartment by myself in a new town far from memories of the past. With my typewriter in tow and stacks of notes and research papers, I set out to complete this book.

At times, feeling sad about the disappointments of the past, I wondered if I would ever find a loving relationship with a man, one that was healthy and caring — in which I could be fully *me*. Would I always be alone? Would life ever feel really good?

Late one afternoon, at the close of a social gathering I'd attended along with 11 married couples, I took time to walk by myself to the nearby beach. As I walked along the sandy path past the tall beach grass, I could hear their distant laughter in the cool autumn air. Soon all I could hear was the soft swooshing sound of the ocean waves on the smoothly packed sand left by the retreating tide. The warm orange sun was setting in the misty evening. As I strode along, I noticed part of a sand dollar poking out of the wet sand.

I uncovered it to discover that it was only half a sand dollar. Further down the beach, I found another half sand dollar, and then another and still another. In time I had my hands full of them. At the time this seemed symbolic to me. I was no longer like the couples I had spent the day with — half of a pairing — a half that, with another half, could make a whole.

I tried fitting some of the sand dollars together to see if any of them matched to make a *whole* one, but none of them did. Before I walked back down the path to my car, I tossed them back into the ocean, thinking, "Maybe someday I'll meet someone who'll be a good fit, a good choice. After all, it only takes *one*."

CHAPTER 18

Healing —
A Shared Experience

There had needed to be a *turning point* in the family to break the multigenerational authoritarian (domination-submission) patterns of the past, and I was determined to make that happen.

Grieving for the Losses

When first on my own, I kept thinking about my disappointments and regrets during what, I later realized, was a normal grieving process. There were no more family secrets from the past that needed to be denied or hidden.

For me, grieving involved letting go of sorrow, pain, and anger from childhood, my marriages, and other events leading up to the present, so that healing could gradually take place. Healing brought a sense of sadness, as I began dealing with the overwhelming loss I felt about a lifetime in which there had been so much tension and distress.

Mourning has to do with forgiveness and completing the past. At last I was able to come to terms with all those years I had tried, but hadn't been able to create, the kind of home environment for my children that I so wished they'd had. In this I was fortunate to have their loving forgiveness. Before going on my own I had always been *afraid* to buck other family members and take full control of my life. But it was different now. I was, at last, fully responsible for myself.

I worked at accepting the legacy of the past, and "releasing" the trauma it had engendered. One by one, I replaced wistful thoughts about wishing things had been different (*"If only . . . "*), with the new resolve, *"From now on . . . ."* Deciding, "Okay, this time I will," helped me focus on the present and future so I could make more effective choices. I was finally able to accept the past when I took to heart this fact: the past is what got us to the present and made us who we are.

While working to establish what was essentially a fresh start, I reflected on what had been the best periods in my life, the bright spots when I was most contented and happy. I wanted to understand why they had felt good, and noticed that they had all been times when I had enjoyed the most freedom. I then considered how I might *recreate* similar circumstances. This approach helped give me a sense of direction.

Self-Care

I signed myself up for a "dancercize" class and started lifting weights to get myself back in shape. I took biofeedback deep-relaxation training and learned quite amazing body control. I also began meditating every morning at daybreak as well as before I went to sleep at night. Meditation brought many benefits and insights including a profound sense of self, of being who I was *meant* to be. Prayer was also a way to determine what was for my own highest good and what direction to take.

I tried a vegetarian diet for a while before going back to a more varied eating pattern, just to test which foods seemed related to feeling my best. I was experimenting, trying out new things and testing myself, including going to health- and growth-oriented workshops and seminars where I met other people who were at turning points in their lives. It was an exciting time, and I felt as though I was opening doors to all sorts of fresh opportunities.

It was unsettling to see how often my first reaction to new situations was "I can't do that." I decided that every time this reaction occurred I would *consciously* replace it with "I *can!*" If my feeling was still an unsure "No, I can't; I don't know how," I would just repeat to myself "I can do it," knowing I needed to change my old defeatist thought and habit patterns.

It was as though I had a strong internal Critical Parent continually telling me I was incompetent and unprepared and an Adapted Child that felt afraid and unsure. In a sense, I needed to build supportive, nurturing "self-talk" that could reassure my Adapted Child that "everything will be okay."

Affirmations

I kept two or three handwritten notes in bold lettering to myself on the front of the refrigerator with such reminders as:

No more crumbs from life.
Does this approach feel good? If not, find another way.
I *deserve* a good life.
I can get what I want.
Plan for the future — *live* today.
Pleasure is not something that must wait.
Be open to new ideas and friendships.
The world is not black and white. Things are seldom either/or.
No more shoulds, oughts, musts. What would be *effective*?
What would be *satisfying*?
Only feel guilty when I let *myself* down.
It's okay to express upset feelings.
Do something spontaneous today!
It's okay to do what I want and need to do.
I can trust myself. *Be* myself. Love myself.
Say "no" to anyone who would victimize me.
It's okay to take care of myself.

Most limitations are self-imposed. There are far fewer actual ones than I had imagined.

Every so often I would take my signs down and put up some new ones — each boldly written with color felt-tipped pens — stating affirmations like those above. I could see my progress as these attitudes became natural to me. Jacqueline and Brenda would comment on my "bulletins" to myself and began making ones of their own for their refrigerators.

I also made a list of things I wanted to accomplish that first year on my own. Although I had no idea how I would go about achieving any of them, at least I had spelled out what I *really wanted* to have happen. This was my "actualization list," and I tried to imagine how it would be when these things actually happened. No matter how uncertain I felt, I began working toward my goals. After several months, I had accomplished some of the more immediate ones.

I noticed that *action preceded feelings*. That is, by behaving *as though I were confident*, it was easier to take appropriate action.

This resulted in some successes, which, in turn, built confidence. After awhile, my automatic reaction to difficult situations became a determined "I'll find a way." My self-talk was changing.

I began trusting myself. When I experienced fear welling up inside me, I would think, "Is there anything here — right now — to be afraid of?" Since there generally wasn't, fear would subside. I had experienced much doubt about being on my own, but here I was enjoying doing just *what* I wanted, *when* I wanted. No more rules! I would remind myself that growth involves taking risks. "A boat is not built to stay in the harbor," I had heard a friend say. I translated that into telling myself to get moving and not place false limitations on myself out of unwarranted fear.

Guilt and Shame

I needed a sharpened understanding of past guilt-producing personal interactions so that I could avoid them in the future. Just a few months prior to separating from my husband, I had spent a month and a half preparing one of my mother's properties for sale, and there had been many guilt-provoking incidents. One had occurred five weeks into the project when my mother asked me to dye her leather camera case and some other things. She indicated that she wasn't going to do this herself because she didn't want to get permanent black dye on her hands. I didn't want to get dye on my hands either, so I offered to get the job done for her instead of doing it myself. To this suggestion, she had sarcastically snapped, "Well, my uppity, *selfish* little daughter doesn't want to help me!"

It had been a minor incident, but the old familiar message had been clear: "You should feel *guilty* and *ashamed* of yourself! You are a bad daughter."

For weeks, every day I had spent most of my time on her projects and had immediately offered to get the dye job done for her. I thought of how the counselor had recently pointed out to me that in my script, guilt and shame play such a large part. My mother was the one who had wanted the black dye applied to her leather articles. Since she was perfectly capable of doing this herself, whose problem was it? *Hers*, not mine. At last I was able to distinguish this.

In the past, I had "rescued" her and done far more than was reasonable in an attempt to minimize her caustic remarks and not feel badly about myself. The counselor had helped me see that interactions with her had rarely been quid pro quo (something in exchange for something else), as in the case of a person providing help that's negotiated and appreciated. She wanted me to take on her responsibilities, an act which amounts to rescue. (*With rescue there are bound to be antagonistic feelings.*)

It had taken me a long time to realize that when you repeatedly help someone who acts helpless and blameless, you can be assured that you'll eventually be condemned and become a victim. If you shoulder someone else's responsibilities when they are capable of handling them themselves, the end result is that the helped person feels victimized and retaliates in one way or another. It had been healthy for me to finally declare my limits. In the "camera dye" incident, I'd made a sound choice and was able to recognize that I had no reason to feel guilty.

I'd grown up feeling that it was selfish to make my own needs a priority. Shortly after this incident with my mother, as I was saying good-bye to a friend, I heard the often-repeated phrase "Take care of yourself!" This time I really heard the words, for it occurred to me that we do not say, in parting, "Take care of others!" We do not wish self-sacrifice but self-care.

Brenda's comments regarding this "dye incident" included her rhetorical question, "Who was selfish?" She pointed out to me, "Your mother feels it's okay for her to protect and take care of herself, but not for you to do the same for yourself. Your feelings didn't count. She let you know in not so subtle ways that if you distressed her she might have a heart attack and die. You were always afraid to set boundaries with her, afraid of upsetting her."

Brenda had become very aware of setting limits. In this same conversation she added, "As I mentioned to you recently, your mother is not as confident and all-knowing as she acts — in fact, I think she's quite the opposite. She probably feels somewhat powerless, and bullied you to hide this from herself."

Searching for Approval

Cohealing helped me comprehend how much I'd wanted my mother's approval back in childhood and ever since. Back when I had been helping her on a daily basis at her home, Jacque was often present and gave me her insights on my mother's reactions. Jacqueline's impressively mature assessment had been that "Your mother feels you owe her your life. Since she can't stand thinking she's not superior to you, she's continually in the bind of wanting you to do a top-notch job for her and then hating you for doing so. In order to deal with these conflicted feelings, she complains all the time and acts disgusted with you. Your actions, accomplishments, opinions, are all being negated."

I was paying attention to my mother's reactions and how they related to lifelong patterns between us. For example, soon after I'd completed renovation work on a property my mother wanted to sell, her realtor phoned saying that he had received an offer. While he was on his way over to the house to present it, she told me, "You do the talking and I'll just listen." But as I proceeded to work out the terms with the realtor, she kept interrupting with comments about her experiences owning property, emphatically telling me to "Keep quiet!" (After he had gone, she explained that it had been important "to impress him" with what she knew about real estate.)

Jacqueline had been in an adjacent room and had overheard the above conversation, so she was aware of what had happened. Later, we talked over the incongruity of my being expected to negotiate a deal at the same time that I was being ordered not to speak! She noted, "Never would she tolerate being insulted like that, yet she expects you to put up with this kind of treatment without complaint."

As I reassessed my mother's reactions to me, her need to downgrade me had been brought home again and again, such as the time Jacque asked me about the proper use of the word "milieu." I said it has "to do with the events surrounding something." My mother, who was present, promptly countered, "No, it means area!"

To clear up this disparity, Jacqueline looked the word up and read aloud from the dictionary. The first definition used the word "surrounding" and the second listed "area." My mother leaned across the table triumphantly. Wagging her finger at me, she said, "You see! I was right, and you were *wrong*!"

Still holding the dictionary, Jacqueline shrugged in my direction with a look of "What can you do?" We talked about the incident afterward. This seemingly insignificant exchange had encapsulated a great deal. It related to my being judged by the repeated theme: *Ah ha! I knew you didn't know what you were talking about!* There had been the usual undercurrent of triumph on her part and basic belief that she knew better and that I was wrong.

According to the dictionary, I'd been successful — according to my mother, I had failed. Because in this case there had been an outside source of reference, it had been clear that her discounting of me was a distortion of reality and that I'd had no reason to feel inadequate. It occurred to me that this type of interaction with her was probably related to my feeling, as a child, that I never did anything of real value.

While growing up I had many opportunities, which I'd appreciated and enjoyed, such as training in figure skating, ballet, fashion modeling, violin, art, even riflery — but despite having learned a variety of skills, I never really felt they amounted to much. I didn't feel my performance measured up; I never felt good enough. I didn't feel the inner me was acceptable. I wanted to feel *significant*, that I really counted for something, but I didn't know how.

Now, years later, my reaction to the "milieu" incident was one of shocked amusement — shocked at how blatant my mother had been, amused at how absurd it was. But I had lacked this perspective when a child, and had felt crushed by her scoffing disapproval. Feedback from the girls during the cohealing process, and simply being able to share my feelings and have them acknowledged, helped me see that my mother was never going to give me the approval I had wanted and that I needed to work on accepting this.

Eventually, I realized that never admitting a mistake, feeling self-righteous and manipulating others with guilt, are all indications of hidden shame. Since these were descriptive of my mother, I wondered whether shame experienced in her childhood might explain some of her reactions as an adult. Gradually, my feelings of sadness and grief related to my mother diminished, a transition that was made easier knowing that her own childhood scripting had undoubtedly limited her responses to people.

Whatever the problems between us, there were many things about her that I admired. She had provided me with an example of a woman who was bright, articulate, and well-read. She had a quick mind, was artistically creative, and feisty in her own way. In spite of limited stamina and strength in her later years, she traveled abroad even into her eighties. She pampered herself and has outlived all of her long-time friends. Now in her ninetieth year, with my father in a convalescent home, she lives alone and functions well, busying herself with hobbies, visiting friends, and managing her investments, as well as carrying on daily routines.

Many of my interactions with her in the past had been painful, but they had been part of the path to the present, and that was feeling better all the time.

Though I couldn't build a comfortable, relaxed relationship with my mother, I did go through an extended cohealing process with my father which basically transformed that relationship.

He had a habit of telling me to both "speak up" and "shut up." For a lifetime I had tolerated this, but now, with the help of Lisa and Brenda, I began keying in on it. I recall my father's phoning Lisa and me one time, asking that we each get on an extension so he could talk to us at the same time. Ostensibly, he was calling to visit and ask what type of used vehicle I planned to buy plus how I had arrived at my choice. After we had hung up Lisa said, "I was counting, and he told you to 'Shut up!' 24 times in just half an hour. Did you realize that?" (Yes, I had noticed!)

Later, Brenda shared with me this insight: "Your father yells at you to 'Shut up!' and you're in a bind because he's often furious if you try to answer his questions but equally mad if you don't. He does the same with me, only less so. It really makes no sense that he so frequently squelches you, because underneath his blustering, it's obvious he treasures and admires you."

And there was the problem of his compulsive talking, which had become exaggerated over the years. In his early eighties, one time when he visited me for a day, he even refused meals because this would interfere with his discourse. During many visits he talked for hours, virtually non-stop, insisting that I not comment but just listen. I enjoyed his reminiscences of past triumphs and adventures, along with his delightful sense of humor and drama, but longed to establish a relationship with him in which we could exchange ideas and converse. So, one time, I asked my father if he was aware of his incessant talking.

He answered that he knew he "talked a lot," commenting that when growing up, he had never got his say at home because his own father had talked so much! This statement about his childhood gave the clue that, in spite of his monologues, he still felt that he had never really been heard. To change the pattern, I began writing letters which I read aloud to him when we visited. This opened conversation. On other days, I handed him a list of six or seven topics I wanted to discuss, or I'd request that the first 15 minutes be devoted to conversation before he began his story telling.

Mostly, over time, I tried to let him know that he was indeed being heard. When he was willing for me to speak, I repeated stories of his life so he would know they were remembered. His story telling was related to his wanting to leave a legacy that would not be forgotten, and he was pleased when I published a slim book of his poetry and prose, which is really quite delightful. It's subtitled "A celebration of the human spirit and the wisdom that comes with age"[1] and has become a favorite with many readers. My father was being heard, remembered, and appreciated. Significantly, we now converse, and he no longer delivers monologues to me or my children, a delight to all of us.

Recalling the violent thrashings my father had inflicted on me as a child, I finally decided to see if we could coheal this past by sharing my painful memories of how frightening this had been. He was receptive, and I spoke to him about my recollections of his verbal lambastings and his hitting me repeatedly, all the while holding me so I couldn't get away. And I talked about how, as a child, the unpredictability of his rages and my inability to avoid them had added to my feeling helpless and apprehensive. I explained that though such outbursts had *spent* his rage, they had *built* unspent anger and resentment in me.

Now, so many years later, I was revealing how his beatings had not only been physically painful, but that I'd also felt emotionally devastated, having wanted so much to feel I had his approval.

Surprisingly, he vividly recalled the beatings his father had inflicted on him but not those he had given me. It helped that he told me how sorry he was for having done this, repeatedly telling me he couldn't understand why he had done it because "You were such a dear little thing." He asked my forgiveness. It was healing to both of us to share our feelings about having each been physically abused, and I finally got beyond the anger I had felt.

He remembered that in his youth, his own father had a raging temper, had beaten him, not let him express himself, and had excessively controlled him. Now my dad became interested in generational patterns and in John Bradshaw's work on shame and guilt, as well as the general subject of codependence. Here he was, in his nineties, reassessing his own childhood. He was gaining new perspectives and greater peace of mind by talking over and working through his own conflicted feelings of having admired his father and at the same time hated him for the abuse. (Even in the tenth decade of life, significant emotional healing can occur!)

In the process of cohealing with my father, my resentments toward him faded, and I was better able to see his gentle, caring side. I found myself recalling the many good times we had shared and concentrating on the things about him that I admired: his determination, courage, ambition, perseverance, and sense of humor, plus his imaginative and enthusiastic approach to life.

Now I more fully understand how much he means to me. I especially treasure his support regarding the major changes that I have made in my life, and his belief in me. Regarding my ponderings on the desire to feel significant, he responded, "You have significance; you don't need to do anything to get this, you already have it."

Six years after my divorce, I met a woman old enough to be my mother. We became dear friends, sharing confidences, mutual encouragement, hopes, fun times. She became my mentor, my aunt Aggie, my *substitute-mom* who is loving, caring, supportive. She wants what's best for me just as I want what's best for her. Neither of us is into controlling or criticizing, rescuing or being victimized by the other. This relationship has given me a chance to see how good it can feel to have a loving motherly response from someone I care about; someone I admire, trust, and enjoy. I treasure having her in my life. She's content and confident, radiating love of people and life itself, although she has health problems and physical restrictions just as my own mother does.

Someday Is Now

Over time, the children and I had developed an easy openness, acceptance, and sharing that was setting healthy patterns for each of us. During a get-together with Brenda, noticing changes that I had been making in my own life, she commented, "I think there's nothing more tragic than not taking care of yourself, not standing up for yourself, not believing in yourself, and not being who you really are. It's great that you're doing all these things. These are the opposite of the messages you received from your parents. I'm so glad to see the crazy legacy of the past has stopped. I'm happy for *you*, and I'm happy for *me*. You're the mother I always wanted."

At the close of this conversation she added, "You were always dreaming of *someday* while leading a mundane existence. You seemed to be caught in endless work and lists of things to do. You could never relax and just have fun. It was as though you were programmed to believe that you're good if you're accomplishing and bad if you're not. It's so nice to see you enjoying yourself."

I knew I would not have made the many changes I did had it not been for the supportive input from my children and others who became an integral part of my life.

New Choices

For years, the children's stepfather had warned me of all sorts of dangers. For example, he had forbidden me to ride in airplanes, thinking them unsafe, and wouldn't allow me such simple pleasures as a walk by myself on the beach. Toward the end of our marriage whenever he saw me leaving the house, he'd warn me, *"You be careful!"*

I now realized how inhibiting such warnings had been and ventured out in fresh ways, like the time the four children and I teamed up for a tropical vacation at an island resort. Jacqueline had arranged for a condominium which was lent to us by one of her friends. We all went scuba diving and boating, and had a delightful time snorkeling for hours among myriads of tropical fish in a tranquil bay. We had a grand experience on a helicopter ride and tried all sorts of new things together. The five of us all had such fun "adventuring" and felt so alive.

There was a sense of release now that eating disorders and other inhibiting and degrading problems we'd been through were a thing of the past — we had finally made it out of what had seemed like an uncharted "wilderness."

For me, real estate investing seemed like an appropriate place to start a career. I had liked working on my parents' property and thought it was an area in which I could build an adequate financial future for myself. With this in mind, while writing this book, I took time out for some real estate courses, went to workshops and seminars on the subject, read extensively, and spent countless hours discussing this type of investing with those who were successful in this field.

For months I looked for a fixer-upper property with a loan that could be assumed and an owner who would carry a note for most of the balance. Finally, near a popular beach, I found a bargain property that was in need of a good deal of repair — a lovely old Victorian plus the cottage next to it. I had my first project with my name on the deed.

It's funny how, as we move through life, we see it from different perspectives, and our values change. In the past, I'd valued having a home and a comfortable bed at night, a well-supplied kitchen and the like, but my life had seemed banal. Now I was living in a cottage that was torn apart, sometimes without heat or windows, and certainly with none of the comforts of the past.

I began what was to be three years of sleeping in a bedroll on the floor, with my work clothes in cardboard boxes at one construction site after another. Meals were basic and uncomplicated, and, if I was warm enough, I felt my creature comforts were being met. I remember starting work on the cottage foundation during the rainy season.

The rain promptly turned the ground to slick mucky sludge. One day, as I lay in a puddle under the floor joists in my yellow plastic slicker — shimming the foundation to make it more level — water kept trickling down my face from my wet hair. I thought how silly I must look, this 53-year-old woman, doing construction work. Yet it felt wonderful to be doing exactly what I wanted. I was enjoying myself and making progress on things that were important to me.

Each step of the way I learned skills needed to carry out the renovation work. I learned basic carpentry and how to mix and pour concrete. I learned to tape and texture sheet rock. I learned some plumbing and various other skills and felt accomplished when I crawled into my bedroll at the end of the day and turned on a heating pad to soothe sore muscles. (The migraines and back spasms were long gone — these were healthy aches of newly discovered muscles.)

I worked long hours, six and sometimes seven days a week, getting a real "hit" off what I was doing. I was making my own decisions and being productive. With this, the stagnation of the past evaporated. This forward momentum made an enormous difference as to how I felt about myself.

One day I realized just how much my basic attitudes had changed. At that time, I was working with a roofer, laying shingles. I don't like heights, but I was up there doing my fair share of the work when he made some flippant and seemingly derogatory comment about my having to earn his respect regarding my work. Formerly I might have given in to hurt feelings, but this day I simply told him what I thought. "I think I have *earned your respect*," I remarked.

He looked at me and grinned in recognition. Nodding, he admitted, "You sure have. You're doing a great job." I had not only gained his respect, but fortunately my own as well.

Since then I have worked for myself in property renovation and, more recently, in land subdivision. I'm well aware that working in real estate for myself has given me an opportunity to be my own boss. This circumvents many of the handicaps that face women who, like me, enter the job market in mid-life for the first time.

I had become engaged at 17 and had moved directly from my parents' home into the responsibilities of marriage and, a year later, of parenthood. Now I felt that I was at last having what in essence was an "adolescence." That is, I was concentrating on personal development, including the search for self-identity and independence. Though this had been much delayed, it was now a priority.

Roommates

Jacqueline stayed with me part of the time I was working on the cottage and Victorian house project. We slept in a little six-by-eight-foot room that was out of the way of construction, each of us with a bed roll and each with two cardboard boxes that held our clothes. We often talked late into the night, laughing and sharing. We were into working hard but having fun in the process.

One evening I'll never forget, Jacque and I were driving past a local lake at sunset. The water was glossy black with brilliant ripples of orange and rose. No one was around to see us. We were both strong swimmers so we stripped down and jumped into the icy waters, splashing vigorously at first until we managed to get used to the cold. Then the two of us swam along the shoreline toward the sunset, delighting in the continually changing colors of the ripples pushing ahead before us. Such fun! It was a night to remember.

Another time, back when I had first gone on my own, Jacque noticed that I was finally doing what was best for me, and she wanted to celebrate my decision. So, with a young man she knew, one midnight we stood by a beautiful river, watching him set off fireworks in my honor. What a lark! How much I appreciated her arranging this special occasion for me. Later she gave me a lovely oil painting of a scene of a river with Fourth of July fireworks bursting above it. She said it was to "commemorate your personal Independence Day."

Jacqueline and I walked beaches together, explored hilly trails, did "jazzercise" to her cassette tapes, and talked and talked. In the evenings while watching television, we sometimes gave each other head and shoulder massages to relax tired muscles and exchange nurturing. It even seemed special to sit around eating fish burgers and fries after the day's work was done, sharing ideas. As I made progress, she was there to give me hugs and say how proud she was of me. So were Brenda and my other two children. They were my rooting section, pulling for me, encouraging me, and letting me know in various ways that they cared.

Part of the healing process involved substituting new images — having fun, delighting, sharing, nurturing, connecting, growing, learning. Close friends, mentors, family were all part of it.

At one time or another, after I was on my own, each of the four children stayed with me for several months. This gave us an opportunity to relate to one another on a new basis, as independent adults who were starting out in our respective careers. What this amounted to was a process of "reparenting" in which each of us built a healthy "Nurturing Parent voice" in our minds, one that was supportive rather than inappropriately critical.

We were stretching out, expanding in new directions — starting new jobs, meeting people, living in new locations — with each of us at that point in our lives when we were working on being self-supporting and making our way in the world.

We began to shed old limitations and to achieve and grow in a wide variety of new directions. In so doing, we each seemed to be opening possibilities for the others. We were being authentic and real, which felt, and was, good for us. The girls have no reason to feel guilty for availing themselves of opportunities that I either didn't have or didn't pursue at their age, because I am vigorously pursuing them now. We have, in a sense, joined forces, and they feel free to initiate and assert themselves, in part because I am doing so also.

Parallel Healing

Although the girls' stepfather did not involve himself in their recovery process, he did seek counseling for an extended period, on his own, after we divorced. He was working at restructuring things about his own life concurrently with many of the changes the girls and I were making in ours; only he was doing this separately. Recent talks he had with Lisa about his own father having been "confrontational and highly combative" revealed fresh insights into how he had both suffered from this as a child and copied that pattern himself as a parent. He told Lisa that he regretted having taken this approach and wished he had done many things differently. He also said that he had come to accept that the past was over and there was nothing he could do about it.

In what also might be part of the healing process, he wrote a note to me saying that he was sorry he had dumped "crap" on me, adding that he felt my leaving him was probably one of the "best decisions you ever made" and that he wished me well. And, though it would have seemed impossible in the past, he and Jacqueline have developed a warm and loving relationship. Her stepfather has come to accept that she's an adult and, as such, has her own life to live. He no longer feels the need to try to control or lecture her. On the contrary, he makes it a point to be supportive and show he cares.

Surprising to both of us, the children's stepfather and I have developed an amicable relationship. When we talk from time to time, he's encouraging regarding my various writing and lecture activities, and complimentary concerning my accomplishments. I appreciate this and find it interesting that when I sometimes mention problems I'm having, he'll say light-heartedly, "Well, at least you don't have me yelling at you any more!" Years ago when we were still married, I would never have thought that one day we would be able to laugh about what were such painful times for both of us, but I guess that's a measure of the healing that's occurred.

Developing Co-Independence

The children and I were each developing our own "wisdom" about what felt good and worthwhile to us. In this process, we found that our confidence had grown and, in time, our independence. Now we live in different towns, but we're still there for each other as friends and family. We've learned to handle the paradox of being *autonomous* while at the same time having emotionally supportive *connections* with each other. This balance with loved ones and friends combines individuation with mutuality in a state of what I came to refer to as *co-independence*. With this balance we can each be our own person and yet know that we are not alone.

My changes, as well as those the children made, were all part of the ongoing cohealing process. This had taken off in earnest *three years after* Jacqueline's midnight phone call. Before that, in interactions with the children, I had responded pretty much as a parent rather than as a parent/friend, Mom/person. It really wasn't until the period in which Jacque and I began working together on my parents' large renovation project that the children and I really opened up to each other. They tell me that in their eyes I moved from being a "mother figure" to being a whole, real person. Cohealing had become a family process in which we were all changing many things in our lives and letting these readjustments settle into place. Now I sign my notes and letters to them: Mom/Hope, that is, "co" (Mom — denoting our special life-long relationship) and "independent" (Hope — denoting my separate personal identity).

In years past, *joie de vivre* — joy in living — had seemed elusively beyond my reach. Now I enjoy myself on a regular basis. Beyond that, I've had peak moments, particularly while walking in the woods, when I felt totally at peace and everything about life and the world seemed okay. Such moments bring *a timeless sense of exquisite wonder* at being conscious and aware in this limitless universe. At such times, everything seems connected in an infinite eternal *"oneness"* of which we are each an integral part. These "mountain-top" experiences help us understand the high points life can reach.

How could I have possibly understood this until I had experienced it myself? The sense of bliss at such times is truly indescribable, overwhelming, and an indication of the full range of human experience. Having these moments of awareness of the interconnectedness of all that is, of complete peace and acceptance, made it clear how limited my previous view of life had been.

Self-Exploration

I was fortunate during the time I was working on self-exploration, to have opportunities to participate in experiments with two of the world's foremost researchers studying intuition and the extended capabilities of the conscious mind. Initially, I took part in designing "remote perception" tests and evaluating their results but, in time, became involved actively in the research, including becoming a subject.

This fascinating field of study gave me new insights into myself and what we humans are capable of knowing, including being able to accurately and consistently perceive things with great accuracy without use of the ordinary senses — unconstrained by space and time, or even by physical barriers that preclude the use of common sensory perception. Until I had experienced this myself, until I had proven it to myself repeatedly, I could not have begun to fathom this *higher consciousness* or the seemingly holographic[2] aspects of time.

Each of us has this intuitive sense — beyond our regular consciousness — and science is progressively uncovering ways to study and teach these capabilities. This research gives us new insights into the *interconnection of all things* and the idea that we are far more than our physical body.

About this time, I was invited to teach a psychology class at a prestigious university that was pioneering in this field. I taught one hour each weekday during summer session, describing the scientific studies in which I had been involved, and the following hour conducted research with the students, teaching them to recognize and use their latent intuitive capabilities. I'll never forget the last day of class when I went to leave (down the aisle to the door), the students filed to the center and each hugged me good-bye and thanked me. The class was a wonderful experience, thought-provoking and challenging, for the students as well as for me. It was also a long way from the years I had stared out my kitchen window while doing dishes, dreaming of a future time when life would somehow be less constrained, more rewarding, and more exciting!

During this period, in connection with some of the research, I had the opportunity to work with equipment that gave me feedback as to what brain-wave state I was in. I could therefore determine when I was maintaining alpha waves, a perception that gave me insights into my meditation. Through biofeedback techniques, I even experienced what it is like to be awake and reduce feedback to the brain to the point where I could no longer sense my body, not even my own breathing. I discovered that with these sensations absent, the mind is wondrously alert.

As I incorporated what I had learned from these studies into my life, I noticed that significant synchronicities[3] began happening with some regularity. We all have a higher sphere of consciousness available to us, and for me, this exposure to research into the extended abilities of the human mind brought fresh insights into the interconnection of all things.

I experience life much differently now from the way I once did. The stagnation and fears of the past seem like a long-ago echo, as though from a different existence. Life feels freer and better than I had ever thought possible. I see not only the world in a new way, but also myself as well. Instead of having a heavy, sinking feeling (like a slightly submerged log), I have gained a sense of lightness and buoyancy. Naturally, life will always have its problems, but it feels abundant, spontaneous, and filled with good possibilities.

Partnership and Purpose

Cohealing, whether in a family setting, with friends, a counseling group, or others, can bring an increased sense of connectedness. Hopefully, it bolsters *compassion* toward ourselves as well as toward others, and a *passion for life*. With heart-to-heart sharing, we move from *longing*, to *belonging*.

While researching this book, I found many new areas of increased awareness. I'm sure that I would never have become so involved in exploring and trying to understand issues that affect women today had it not been for my own daughters' illness.

Since early in my teens, I have had a feeling that there was some sort of overall purpose to the events in my life. Though up close they seemed fragmented, from a long-term perspective they seemed to be moving consistently in a purposeful direction. I do not regret anything that happened and feel as though life is somehow unfolding as it should. Writing this book and another that is underway, going on speaking tours, and doing other related activities are my commitment to making a difference.[4]

I've found also that relationships are nurturing if they foster trust, acceptance, respect, and touching the world at many points. Such relationships fill the need for connectedness because they're based on mutuality and partnership[5] rather than on dominance and submissiveness. People with this open outlook are the ones I cherish in my life. There needs to be equal power between people to have intimacy, with both getting their needs and wants met.

By concentrating on *opportunities* rather than on fears and limitations, I'm often surprised at how *many* good possibilities there are in any given situation. I remind myself that "Life's an attitude" and that responding to situations assertively and creatively makes a positive outcome much more likely.

As my life became more fulfilling, so did my daughters' lives. Such is the cohealing process. We each had contributed to the others' feeling freer and less threatened. These days, the sky's the limit as far as what we decide to do. I was pleased that they liked seeing me develop a strong sense of direction and purpose.

I had needed to learn to be comfortable alone. When I had been married, the thought of being by myself had been problematic because I had never lived on my own. But I found that it was quite acceptable and allowed a great deal of freedom. Days were satisfying; I was content. I no longer felt like part of me was missing but that I was whole.

Though I was not feeling needy, I gradually became open to meeting a man someday who would be a "half sand dollar" that would fit well with the "half sand dollar" that I am. I knew that if we each felt complete within ourselves, we would have the foundation for a *co-independent* relationship in which we could share affection, trust, and a feeling of partnership in which we could each maintain our own identity, yet have a sustaining intimacy and closeness.

I recall a night five years ago, when I was living on my own. I had driven to a favorite beach. It was about ten o'clock, and the stars were out. Because of a recent storm, there were huge waves crashing against the rock cliff in front of where I had parked. There was a full moon, and the scene was exquisitely beautiful. I was listening to soft music on the car radio and, though savoring the moment, I had thought how much I would like to be sharing it with a man with whom I had a loving relationship. Feeling ready for this, I thought, must be another sign of healing.

These days I find that music, sunsets, a child's smile — along with other day-to-day events — are all the more gratifying when shared with others. I enjoy my work and find a sense of purpose in it. In the past, when I had daydreamed of "someday" when things might be better, I never thought that life could feel as good as it does now.

Route to Wholeness

It's been seven years since Jacqueline made a commitment to health. Today all four children have challenging careers in which they're successful and respected. Jacqueline and Brenda have learned to look out for their own best interests. They have congenial friends and are leading satisfying lives. I'm thankful that they eat healthily and take good care of themselves. Fortunately they feel no permanent aftereffects from former eating disorders.

Interestingly, Roger has had a strong influence on his sisters as well as on me. When living together in the Alaskan wilderness, Jacqueline, Lisa, and he shared all sorts of adventures, and later he lived with Brenda in California, so he also became involved in the family's cohealing process.

He was in college when I finally decided to get a divorce, and though he had spent his youth with his stepfather, he was never troubled by the problems that beset the girls. He's a personable young man, ambitious and directional in his career, but he "takes life in stride." He deals with disappointments and frustration in a pragmatic, level-headed way without any of the irrational, angry, emotional outbursts or displacement of blame onto others that his father, grandfather, and stepfather had exhibited.

All three sisters adore their brother, and each told me years ago that he was their example of the type of man they would like one day to marry. Though he's the youngest by several years, he's more like their "big brother." He's a man they trust, feel comfortable with, can rely on for supportive caring and advice, and with whom they can share good times. His congenial, easy-going personality reassured them that other men like him were out there, and also that they knew what felt comfortable in being co-independent with a male. I'm thankful that the legacy of dictatorial controlling-male influence in the family has not been passed on to this generation.

Growing up, Roger had been spared many of the unreasonable and raging dictums directed at the girls and had come in for much less paternal control, simply because he was male. Also, because he was born two months after I separated from his natural father, he never knew him. He now has a lovely wife, and they have a comfortable, caring marriage.

We have egalitarian relationships within our family as well as with other people and are no longer under a patriarchal set of family rules. Having escaped such rules, we finally have the freedom of choice that we so craved.

It is, of course, impossible to tell what our lives would have been like had we not taken a detour through the uncertain, often terrifying terrain of these eating disorders. I do know that traveling that route and learning to solve the problems of the past and present profoundly improved not only the lives of my children, but also mine as well. The seriousness of the illnesses had made it vital to change, and it's these changes that have expanded and enriched our lives.

Although I have written this from the point of view of a mother, some readers will be fathers, husbands, sisters, boyfriends, or wives, daughters, girl friends, or other loved ones, or counselors — people concerned about someone with obsessive-compulsive problems, addictions, and other traumas that need healing. Some of you have these difficulties yourself. Each of you will read this from your own viewpoint. Because we are all concerned about an individual (self or someone else) who is suffering compulsive-addictive problems, we share a common bond.

I know the dreadful anguish one can go through when caring about someone with these disorders, for I have seen and lived the trauma. I hope our experience has provided you with some helpful insights into recovery. My heart goes out to you as you work your way along this path.

I think the most important message is love — love of self, love of others, love of life itself.

CHAPTER 19

Cohealing and Co-Independence

As we move through the synergistic cohealing experience, in which all involved benefit, it becomes apparent that our actions are based on responding appropriately regarding our own interests as well as the interests of others. Those who are part of our *cohealing network* support this healthy behavior. It also becomes apparent that we are always in the process of healing and growth, of overcoming and, hopefully, of experiencing life more fully.

Cohealers

Cohealers are not obsessed with changing or controlling others. They act responsibly on their own behalf and let others do the same. They are people who, when we're with them, help us feel good about ourselves, and we do the same for them.

As cohealers we let each other know that "You matter to me. You're special and appreciated; your feelings, thoughts, perceptions, and desires are okay, just as you are okay." Cohealers hold us and hug us warmly, and in this protective setting, we are permitted to practice being in touch with our authentic self. Cohealers offer each other attention and concern. They help us to feel valued, accepted, respected. They are people who share fun, laughter, and tears. They nurture and help each other and believe in each other, knowing that we all have an innate desire to "count for something," to feel that we have made a contribution that gives life meaning and depth. Like us, other cohealers are in the process of self-discovery.

By being cohealers, we develop a *reciprocal relationship* in which all benefit and feel comfortable. In this exchange, cohealers sometimes offer helpful comments, sometimes just listen. They validate our reality by respecting our perceptions and feelings. They allow us to grieve for our losses, release our sadness, anger, and other distressing emotions, so that we can heal and grow. They are people with whom we can reciprocate by providing this same supportive, concerned interaction. Cohealers and mentors can help us expand our horizons and gain a sense of mastery and assurance that we are indeed special and worthwhile. We need them to validate our traumas, understand our pain, and help us feel acceptable.

Our part, as cohealers, can include quality time spent together, plus active *real* help (asked for and acknowledged), not *rescue*, in an exchange where everyone involved benefits. As cohealers, we ask ourselves, "How do I interact with my wife, husband, sister, brother, daughter, son, friend, client? Do I encourage her, or his, spontaneity and creativity? Dignity and self-worth? Self-respect and growth? Safety and inner peace? Feeling special, lovable, valuable?"

Cohealing can take place with counselors and participants in cohealing self-help support or therapy groups, as well as with supportive relatives, roommates, friends, and others who make it safe for us to express ourselves. This is an essential ingredient in the process, finding people with whom we can safely reveal our inner selves. For, by revealing our innermost being and finding acceptance and appreciation for who we are, a burden is lifted. Being loved just as we are "unfinished and still learning,"[1] frees us to accept ourselves. Compassion and respect, combined with mutual support and sharing, are fundamental ingredients in the *cohealing process.*

Individuals working to overcome a legacy of past abuse, of dysfunctional family patterns, and compulsive-addictive behaviors need cohealers who believe in their ability to responsibly handle their own lives. We benefit by having a combination of people in our recovery network, including professionals with special training, experience, and success in helping people with similar problems, and cohealers who are working through the healing process themselves and who share it with us.

Exploration of core issues, along with development of growth-oriented attitudes and approaches to personal relationships, generally requires working with a mentor-counselor who is well versed in this work, as well as family members who are committed to the cohealing process.

Cohealing Network

While Jacqueline was still bulimic, Lisa, Brenda, and I, each separately, went to various workshop groups, using these settings as a place for cohealing with people outside the family. By listening to the often traumatic personal stories of others in these groups, as well as by discussing our own feelings of distress and getting feedback, we each gained new perspectives and benefited substantially.

Individuals who are suffering emotional distress need to ask for and accept assistance. If they've retreated into themselves, we need to reach out to establish *connectedness,* the "co" part of being *co*-independent. We can let them know that "I love you and want you to feel loved. I want you to be gentle with yourself. You're a very special person to me, and I treasure you. I want you to be happy and enjoy life." Communicating these feelings comes more easily when we feel similarly about ourselves.

Love is the greatest healing force of all, as well as one of our most basic "hungers." Within the family, we can hope that love exists, but if it doesn't, then we must seek it from other, caring people that we can choose to include in our lives.

In selecting people to become part of our recovery network, we need to seek out those who have consistently shown they are capable of being helpful and to whom it has proven appropriate to risk confiding our concerns. These individuals have a genuine commitment to "being there" for us, and we feel similarly toward them.

We can't expect a parent or other relative, friend or companion, sponsor or counselor, or even a cohealing group to provide all of the resources that we need to recover. For this reason, we need to find a variety of appropriate people to become part of our cohealing network. We may find that some who are the most helpful have been through a similar process of healing after having grown up in a dysfunctional home. We can learn from their experience and example and thus gain confidence that we can do the same. Others in our network will undoubtedly be in stages of the recovery process similar to ours such that we find ourselves moving through the process concurrently, each at his or her own pace.

By forming a cohealing network, we in essence build a supportive co-independent substitute "family" for ourselves. We can't choose our blood relatives, some of whom may have been toxic to us, but as adults, we can select wisely whom we include in our lives.

Those who grew up in a dysfunctional family may find considerable reluctance among family members to change, along with the reaction, "I didn't have anything to do with this bulimia thing so don't bug me about it!"

Here the bulimic or anorexic individual is seen as the only one who needs changing. If so, it may be necessary to move forward through the healing process without them. Some family members may, in fact, even try to dissuade the individual working toward recovery from making the very changes needed to achieve it. Being close to them on a regular basis may, therefore, prove detrimental. Nonetheless, exploring the healing process with them can always be held as a future possibility, for in time, various members may see the compulsive eater's problems in a larger context and begin to relax their resistance to pursuing their own healing. This self-protection and justification can gradually give way to a sense of freedom to explore, and to the rewards that come with growth.

It definitely helps if the *cohealing mind-set is understood by family members*, because such understanding helps remove their resistance as they visualize cooperative progress toward individual fulfillment.

In much of the literature on codependence, emphasis has been placed on "detachment." Used appropriately, detachment is helpful when it involves relinquishing negative attitudes and habits, destructive relationships, reliance on detrimental substances, and unwarranted emotional neediness. (In our case, divorce was part of detachment, as was Brenda's decision to restrict interactions with her stepfather to infrequent correspondence. The process can take many other forms, most of which are less extreme.)

Descriptors

Codependence and *codependency* are relatively recent terms, created little more than two decades ago to describe age-old problems. There are many definitions for codependence, but in general they refer to learned self-destructive habitual responses that develop out of having lived in stressful, dysfunctional relationships for a prolonged period. Codependence involves other-centeredness, being constantly emotionally needy, overly reactive, and overly, or unhealthfully, dependent.

Clear and appropriate terms (such as codependency, compulsivity, and addiction) highlight what we are aiming to overcome, clarify our choices, and make it easier to stay on course toward recovery.

Language affects our attitudes and feelings, our self-perception, creating mental pictures, fostering ideas, revealing concepts. Descriptors, the words we use, affect our thought processes, rounding out and molding our reasoning, transforming and shaping it. They give perspective, help us analyze our motives, goals, feelings, and much more. When our language is limited or inaccurate, our communication is restricted, as well as, in a sense, our conceptualization processes.

Since *"dependence"* is a state of being controlled by or subordinate to someone or something else, it describes an unhealthy condition of emotional neediness in which the individual's circumstances are largely determined by factors other than personal choice and free will. So when we are referring to and trying to conceptualize relationships that are *not* codependent, it's helpful to avoid the word dependent in the descriptors used. Early on, when I found myself using the word "interdependent" to describe *healthy ways of relating*, I realized that it does not accurately describe that condition.

"Inter" indicates between or among; thus, inter*dependence* refers to *dependence* between ourselves and others and emphasizes the dependence aspect of relating — neither indicating whether this relating is healthy or unhealthy, compulsive, or destructive. Healthy relationships, however, have a balance between being connected and independent.

Using a word that is based on the concept of dependence to describe healthy relationships that are, on the whole, comparatively free of the loss of control that comes with overdependence is confusing. Nor does it create accurate mental pictures of what we are seeking to achieve.

In sum, there is a downside to trying to fit the word "interdependence" with descriptions of healthy relationships, since its base concept is dependence and of being controlled from outside ourselves. If our goal is to describe relationships that are not compulsively dependent, not codependent, but rather healthy ones, then "interdependent" and similar terms don't serve the purpose because they are less than accurate descriptions of the condition that we are trying to contemplate or discuss.

For instance, the term "undependent" has sometimes been used to describe relationships that are healthy and not codependent, but this word also has drawbacks since it fails to indicate the *shared* part of relating (the *we*), referring only to the separate nature of the individuals involved. *Undependent* is a poor description of the process of maintaining nurturing intimate relationships. It may also subconsciously be associated with being "undependable" and similar negative concepts.

We have needed some other way to describe and think about healthy relationships, a word that conveys both the interconnectedness and the individual self-identity aspects of healthy relating.

Co-independence provides us with a word, and a concept, that accomplishes this clearly, directly, and understandably. It describes both the co(mutual) and independent (separate identity) aspects of healthy relating and provides a mind-set that helps overcome codependence. We need to think in terms of building *co-independent relationships* based on maintaining mutual cooperation while staying firmly with who and what we are, want, think, prefer, and choose for our own life. This mind-set establishes a mood, a perception, that emphasizes both the principle of cooperation and of individuation, including recognizing that we are each responsible for ourselves and for how the story of our lives is written day by day.

When we are relating in cooperative, mutually beneficial ways while maintaining our uniqueness, we are acting as co-independents. Thinking in terms of being co-independent helps us focus on healthy resolutions to problems of codependence. It helps us conceptualize building a common bond while still maintaining our separateness. While codependence stresses unhealthy compulsive dependence, co-independence clearly delineates cooperation and mutuality, combined with being independent individuals.

Codependence

Codependence has to do with lives that seem unmanageable, painful, fearful, deprived, and rule-bound. It has to do with feelings of sadness, frustration, deprivation, anxiety, resentment, guilt, and self-pity. In addition, it frequently involves anger and blame, excessive sense of obligation, obsessive worry, controlling and feeling controlled, and in some cases, of having been sexually molested, physically abused, and/or raised by an alcoholic parent.

Compulsive-eating disorders have parallels with alcoholism; in both cases, those in close relationships with someone suffering these problems often have codependent coping patterns. As an individual's eating distortions become more unmanageable, people in her environment tend to find their own lives becoming progressively more distressing: all too often they become reactive, absorbed in her problems, and obsessed with helping her, no longer expecting her to do for herself that which she is capable of, and ought to be, doing. These self-defeating patterns of relating to a compulsive eater reduce our ability to have a warm constructive relationship with her, and would be termed codependent.

Those who are codependents maintain hidden lives behind the more obvious problems (such as alcoholism, bulimia, or drug addiction) and suffer their own agony and torment, their own sense of being out of control. When we become so other-directed that we fail to be appropriately self-directed, when we rescue and struggle with trying to control the actions of the compulsive eater, we are in codependent territory. (Taking appropriate care of dependent children is our responsibility and is not to be confused with compulsive caretaking or "rescuing" of adults.)

Codependents are unable to function effectively themselves due to overinvolvement with someone else's behavior and needs to the point of disregarding important issues in their own lives. This overdependence on others weakens the codependent's own self-identity. Thus, codependence is associated with extreme attachment to, or long association with, an individual who has a chemical or other chronic dependence.

Codependence refers to dysfunctional behavior and character traits that inhibit individuals from initiating and maintaining healthy relationships. We can think of codependence as learned maladaptive behavior that decreases the ability to form mutually satisfying, co-independent relationships.

Codependence and compulsivity, addiction and related problems have a cross-generational aspect to them. As children, we make decisions about how to react to our environment in order to survive, and these patterns continue into adult life even though they may be ineffective, self-defeating, and inappropriate. When our basic needs went unmet as a child, as well as when we were abused physically or psychologically, we continue to be affected by those childhood emotional wounds as adults. It's as though we were on automatic, being driven by the past, instead of making appropriate choices based on the here and now. In our relationships (including raising our own children), we tend to carry on the generational patterns learned in childhood.

Low self-esteem, along with long submerged feelings of fear and distress, are often the result of having been shamed, discredited, overly controlled, or otherwise mistreated as a child. Dysfunctional families are frequently referred to as "shame-based," and compulsive behavior grows out of hidden shame. When our "inner child" (sometimes called our "real self") is not adequately nurtured or allowed free expression, a co-dependent self develops. This is associated with assuming a victim role.

Codependence is common in those who either are being, or were, raised in dysfunctional families with compulsive-addictive problems, authoritarianism, chronic illness, shaming, abuse, or abandonment. Compulsions, as we have seen, are irresistible impulses to act in certain ways regardless of how illogical the motivation might be.

Codependence grows out of emotional pain, the denial of innate responses, feelings, perceptions, and needs, and is related to losses that the individual has been unable to deal with and accept. Life feels painful, even out of control. Only when this emotional pain is healed can we know who we really are and live freely, abundantly, and creatively.

We were well along in the cohealing process before I realized that the problems we had been working to overcome were *those of codependents*, and that it was codependence that we were gradually replacing with healthy co-independent patterns. In the past, I had so associated codependence with alcoholism that I hadn't seen the parallels with our situation until after we had already made major strides in our recovery.

Within our own family system, codependence had taken a number of forms, and behind each form had been the excessive need to *control*. In my own background, there had been compulsive rage and physical abuse, along with lecturing, shaming, moralizing, and compulsive talking, by my parents. There had been manipulation by my mother, who used shaming and criticism as a means of control. Both parents had stifled their children's independence and individuation.

When I read the statement "Shame is the trademark of dysfunctional families"[2] in Melody Beattie's book *Beyond Codependency*, I was carried back to my own childhood and the shame that I had experienced. Beattie stresses the point that "shame is a tool for controlling behavior."[3]

My own children's natural father (who had been physically abused as a child) had used manipulation with them and with me to create distress. Later, with their stepfather (who had grown up with parents who relied on a combative, confrontational approach to child-rearing), the children had been subjected to compulsive rages, rule-setting, and moralizing. Both father and stepfather had been "addicted" to power and control.

Abusive power is "frequently hierarchical" as well as "a cover-up to shame," according to John Bradshaw, who talks about those who set "inflexible rules about how . . . other people should act."[4] He describes angry behavior that results in shouting, cursing, or condemning others and explains that people who are shamed as a child have a "fear of abandonment," as well as insecurities and the need to cling to what they have.[5] Perfectionism, arrogance, rage, moralizing, judging, blaming, and a host of other emotional outlets are ways of transferring shame to someone else.

Much of this "shame-blame" takes place at the dinner table.[6] I know this was certainly true in our family. The dinner hour was a troubled time in which the children's stepfather dished out not only food, but also orders, criticisms, and blame. Any minor infraction could cause a violent blowup, at times resulting in the child being ordered to bed without dinner. No matter how I tried to make mealtimes pleasurable, I failed miserably. This left us to wonder at how the tension of the dinner hour, during Jacque's childhood, might have later influenced her eating patterns.

Whatever form it takes, by acting shameless and self-righteous, the individual is passing his, or her, own sense of shame on to those on the receiving end of this behavior. Children who grow up taking the brunt of such ridicule and criticism suffer the agony of humiliation, guilt, and powerlessness, such that the pattern gets passed along to a new generation.

Control takes many forms. Some people work at controlling others' "thoughts, feelings, and actions" as a way of protecting the self against unresolved emotional turmoil.[7] Thinking about my husband's rules, I couldn't miss the parallel with the home situation in which the children had been raised.

Being controlling, as well as being controlled, destroys equality, comfort, and safety. It destroys the free sharing of thoughts and emotions. It destroys acceptance of who we really are, and in the process, it destroys real intimacy.[8] When I read that perfectionism "says you shouldn't perceive, think, feel, desire, or imagine the way you do,"[9] I thought of how many times my genuine emotions had been invalidated during my marriages. Now I could see that our family was not unusual but shared codependence patterns with countless other families.

Recognizing this, I was even more convinced that we can become so trapped in guilt, shame, and old habit patterns that we don't allow ourselves to make healthy choices — until we go through the process of cohealing.

Every family member affects the others, and in dysfunctional, codependent families, all are addicted to the interactions in the family system. Those who are not in controlling roles in these families are unable to get their needs met, so quite naturally they feel emotionally hungry and needy. For today's females, these negative emotions have a way of developing into eating-related problems.

In our family system, I had accommodated and placated in what is referred to in codependence terminology as an "enabler" role. In my struggle to feel secure and acceptable, I had stayed in situations that weren't good for either me or the children, something they recognized and that Brenda had particularly resented. I had set an example of submissiveness and dependency, an example the girls certainly didn't want to follow.

Codependence has been associated with such things as being perfectionistic, self-righteous, inhibited, destructive, judgmental, hard to please. Frequently codependents are mistrustful, have painful relationships, experience lack of intimacy, and display general avoidance and denial of feelings. Other signs of codependence include aggressiveness and/or passivity, blaming, pretense, grandiosity, and a compulsive search for control. Many codependent attributes are those of the Critical Parent.

Cohealing involves understanding and releasing the emotional distress buried in our consciousness from childhood, modifying our behavior, progressively expanding awareness of our spirituality, and generally experiencing healthy patterns. With this transformation, our resilience is enhanced, our optimism expands, our ability to experience healthy love is increased, and we begin taking control of our lives. We are no longer acting out a "role" that we learned in childhood but at last own our life. We find a sense of what's been referred to as "empowerment," which enables us to treat ourselves and others with kindness and respect. We each need this process in order to heal both past emotional wounds and whatever distress we are experiencing due to our present circumstances.

Co-Independence

Because compulsive family patterns are systems of control, individual members need to establish new patterns of connection without the obsessive need to control. Within the family, with friends and colleagues, to understand the nature of this growth from dependence to healthy, satisfying relationships, it is useful to think in terms of co-independence because such thinking underscores the combination of individuality with mutuality that provides the balance required for optimum functioning within personal relationships.

Co-independence is the essence of healthy relationships, the alchemical ingredient that bridges the healthy need to combine autonomy and intimacy. We need to depend on and trust others. The co-independent perspective creates mutually supportive interactions that maintain individual identity. This concept, and indeed the term itself, draws attention to the truly cooperative nature of harmonious relationships. The term implies (on a personal level as well as a more general one) the interconnectedness of all things. It recognizes cooperating with, rather than controlling or struggling against, and fosters positive concern for both self and others.

We all can benefit from co-equal, co-independent relationships. They are the basis for feeling good about ourselves and establishing healthy connections with others. (See: Reclaiming Our Rights — Egalitarianism and Partnership)

Co-independent characteristics include: being able to grow within relationships; taking comfort in exploring feelings; being capable of trust and mutual support; having a network of friends and interests; expressing spontaneity as well as openness to new possibilities; maintaining one's own identity; honoring individual self-worth; respecting healthy limits (sometimes referred to as boundaries); nurturing and feeling good about ourselves as well as others; having freedom to be and become, accept and allow; being valued for who and what we are as we grow and change; plus validation, forgiveness, kindness, patience, and awareness. It also involves having fun and being playful, with the ability and willingness to discuss and negotiate mutually satisfying approaches to getting individual, as well as joint, needs and wants met. These components of healthy relationships fill our most basic needs for companionship and love.

By building co-independent relationships and healthy self-regard, by learning appropriate problem-solving and conflict-resolution skills, by developing a sense of completeness and personal identity, we build a good life for ourselves. Others whose lives we touch benefit from this as well. How much connection is present depends both on the relationship and the mood at the time. Casual acquaintances have little of the "co" aspect, but in relationships that become closer, more intimate, this sharing becomes deeper and more profound. Yet even then the degree of this closeness will vary considerably over time.

Prevention of Codependence and Addiction

As for obsessive and health-damaging dieting, purging, fasting, and bulimic symptoms, these are alarmingly common among teenage girls and young women. In fact, recent findings have shown that restrictive weight-loss dieting starts early among girls, often by ages seven or eight, in an effort to limit their size. By their teen years, a significant number are obsessively concerned about their weight and suffer bulimic symptoms.

Many parents undoubtedly think, "This could never happen to my daughter." Unfortunately, countless others who must have thought this were wrong. If some outward sign were readily visible, indicating females with bulimic or other self-destructive compulsive-eating symptoms, we would be shocked into sudden awareness of the *staggering, growing tragedy* of these problems. Parents need to understand the overlapping, cross-addictive aspects of compulsive behavior, which often include not only eating disorders but also such additional problems as alcoholism and drug addiction.

Bulimia is considered to be socially communicable, and young daughters are being "exposed" to other young people who, because they are bulimic, eat all they want whenever they want and counter this overindulgence with purging, therefore never having to suffer the consequences of weight gain. This is especially true in campus living groups, among athletic squads with weight limits, and dance classes.

A large percentage of our female population have an obsessive over-concern with their weight, dislike their shape, and suffer the detrimental psychological consequences of constantly struggling to be lighter and more slender than is genetically suitable for them. They are vulnerable to the lure of bulimic indulgence and "weight control" by purging.

Since recovery from eating disorders is frequently a long, drawn-out process and because more women are continually becoming ill, the major impact on today's women and their families becomes apparent, as does the need for *prevention*. Prevention needs to be made a primary concern of all parents of young daughters, yet there's been an amazing lack of materials on the subject. A major key to prevention, naturally, is helping individuals build a strong sense of personal worth, power, and security — which goes along with feeling competent and in charge of one's life. When parents create co-independent patterns at home, they encourage their children to do likewise — which builds their self-esteem as well as their *resistance* to self-defeating behaviors including compulsions, codependence, and addictions. Co-independence could well be the center of most prevention programs since it is *the* basis for individual well-being as well as for healthy relationships.

Transformation

Consciousness is expansive rather than limited. It is interconnected rather than separate. Reality might best be described as being like a hologram, with ourselves as part of the totality of all that is.[10] The deeper we delve into higher consciousness, the greater the wonder we perceive. Life should not be approached as a problem that must be solved or a struggle that must be endured, but rather as a wondrous mystery to be acknowledged and lived.[11] The self-reflectiveness of the healing process can so expand our awareness and transform our consciousness that we feel renewed and regenerated, at last able to live more creatively and freely. For many, there is a new feeling of spirituality and attunement to the joy and wonder of life.

We will still need to deal with life's disappointments and tragedies, pains and problems, but hopefully, in recovery we learn to live day to day with a new found meaning and purpose that helps us maintain an overall sense of peace, genuine optimism, and thankfulness for what is worthwhile and good. Spiritual well-being is essential to health, for it has to do with both our essential self and our relation to the universe.

Cohealing and co-independence set the stage for us to develop the courage to be ourselves and provide a path for acting on our personal rights. Co-independence stresses a partnership approach, along with recognizing the right to move freely toward what is our own highest good, as long as this does not impinge on others' similar rights. Any other form of relating disallows this. Ranking some individuals above others presumes that their needs, desires, ideas, and motives are preeminent. The co-independent stance encourages equal justice and well-being for all concerned, along with a stewardship approach toward our world habitat.

"The principle of linking rather than ranking" was extensively described by Riane Eisler as the "partnership model" in *The Chalice and the Blade*, a book devoted to "Cultural Transformation."[12] Basic to this "cultural evolution"[13] is cohealing, for this process fosters our gaining the insights and awareness necessary for us to become willing to consistently and dramatically work on overcoming the damaging legacy of our shared past so that we can establish new partnership attitudes and approaches to our lives. It encourages the healing that needs to take place in our families, our communities, and beyond, so that people of all backgrounds can come to realize the benefits of working together to release themselves from acceptance and perpetuation of the dominator ethos while working to build a world based on partnership and co-independence.

Cohealing helps us relinquish our hierarchical past, a transition that transforms our attitudes. This creates a mind-set for accepting partnership and co-equal relationships between individuals, and between groups, whether they be separated by religious, ethnic, racial, national, or other "artificial" divisions. It is a process through which we can visualize how to work cooperatively on understanding and healing divisions and dysfunctions caused by our present dominator social system. This prepares us to accept, and even welcome, the new freedoms and responsibilities of an egalitarian, partnership social structure. The cohealing process can be seen as a transformational experience, one that creates the framework in which co-independent partnerships can flourish.

Conflicts between the dominator paradigm and emerging egalitarian values create stresses that foster eating disorders among females. The dominator ethos contributes to all manner of human misery. For millennia, we humans have acted on the premise that it is our destiny as a species to dominate the globe and all other creatures. We talk of conquering space, subduing enemies, "wars" against all manner of social problems. This attitude of conquering and subduing has been preeminent. Yet, if it continues, we will destroy the biosphere, making our planet uninhabitable. Our only hope for survival is to work together to restore and preserve our fragile and badly damaged environment.

Cohealing is inclusive rather than exclusive, holistic rather than divisive, and based on transformation rather than on dysfunction. It facilitates the formation of attitudes that accompany a partnership attitude toward where and how we fit into the scheme of things and a willingness to be part of the process of recovery, growth, and improvement. The future must lie in interpersonal healing, beginning at its most basic level — with each of us working to transform the ethos of aggression and domination to one of mutuality. Never before have our social systems been as interconnected worldwide, and never before have we been so badly in need of constructive efforts to firmly establish egalitarian values.

The coequal, co-independent mind-set, when it is present, promotes authentic communication and a feeling of safety, inviting self-actualization and self-acceptance. It prompts trust and intimacy, integrity and personal responsibility, thus providing a basis for healing and for hope. Clearly, a dominator system is the opposite of cohealing, which is cooperative and intuitive, not combative or controlling. The cohealing response is essential to establishing a partnership paradigm. Recovery from the abuses of the dominator system will require a fundamental cohealing response marked by constructive attitudes, approaches, and ideals. With such a response, we can establish an ethos that honors diversity and self-determination while stressing cooperation.

Rather than emphasizing power over one another, we need to develop a sense of personal control to achieve our own potential without infringing on the rights of others. Cohealing allows us to move forward together, so that as we redefine ourselves — growing toward wholeness and increasing our life satisfaction — others whose lives we touch may be beneficially influenced by the changes in our lives. Like a spiral spider web in which each delicate strand is an integral part of the whole, *reality* needs to be viewed as a *whole* in order to understand its pattern and integrity. Cohealing and co-independence give us avenues for thinking in terms of oneness and of our being an integral, inseparable part of the whole of humanity and indeed, of all nature.

I've written a small, open-anywhere book titled, *Thrive! You Have a Right to Thrive . . . Not Just Survive.* It expands on the ideas introduced in "Reclaiming Our Rights" (in the Notes section of this book). If you've been allowing others to take advantage of you, manipulate, intimidate, or abuse you — this book was written for you. This quick-read volume provides numerous "Rights Reminders" and 12 "Key Concepts" to help you stand up for your rights and needs, and teach others to treat you with respect. It offers proven strategies to help you create relationships that are more equitable, satisfying, and loving. In its pages, you'll undoubtedly recognize yourself, your family, and your friends and gain valuable insights into power imbalances in your relationships. *Thrive!* shows how to rebalance your relationships and become healthily *co-independent.*

We Would Like to Hear From You

We would like to hear from you at the *Center for Cohealing.* Write to us at: Center for Cohealing, 4546 El Camino Real, B10 – Suite 150, Los Altos, CA 94022. Although it's not possible to answer all correspondence, we welcome your insights and perspectives, problems and resolutions, ideas and concerns.

Additionally, a COHEALING GUIDE is being assembled for use by individuals, families, professionals, as well as Cohealing and Co-Independence Groups. We invite you to join in contributing ideas, suggestions, and practical applications to this project. This is a joint, growth-oriented adventure and we look forward to your participation.

If you are with a Cohealing Group, please include the name of your self-help group, location, and coordinator's name so that it will be possible to keep track of your progress. Professionals who are using Cohealing Therapy Groups in their practice are invited to share their experiences and suggestions for the GUIDE.

Notes

Reclaiming Our Rights

Open discussion among co-independents is essential for healthy relationships to develop and thrive. Here are some ideas to stimulate sharing that can foster cohealing and form the basis for co-independent interactions. The rights given below are your privilege and point the way to develop and free that spark within you — your higher self.

PERSONAL RIGHTS (Permissions)

Exercising our personal rights builds a sense of freedom to accept and *take good care of ourselves.* This list is helpful as a basis for discussion of personal rights as well as for determining whether we accept these rights. Accepting and acting on our personal rights builds confidence, equalizes our relationships, helps us deal constructively with anger, and promotes effective self-expression.[1] Acceptance of our innate human rights is critical to getting our needs and wants met on a consistent basis. Do I (we) accept the following:

IT'S OKAY TO:

- Love and accept myself, recognizing that I am a lovable person.
- Trust and believe in myself, knowing I am important, worthwhile, and valuable.
- Be patient and tolerant with myself.
- Care for myself, taking time to pursue my own happiness and well-being.
- Lift myself up rather than put myself down.
- Act in my own best interests, doing those things that help me feel good about myself.
- Experience all of my feelings, including, anger, grief, sadness, resentment, and fear.
- Trust my own perceptions, thoughts, judgments, intelligence, strength, and experience.
- Set my own priorities and take action to achieve them, and accept responsibility for the outcome.

- Try a variety of things, take calculated risks, make "mistakes," and learn from them.
- Have my own activities and healthy co-independent relationships, including friendships of my own choosing.
- Communicate directly and effectively, and not feel the need to give justifications or excuses for my actions.
- Say "no" to things I do not want to do, refusing unreasonable demands from anyone.
- Expect my communications to be really heard.
- Identify, discuss, and resolve mutual problems.
- Disclose when I don't know, understand, or feel ready to decide.
- Expect to be treated with compassion, dignity, and respect.
- Refuse to tolerate hostility and disrespect.
- Ask for what I really want.
- Not sacrifice myself unduly for others.
- Feel free to sometimes change my mind and make this known.
- Avoid unpleasant people.
- Not take on duties and obligations that belong to others.
- Avoid conforming unquestioningly to other people's expectations.
- Choose my own standards and values.
- Expect equal justice, opportunity, and protection.
- Ask for and receive fair pay and compensation.
- Succeed and take credit for my successes.
- Expect my contributions to receive appropriate recognition.
- Take initiative, be assertive, and strive to live up to my potential.
- Be imaginative, innovative, and spontaneous.
- Grow and be open to change.
- Be outgoing, playful, and sometimes unconventional.
- Live more fully now, and not wait until later.
- Seek and expect love, support, help, acknowledgment, meaningful work, and all the other elements that go into building a good life for myself.

Since these rights belong to everyone, just as we should not deny them to others, we should not deny them to ourselves.

Rights bring with them certain responsibilities, such as: "I am responsible for my own welfare and for acting appropriately." Along with this we need to believe that we can take care of ourselves and work to achieve this, while living fully today and planning for the future. Caring for dependent children is a responsibility, but we need to remember that we are not responsible for our grown children. They are responsible for themselves, just as we're responsible for ourselves.

Women are particularly prone to denying themselves *permission* to love and accept themselves, look out for their own highest good, or exercise all the other personal rights listed above. Many of them live narrow, constricted lives, feeling anxious and dependent. All too frequently, they're overly adaptive, insecure, indecisive, conflicted, and restrained. Beyond this, countless women fear taking on all the rights and responsibilities of fully mature adult living, and stay in "codependent" relationships that hamper the growth of their individuality, their identity. They settle for the false sense of security of dependency, a trap that keeps them mired in inertia and inhibitions.

Unsureness and indecisiveness hold them back. They can release themselves from this inhibiting past and present by moving through the cohealing process and learning to form supportive, growth-oriented co-independent relationships. (This is especially true of those with eating problems, who must overcome a legacy of being too adaptive, other-directed, self-critical, perfectionistic, fearful, and dependent. A host of inhibiting presumptions and justifications have kept them in self-defeating patterns that need to be relinquished.)

Those who are hemmed in by inhibitions and prohibitions limit their willingness and ability to look out for their own interests. *Permissions are the opposite of prohibitions.* For this reason, the rights listed are stated as permissions, as an initial approach to working on accepting and acting on them. At first, it may seem unsettling, even scary, to begin acting on our personal rights, but by facing our fears we gain courage to make positive changes that can greatly improve our lives.[2] As we move from dependency to autonomy and self-respect (and in so doing, accept our personal rights), it gradually seems acceptable and even logical, to begin each of the above statements with, "I have a right to . . . "

Each of us deserves to be treated well and have our personal rights respected. Once we wholeheartedly accept that we do indeed have personal rights, we can begin acting on them and teaching others to honor them.[3] We need to continually keep our rights in mind and acknowledge this awareness to others so that they will respect them and us. Anytime we feel ready to silently suffer unhealthy pressures and influences that ignore our rights as individual's and weaken our self-respect, or go "along with unkind, disrespectful treatment that makes us feel devalued," we need to remind ourselves that *we deserve better*, as noted by Sue Patton Thoele, in *The Courage To Be Yourself*.[4] We each deserve to build a good life for ourself and to develop a sense of who and what *we desire* to be. We need to listen to *our inner* guidance as to what is consistent with our own highest good, because this stance helps us choose satisfying ways of thinking and acting.

If "permissions" to *reclaim your rights and your life* are something you feel you need to work on, you may want to create your own list of positive statements that are affirmations of your right to be yourself and become the person you choose to be. Read these to yourself, write them out, put them where you see them regularly, so that over time your "inner self-talk" becomes life enhancing and *allowing* rather than limiting and *prohibiting*.

AWARENESS

Choices that help us overcome the legacy of societal values that handicap us are based on *understanding and heightened awareness*. They must be made by developing a critical eye regarding cultural messages that are negating and demeaning. The following checklist and questions increase our awareness of stereotypical attitudes toward the genders (particularly in the media, but also from countless other sources). We need to ask ourselves: is the kind of thinking loaded with contrived inconveniences that promote self-dissatisfaction and self-defeating attitudes, and involve completely unnecessary expenditures of time and money? Or is it, instead, supportive of self-worth? Is the approach (1) *Beneficial?* (2) *Useless?* (3) *Harmful?*

WHAT VALUES, CHARACTERISTICS, AND ASSUMPTIONS ARE BEING CONVEYED?

Natural, enduring, consistent	Cultural, transient, seasonal
Self-accepting, satisfied	Not good enough as is, dissatisfied
Effective, practical, competent	Ineffective, impractical, incompetent
Self-actualizing	Inhibiting, self-limiting
Personal identity	Role identity
Genuine, real, authentic	Artificial, illusory, unauthentic
Important, meaningful, valued	Trivial, silly
Mature, intelligent, assertive	Childlike, passive
Expressive, individualistic	Matching a typical model
Realistic, necessary	Contrived, unnecessary
Comfortable, freeing	Uncomfortable, restrictive
Powerful, self-directed	Fragile, acquiescing

Surely we deserve to look for, and incorporate in our lives, those values that are enduring, practical, comfortable, meaningful, effective, liberating, and supportive of self-actualization. Certainly, we have a right to look out for our own best interests in the long run.

OUR RIGHT TO GOOD HEALTH

Proper eating and nutrition are basic to good health. Starting in childhood, females are subjected to pressures that promote acceptance of unhealthy eating and dieting practices aimed at trying to control, or reduce, their size. We each need to find constructive ways to deal with these confusing influences. Talking about them, sharing feelings and concerns, can be a step in this direction.

It can be helpful to approach this from the standpoint of a "triad" having as its three elements:

- Society's continual cultural pressures on females to purchase food, prepare it, and over-indulge in eating it.
- Simultaneous pressures to diet, lose weight, and buy skinny fashions.
- The guilt, frustration, and self-recrimination this crazy-making conflict causes (plus for some, the dangerous purging "solution" that allows them to indulge and lose weight at the same time).

We can think of this as the *Bulimic Triad* in which the bulimic has integrated two major opposing social messages, both fueled by billion-dollar industries, and complies with both concurrently. She can eat more than her body requires as well as be thinner than is natural, by purging her system of unwanted calories. Whether this purging is attempted by regurgitation, diuretics, amphetamines, laxatives, or other means, these aberrations are related to cultural pressures that are not only at odds with each other but also at odds with what's healthy!

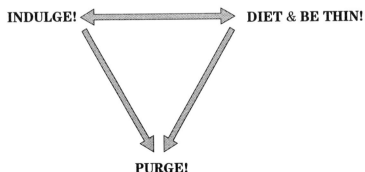

INDULGE!   **DIET & BE THIN!**

PURGE!

We need to ask ourselves how we and those we care about can consistently counteract these opposing influences in ways that are satisfying and healthy. How are we handling such pressures and how can we do better? It's our choice and our responsibility to find effective ways of coping with them so that we do not succumb to unhealthy life-damaging behavior and needlessly frustrate ourselves. We deserve good health and to have eating be a comfortable part of our lives. In addition, we have a right and responsibility to feel good about, and take proper care of, ourselves.

EGALITARIANISM AND PARTNERSHIP

For those who wish to exchange ideas on what it means to be co-independent and how to build this type of relationship, here are some thoughts for possible discussion.

Co-independence is based on each party retaining her, or his, own identity. It's founded on *equality, parity,* and *balance* in relationships. The opposite of this egalitarian approach is one that is unequal, lopsided, or unbalanced, with one or more parties not having equal rights or opportunity to get their needs and desires met. We can ask ourselves how our interactions compare with these two approaches to relating.

Looked at from the standpoint of justice, co-independence intrinsically relates to fairness and equity. It has to do with seeing that everyone concerned is honored and respected. Injustice relates to inequity and unreasonableness, to having one's rights violated or being wronged. Taken from this perspective, *wrong* indicates unfair and partial, one-sided and unjustified as well as objectionable and injurious. It's appropriate to consider whether our relationships are equitable and based on trust.

Linking the concept of *justice with freedom,* consider what it means to be free to do what we like and act on our rights. Co-independence has to do with acting in ways that foster one's own highest good and self-development, and the attainment of one's self-chosen objectives. It contributes to forming a sense of freedom and autonomy. Do our relationships provide this sense of personal freedom in addition to supportive closeness, both essential to our well-being?

No solid, co-independent interaction can be established without trust, for we need to know that we will be respected and our mutual agreements and understandings honored.

The mutuality aspect of co-independence confers dignity and respect as well as fosters self-esteem. It gives a sense of shared commitment, of "being there" for one another. It's based on fairness and regard for each individual. The reverse of this is authoritarianism, which is founded on privilege and demand, a rank ordering based on the unequal status of those involved. Instead of the respect and mutual regard that are found in co-independence and partnership, authoritarianism in personal relationships involves variations of disrespect, disparagement, shame, insult, disregard for personal rights, discrediting, and debasement. At its extreme, it is a contrast of privilege on the one hand and futility on the other.

Females can ask themselves whether they relate more closely to the "co" principles of co-independence, viewing a co-equal partnership as gaining power, status, and connection along with greater self-reliance and personal responsibility.

Conversely, males can ask whether, having been raised in a hierarchical social system, they may view the "co" aspect of co-independence as a loss of independence and perhaps also of freedom and status. They may more easily relate to the "independence" principles of co-independence and find they need to concentrate on the benefits that can be derived from greater connection, cooperation, and mutuality, while females may need to concentrate more attention on the benefits that can be derived from greater emphasis on identity issues, self-sufficiency, and acting on personal rights.

By sharing the exploration of such issues, we can create a climate for accepting the partnership approach to relating, and see the unlimited benefits that accrue. Both genders gain by achieving a *balance*, by sharing responsibility, and by overcoming our personal and hierarchical social patterns of relationships based on domination.

In discussions, we can consider what the concepts of *freedom, justice, mutuality, trust, dignity, respect, worth, equal protection, and related concepts mean to us personally, and can explore what we want for ourselves, for those we personally care about, and for all others of these and future generations.*

Extent of the Problem

In many westernized countries, there's been an alarming increase in the incidence of females suffering from self-image and eating-related problems during the past[1] quarter century. Though experts in the field agree that the incidence of bulimia and other eating disorders is unknown,[2] there's little agreement on its extent other than that these problems are quite common in females[3] yet uncommon in males.[4] Many medical professionals, however, describe the situation as "epidemic"[5] particularly among younger women.[6] For this reason, currently there is a desperate need for *cohealing support programs* aimed at dealing with this tragedy.

Eating disorders have become a sign of our times and have appropriately been referred to as "a distinctive form of female suffering," with bulimic behaviors, in particular, said to be prevalent.[7] Doctors William White, Jr. and Marlene Boskind-White, specialists in eating disorders, reflect this situation in their descriptions of bulimia as being "widespread," "rampant," and a "major health threat" involving a "staggering" number of females.[8]

Without our realizing it, we've gradually become accustomed to hearing about girls and women with bulimia or anorexia — from our friends, acquaintances, and of course, the media. The *overwhelming impact on the lives of today's females and those who care about them is seldom understood* yet such awareness is essential to understanding the root causes and addressing them. If for instance, *every* female with significant bulimic or self-starving symptoms were to have her hair turn green overnight, *then* we'd suddenly be shocked into an awareness of the massive numbers caught in health-damaging, life-distorting food-related disorders. And it would become apparent that this is not occurring in a vacuum, but is the result of conflicting, confusing, and often negating social pressures experienced by today's females.

Prevalence

The statistics fail to indicate the turmoil and anguish felt by those who express their distress in the form of tortured eating behavior.

Figures in the range of *one in five* are frequently given as the number of young women in this country with "self-destructive" eating patterns,[9] but behind whatever figures are pinpointed, are millions of individuals who are suffering a profound identity crisis, an overwhelming lack of self-confidence, a torment born of the conflicts inherent in societies that bid women to become full members of the culture but define this in masculine terms and base it on hierarchical principles. The agonized feelings of *alienation, confusion, and inadequacy they're experiencing, and the root causes behind them, are the real story that needs to be addressed.* Yet we must look to the statistics regarding eating disorders as an indication of the numbers involved.

Though there is no agreement among experts on the prevalence of eating disorders, some broad outlines can be sketched. For instance, recent surveys show that *preschool* girls are already aware that thinness is considered beautiful in women. Dieting starts early, with 80 percent of our fourth-grade daughters so concerned about their size and weight that they are already dieting. And by age ten, fully 90 percent of our young daughters are estimated to be dieting in an attempt to limit their size.[10] Dieting is often the initial sign of far deeper problems than worries over shape and weight, and all too often is the prelude to a lifetime of distorted eating patterns, self-image problems, and a self-limiting approach to life.

A recent prevalence study of high school girls and college coeds showed that currently *6.5 to 18.6* percent are bulimic and that one to four percent are anorexic.[11] There is general agreement among health professionals that the incidence of bulimia and of bulimic symptoms is greatest under the age of 30 to 35. But considerable disagreement arises in statistical reporting regarding prevalence because some researchers have included borderline maladaptive eating patterns in females while others have used very specific diagnostic criteria for what they consider a "case" of bulimia or anorexia. This, in part, explains why, though there is general agreement that distorted eating attitudes and behavior are common, the statistics vary widely.

While a much higher incidence of bulimia has been reported in some research,[12] in other reports using limited, highly specific diagnostic criteria, investigators have reported around 7.2 percent of the young women questioned were "clinical bulimics" or "near bulimics."[13] Still others in the field who've researched particular food-related disorders, have reported finding that among high school girls, of those who have compulsive eating problems, 38 percent compensate for binges by fasting, 17 percent by excessive exercise, 12 percent by diuretics and/or laxatives, and nine to ten percent by vomiting.[14]

In addition to surveying those who are *currently* having problems, some investigators have considered the percentage who have had significant problems at some time in the past, while others have tried to estimate what percentage of women are likely to *become* bulimic at some time in their lives. Discrepancy in the statistical reporting of the prevalence of bulimia and other eating disorders also stems, in part, from differences in how researchers choose to define a particular "syndrome" they are examining, the accuracy of their questioning methods, how stringent the criteria are for specifying a "case" in their study, plus their particular sampling techniques and other variables.

Epidemiology

It's been reported by some investigators that bulimia is significantly less common in black high school students than white[15] or in black college coeds[16] than white, but conflicting reports state that the percentage is about equal among black, white, and other racial backgrounds.[17]

Recent studies of minority women have turned up alarming statistics suggesting that prevalence figures from the past were significantly underestimated, partly because less affluent minorities seem less likely to seek treatment[18] and therefore be noticed.

A case in point is research into eating patterns of native Americans and Hispanic females. One examination of American Indians and Southwestern Hispanics produced findings that indicate a "substantial" rate of disordered eating — with 11 percent meeting the criteria for a diagnosis of bulimia as defined by the Diagnostic and Statistical Manual of Mental Disorders (DSM-III).[19] Another survey of Native Americans "revealed that 74 percent" of the girls and women "were trying to lose weight" and that of those on weight-loss diets, 75 percent "were employing potentially hazardous techniques."[20] Further, these survey results indicated that 24 percent of those who were dieting were also resorting to purging.[21]

These researchers point out that minority women are often reluctant to seek treatment for their "pathogenic weight control techniques . . . which are likely to be injurious if practiced over time," such as "self-induced vomiting, fluid deprivation, prolonged fasting, laxatives, diuretics, and diet pills."[22] More than *half* of those surveyed were using health-injurious methods. This included the more than 20 percent who resorted to one or more methods of purging.[23] Twelve percent of the Native American girls and women studied purged by vomiting, six percent by laxatives, and another six percent by diuretics.

Beyond this, their attempts at weight loss included skipping meals, eating only low-calorie foods, spitting food out after chewing it, taking steam baths and saunas, following special limited diets, and substantially increasing exercise.[24] In contrast to this female struggle to trim down, Hispanic and Native American boys reported wishing they weighed *more* than they currently did.[25] Indications are strong that dangerous means of weight control are not limited to Caucasian women and that when we define this as a major health problem in westernized countries, this applies across the board to women of widely varied social, racial, religious, political, and ethnic backgrounds.

Our lack of awareness of the pervasiveness of eating-disorder symptoms among women is, as pointed out, largely due to their being concealed. But despite statistical disparities, at some point in their lives, many women come close to the pathology found in bulimia. Certainly, at any given time, bulimic symptoms and other food-based compulsions, are relatively common in our female population. *There are at present invisible millions with secret selves they feel are unacceptable, leading secret lives enslaved by distorted food-related behavior they dare not let others know about, afraid they would be thought foolish.* Though many do not have a full-blown syndrome, clearly their symptoms indicate unhealthy patterns that need to be addressed and overcome.

These individuals are part of the population of women who struggle with *gradations* of eating disturbances, a large share of which are considered "subclinical." They continually struggle to subdue their craving for food and frequently suffer from intense feelings of inadequacy.

Eating Behavior Continuum

Looked at more closely, these gradations[26] can be considered as behaviors along an *Eating Behavior Continuum*. Segments along this continuum might be thought of as including (beginning at the extreme range of illness):

Anorexia — for describing those who in their emaciated state, restrict their food intake and may or may not binge and/or purge;

Bulimia — for describing those who frequently and persistently binge and purge;

Episodic Bulimia —for describing those who periodically binge and/or purge but aren't continually involved in these behaviors, and are considered by some to be potential pre-bulimics or pre-anorexics;

Noncompensatory Overeating — for describing those who use no consistent reliable means to control their weight and who may or may not binge;

Chronic Dieting — for describing those who repeatedly gain weight, then go on restrictive diets or fast, to lose the same pounds over and over again;

Corrective Dieting — for describing those who are working on reestablishing a healthy weight and overall well-being;

Occasional Dieting — for describing those who are healthy but overeat and gain from time to time (such as on trips or during the holidays), but soon cut back and return to a normal weight;

Healthy Eating — for describing those who eat and think about eating primarily when they're hungry, maintain good fitness and a healthful weight year after year with no particular effort or concern, and are content with their bodies.

Females who find themselves at the healthy side of the continuum are indeed fortunate, and in westernized countries, they are certainly among a relatively small minority. The situation has been worsening in recent years, with fewer and fewer women firmly established in the latter part of the continuum.

A great many women find themselves in the *Chronic Dieters* range of the continuum — gaining, cutting back, resorting to restrictive dieting, relaxing their routine, and regaining *again* (a never-ending market for fad diets of all kinds). "Diet junkies" who continually wish they could lose five or maybe even ten pounds, may experiment with various means of purging and "binge" on foods they try to resist (though the quantities may, in fact, be relatively small). Rarely do they come to the attention of medical professionals because they don't stick with any "aberration long enough to cause obvious damage."[27] And they never get so thin as to be noticeably ill. Yet the physical, emotional, and mental drain this entails is ongoing and substantial, with our wondering what might be accomplished if all the attention and energy that was being put into dieting and worry over eating and weight were diligently directed at developing individual potential and global harmony.

Individuals may find themselves moving from one part of the Eating Behavior Continuum to another, or notice that they combine traits of more than one segment of the spectrum. But individual patterns aside, it's recognized that weight-loss dieting commonly leads to irritability, food craving, depression, and body defenses that may result in a higher percent of body fat *after* dieting than before. These elements frequently combine to precipitate binge-eating as well as purging.

Of course, no one moves suddenly from healthy eating to being clinically ill with bulimia or anorexia. The progression from health toward illness is taken imperceptibly, a step at a time. This path spans from complete wellness through increasing degrees of distortion to *life-threatening illness*. Unfortunately, there's no way to tell when an individual has stepped over the *invisible line* from distorted eating to addiction.

We need to recognize not only that eating disorders have become pervasive among females but also that this largely hidden epidemic is symptomatic of the more basic problems that women are struggling with in cultures that are experiencing the unprecedented stresses brought about by conflicts between entrenched dominator/hierarchical social systems and pressures to establish more egalitarian/partnership values.

Obviously, new, more effective approaches are needed to prevent eating and weight disorders as well as to promote recovery from them. The principles of *cohealing* provide an appropriate approach for accomplishing this. Beyond this, we need to use the cohealing mind-set in a cooperative, shared search for ways to address the dire social, economic, and environmental ills that civilization is facing today so as to establish systems world-wide that are conducive to social harmony, ecologically sound practices, and the individual well-being of those alive today as well as of those who come after us.

Glossary of Terms

Eating disorders contain common obsessive elements, among them: fear of eating combined with an intense desire for food, distress over excessive appetite combined with guilt and shame after having eaten, dread of gaining weight combined with a compelling need to diet, purge, or even starve for extended periods. Those with eating disorders use food as a means of avoiding distressing feelings and thoughts.

In contemporary westernized culture, the ideal of female beauty has become progressively slimmer while the weight of the average woman has remained relatively constant. Therefore, women have found it more and more difficult to feel good about their bodies or believe that they could ever come close to that ideal.[1] As a consequence, obsessive weight-loss dieting has become commonplace.

Eating disorders are "complex behavioral disturbances."[2] They have long been reported in medical literature, with references being made to such problems as anorexia nervosa and obesity. Bulimia, however, is a different story, for it is a psychosocial disorder that only recently has been recognized as a significant health concern.[3]

People with eating disorders obsess about food as well as about their shape, but they deal with these concerns in different ways. Some overeat and become obese, others abstain and become anorexic, while still others binge and purge, managing in this way to maintain a relatively normal weight.

Categories and terminology need to be thought of as having a certain fluidity since many individuals move through *various* *"phases"*[4] of eating disorders. These may involve progressing from dieting to starving, to bingeing and purging, or to overeating and gaining weight, and then perhaps recycling back again through one or another of the previous symptoms. Eating disorders are, by their inherent nature, neither rigid or well defined.

Indeed, one of the downsides to labeling disorders such as bulimia is that individuals with "bulimic symptoms" may feel that their behavior has been legitimized as an illness and that they are therefore powerless victims with little ability to pull themselves out of the victim role.[5] In a sense, such thinking places responsibility on the disorder instead of on the person who is choosing to continue bulimic patterns.[6]

Eating disorders need to be viewed in context, with consideration paid to the environment — cultural, societal, familial, personal —in order to determine which continuing problem situations (including an individual's social network, daily events, and other stimuli) are affecting behavior. This approach emphasizes the conditions of the individual's daily existence that most likely contribute to the disorder, rather than emphasizing particular symptoms. Yet, a symptom approach is basic to establishing the criteria by which particular illness categories are defined.

Currently, most eating disorders are conceptualized as distinct illnesses, as opposed to considering them as overlapping, fluid, inconsistent, and existing along a continuum of related elements. Also, at present, there is no satisfactory means of relating the different forms of eating disorders to each other. With this in mind, it is easy to see that significant problems in defining these disorders exist.

Over time, the forms of eating disorders and their manifestations have undergone various transformations, which again calls for updating and redefining what constitutes a particular syndrome.[7] For instance, some researchers feel that in defining bulimia, more emphasis should be placed on attitudinal aspects of the disorder than on behavioral ones and that frequency of the criteria need to be given greater consideration.[8]

Since any "cut-off point" in defining diagnostic criteria is arbitrary[9] (in reality humans do not fit in tight categories), various approaches for dealing with this have been suggested. Consideration has been given to recognizing "pre-anorexic" or "pre-bulimic" states, or to classifying those who show "most of the features" of these disorders as exhibiting the presence of criteria associated with "partial syndrome."[10]

This all has to do with defining what is considered a "case," and for some time researchers have been "fumbling for appropriate definitions . . . (of) eating disorders."[11] Combined with this confusion is the need to maintain adequate flexibility in diagnostic criteria so that "borderline" conditions are considered.[12]

Since bulimic behaviors are common in females,[13] practical methods need to be developed for detecting *vulnerability* by understanding the most common *predictors*. Intervention needs to begin at the earliest possible stage when initial symptoms are present. Prompt treatment and follow-up are of course important, but even more essential is the logical and practical need to address the almost untapped field of prevention. Since bulimia is associated with significant life impairment, this task is of utmost importance and urgency.

There is considerable disagreement on what might be the optimal definition for each of the most common eating-disorder categories. According to researchers in the field, this has led to a lack of uniform criteria for classification of such disorders, though there are continuing efforts to classify them. In the meantime, we need to have some idea of how terms are being defined. To facilitate this, here are some broad outlines:

ANOREXIA NERVOSA: Anorexia nervosa is characterized by the "relentless pursuit of thinness"[14] and by deliberate self-starvation, along with rigid, extreme attempts to control appetite.

"Anorexia" is commonly used as a shortened form indicating anorexia nervosa, though the word itself indicates lack of appetite (which is misleading, since this doesn't occur until the later stages of illness).[15]

This pathological, chronic disorder,[16] primarily defined by its physical symptoms, has profound psychiatric ones as well. These include an intense and irrational fear of becoming obese (which persists in spite of weight loss), refusal to maintain a minimally normal body weight, a distorted body-image (with the subject continuing to protest that she is fat though she is overly thin), and loss of menstrual periods (amenorrhea) or failure to commence them in puberty. Some definitions have included the loss of 20 percent to 25 percent of body weight as a criterion for diagnosis. Hyperactivity, in spite of weakness, may also be present, along with such other symptoms as obsessions about food, depression, hair loss, low pulse rate, constipation, and intolerance to cold.[17]

Some anorexics restrict food intake and do not binge or purge, while others restrict intake and purge but never binge. Still others binge and purge and may also restrict intake (sometimes referred to as bulimia nervosa).

The anorexic's intense fear of becoming fat does not subside when she becomes slender and even emaciated.[18] While others worry about her starved condition, she may still deny that anything is wrong.[19] Anorexia is most commonly found in adolescent girls, though it has been reported in early childhood and throughout adulthood. The deliberate self-starvation of anorexia that results in significant undernutrition, is achieved either by restricting intake or by purging. For this reason, anorexics are often grouped into those who are "restricting" versus those who are "bulimic."[20]

I used anorexia to describe the starvation phase of Jacqueline's illness, when anorexia nervosa was the medical diagnosis.

BINGE: In this book and as commonly used in reference to eating disorders, a "binge" refers to *an episode of uncontrolled eating*, during which large amounts of food (usually high-calorie) are consumed within a relatively short period of time. What distinguishes the binge from normal eating is the feeling of compulsion — the seemingly irresistible impulse to eat. Binges are often followed by a sense of guilt and of being out of control.

Many professionals consider binge eating to be a form of bulimia, or simply that bulimia *means* binge eating.[21]

BULIMIA: Some authorities use "bulimia" to describe only those who suffer from food addiction and regularly binge but do not purge. The term "bulimarexia" was coined (by Marlene Boskind-White and William White, Jr.)[22] to designate bingeing followed by vomiting, fasting, and/or purging by other means.

The term "bulimia nervosa" has been used to describe recurrent episodes of bingeing that are accompanied by a feeling of lack of control (with a minimum of two episodes of bingeing a week for three months or more), weight-control attempts by self-induced vomiting, stringent dieting, vigorous exercise, fasting, or use of diuretics or laxatives, and persistent overconcern with body weight and shape (as discussed in Part II of this book).[23] The term bulimia nervosa has at times been applied to those anorexics who binge-purge and may sometimes restrict intake,[24] those with an irresistible urge to binge and purge regardless of their weight,[25] those who previously met the criteria for anorexia but are no longer emaciated,[26] and other variants.

Bulimia is characterized by both behavioral and physical symptoms, among them repeated episodes of binge eating (generally of high-calorie foods ingested in a short period of time). These are frequently followed by attempts to counteract the overindulgence by self-induced vomiting, use of diuretics, laxatives, emetic abuse, enemas, compulsive exercise, fasting, or other means.[27] The individual is aware that her eating patterns are abnormal and, as a result, worries about herself. She usually feels ashamed of her "secret."

All bulimics binge repeatedly, although, as we have seen, according to some definitions, they do not necessarily vomit. They are sometimes referred to as purging or non-purging bulimics.[28]

Binges are often terminated by drowsiness, an interruption in the eating process, or abdominal pain and are closely associated with feelings of guilt, disgust, self-depreciation, and depression. The bulimic repeatedly attempts to control or lose weight and, in so doing, suffers frequent weight fluctuations. Bulimics are generally of relatively normal weight, though they can vary from excessively thin to moderately overweight.

Symptoms of bulimia include: menstrual irregularities, swollen neck glands, fear of not being able to stop eating, solitary inconspicuous eating, preoccupation with body weight and fear of becoming obese, obsessive rumination concerning food, disturbed attitudes toward body shape, dehydration, nutritional deficiencies, preoccupation with becoming thinner, sore throats, erosion of dental enamel, and drinking large quantities of water.[29]

Frequently, the individual has a tendency toward being a perfectionist and her bulimic problems begin as a reaction to the deprivation of weight-loss dieting. Though food restriction is originally undertaken in an attempt to establish greater control over her life, ironically, *lack* of control sets in as bulimic symptoms develop.[30]

Bulimia involves a learned set of behaviors and therefore is based on habits that can be changed.[31] Its maladaptive patterns are clearly related to recent standards of westernized culture.

Eating-disorder symptoms overlap, and bulimia covers a wide range of behavior. Both anorexia and bulimia are appetite behavioral disorders that are essentially defined by specific diagnostic criteria, as in the *Diagnostic and Statistical Manual of Mental Disorders (DSM-III)*, by the American Psychiatric Association.[32]

Because of the confusion over terms, I felt it best to stick with the term bulimia in referring to the period when Jacqueline was maintaining a relatively normal weight but was purging after having eaten what she considered binges (of varying quantities). During this time, she met the psychological and other criteria for bulimia.

COMPULSION: An irresistible urge to act in ways that are against an individual's better judgment and personal wishes, constitutes compulsion. Compulsions are commonly irrational and repetitive, involving a mental state in which the individual feels compelled to perform certain behavior.[33]

FOOD ADDICTION: Strictly speaking, addiction is overdependence on a drug. Though the criteria are disputed, in general they relate to psychological dependence, substance abuse and overuse, craving, and an inability to resist the addictive substance in question, in spite of recognition that it is harmful. One of the recommendations for sidestepping problems involved in the use of the term *addiction* in non-drug situations is to use the term *dependence*.[34]

Dependencies have to do with habituation, a psychological reliance on something or someone. This dependence is characterized by continued involvement even when there are serious adverse consequences. Those with eating problems often develop significant maladaptive behavior in several areas, such as abuse of laxatives and/or other drugs, alcoholism, purging, or ritualistic and excessive exercise. However, since we are all dependent on food to maintain life, it is probably preferable to recognize the addictive aspects of food-related problems by using the term *addiction.*

Food addiction has psychological as well as physical components. In common usage and in this book, addiction describes *preoccupation with food* as well as obsession with the anticipated pleasure, and/or emotional relief, that eating will bring. The compulsion to repeatedly consume excessive quantities of food against one's better judgment, along with loss of control over consumption once eating has begun, are symptoms of an eating disorder. Foods most often associated with addiction are those with sugars, starches, and fats. Binge-eating episodes are usually followed by self-chastisement as well as feelings of guilt and shame. Addictive behavior in relation to food is one of the fundamental problems that bulimics share.

OBSESSION: Thoughts, feelings, and ideas that preoccupy and invade one's consciousness over an extended period of time, which are usually upsetting and persist in spite of efforts to be rid of them, are hallmarks of obsession.[35] Combined with this preoccupation are anxiety and tension, plus an awareness of the inappropriateness of these emotions and related thought patterns.[36]

PURGE: In this book, "purge" is used to describe both *self-induced vomiting* and the *use of laxatives.* Purging methods used to rid the body of substances thought undesirable frequently include taking diuretics and other drugs. In this context the purge is often associated with a sense of having cleansed the body, not only of food, but also of calories and "impurities."

One of the confusing factors regarding criteria for defining eating-disorder syndromes is that some are psychological and behavioral while others are physiological. Definitions are continually being revised, and countless women who have life-impairing and even life-endangering eating-disorder symptoms fail to fulfill the complete criteria for any of the current medical definitions. Since a syndrome is the concurrence of a group of symptoms associated with a disease, identification of syndromes aids in identification of causes, prognosis, treatment, and evaluation of outcome.

It would seem that the current definitions are too restrictive and that optimum ones have not yet been developed. For instance, the variety of abnormal eating patterns included in the description of bulimia is thought by some to be too restricted, so that many who need to be treated are excluded from proper diagnosis and care. Because the intensity and frequency of symptoms may vary, it has been suggested that the term Episodic Bulimia might better describe some manifestations of this eating disorder.

Compulsive overeaters are generally obese, whereas bulimics generally are not, but their cognitive and behavioral characteristics related to weight, shape, and eating have considerable similarities.[37] Some clinicians include a category that they call the "fat/thin disorder" to describe continual obsession about food as a distraction from troublesome feelings.[38]

The similarities between and overlapping of symptoms, plus the movement of individuals from one constellation of symptoms to another — all indicate a continuum, a spectrum, that covers the full range of currently independently defined eating disorders. What we refer to as eating disorders probably makes up "only a small part of spectrum," according to Preston Zucker, former president of the American Anorexic/Bulimia Association.[39]

Medical consequences of bulimic behavior and related compulsive-eating patterns include difficulty swallowing, lesions in the esophagus, internal bleeding, anemia, electrolyte imbalance leading to heart failure, infertility, lack of breast development in adolescence, kidney failure, gastric ulcers, loss of ability to think clearly, plus other symptoms related to undernutrition that have already been mentioned. Other medical consequences involve complications in pregnancy along with fetal and obstetric abnormalities.[40]

Whether an individial's symptoms include fasting, extreme dieting, bingeing, undernutrition or overnutrition, hyperactivity or inactivity, abstinence or purging, theoretical considerations relative to precise definitions for diagnosis must be counterbalanced by the pragmatic need to get the individual who obviously needs help into appropriate treatment.

Considerations
in Selecting a Therapist

There are many different approaches to treating eating disorders, and no particular way has been proven effective in all instances. Therapy is important for those with eating problems and is usually advisable for family members with whom they are living, including parents, siblings, or husbands.[1]

It is best to get a number of referrals and interview each of them, asking such questions as:

- What is your training and are you a specialist in the eating problems for which we are seeking treatment?[2]
- How long have you worked in this specialty?
- Are you licensed by the state, and what certification do you have in the mental health discipline?
- What results have you had in terms of the long-term recovery of those who have been your clients?
- What is the anticipated duration of treatment and the cost involved?[3]
- Would you plan to work not only with the client, but also with other family members as well?
- Are family interactions, along with the concerns and problems of individual members, part of the therapy process?
- Would your aim be to assist family members in making changes that could benefit them as well as contribute to the client's recovery?
- Would you be comfortable with the client and/or family members attending outside support-group meetings and participating in other similar programs aimed at breaking down the isolation, fear, hopelessness, detrimental patterns, and other problems related to the eating disorder?

- How would you handle those times when the client might not want other family members to be seeing you? Would you then recommend another therapist to meet with them?[4]

- Do you develop contracts for you and the client to work on together to accomplish specific goals within an agreed-on time frame?[5]

- Would you work closely with medical specialists on the case? What understanding do you have of the medical implications involved? Would you expect a nutritionist, dentist, or other specialist to be part of this recovery network?

- What therapeutic approach would you be taking? Does it concentrate on:

  Teaching new tools for problem-solving?
  Identifying feelings and gaining insights into why the eating disorder developed, plus possible reasons it is being maintained?
  Developing assertiveness and self-direction to overcome passivity and dependency?[6]
  Using a "feminist" approach that recognizes socio-cultural factors as relevant to the problems?[7]
  Establishing new patterns of behavior?

- Is there some other combination of techniques that you use?

- Would you expect to educate patient and family about the eating disorder so that a better understanding of the problem can be developed?

Interviews with potential therapists including those in the medical profession, should — if a practitioner is to be considered — give a feeling of confidence and comfort, as well as the possibility of building mutual trust and a good, ongoing relationship between care provider and client. Family members will want to discuss their impressions and reactions to the professionals contacted. Which therapist seems to be the best choice, and why?

Interviews need to generate a sense of rapport, "a spark" of interest.[8] Addictive eating behavior is a defense against chaotic nameless fears and buried conflicted emotions, which makes it difficult to relinquish. A feeling of compassion on the part of the therapist or therapists (if more than one is to be involved), physicians, and other professionals is an important ingredient.

Many treatment approaches have *proven effective*, though it often takes time to see results. Sometimes in addition to counseling and medical care, art and music therapies are helpful, along with nutritional instruction and such things as women's studies,[9] and other forms of input that contribute to self-development and confidence. Even after an extended period of severe illness recovery can occur, giving us good cause for hope.[10]

If disagreements with the therapist arise, talk them over before considering discontinuation of the sessions. However, if after having consulted with a therapist (or other medical professional) over a number of meetings, you as client and family do not feel comfortable with the treatment techniques, services, or individual involved, or with the progress made, ask for a recommendation regarding another professional you could consult for a second opinion. Also, if after consistent effort, you feel unable to work with a particular practitioner, you are not compelled to stay with that person and should consider looking for someone who better meets your needs.[11]

In your search, it is wise to look for a therapist who conveys hope and the message "I believe in you and your ability [to recover.]"[12]

Successful counseling "depends largely on therapists' ability to mobilize patients' resources to heal themselves,"[13] as Dr. Moshe Talmon, a psychiatrist and author on treatment modalities, has noted. Therefore, it is of utmost importance that the therapeutic approach be directed at mobilizing the "patient's *positive expectation*" of improvement and optimal health.[14] One of the "most significant ways" that a therapist can assist the patient is by empowering her with the knowledge that she does indeed have the "option to recover," a choice that she can be supported in making.[15]

Professionals and non-professionals, teachers and sponsors, counselors and friends are among those who can act in a mentor capacity. Mentors help us transcend previous limitations. With this in mind, the overview on the following page can stimulate discussion of what the role of mentor involves.

MENTOR

A mentor is a trusted and faithful advisor who provides supportive help — a counselor who has our best interests at heart. Mentors teach us in new ways but do not preach to us. Instead, they promote self-exploration, initiative, and effective behavior. They encourage autonomy along with self-acceptance. Mentors look for the best in us and encourage it to grow. They influence us on the mental, emotional, and spiritual levels.

Mentors are sensitive listeners who ask appropriate questions like, "How are you feeling? What do you want? What are your options?" Mentors provide beneficial feedback and are noncritical. They do not moralize or threaten, interrogate or pry. A mentor's help is compassionate and caring. It nurtures freedom and personal choice, giving us tools for learning and for reaching our goals.

Mentors are facilitators who offer us information and encouragement, but we are the decider and doer. They support personal accomplishments as a way of developing competencies and self-assurance. Mentors make it easier for us to become the person we want to be. They offer us an invitation into the ways of the world and teach us skills to help us prosper.

Mentors accept us for who we are and honor our dignity and worth. They assist us in our passage from one stage to another in our growth and maturation. They show us connectedness and separateness in appropriate balance and do not make us dependent on them.

Mentors help widen our horizons, expanding our awareness both internally and externally. They elevate existence so that we transcend old limitations and move to new levels of self-discovery and satisfaction.

Dedicated to all mentors, teachers, and sponsors
who help us along our path,
Hope Sinclair.

Resource Agencies

Support groups have been organizing across the country in recent years so that there are now resources of this type in most communities. The following national associations provide a variety of services, including eating-disorder information, referrals to therapists, physicians, and support groups, newsletters, workshops, speakers' bureaus, counseling services, conferences, and other related services.

American Anorexia / Bulimia Association (AABA)
293 Central Park West, Suite 1R
New York, New York 10024
(212) 501-8351

Anorexia Nervosa & Related Eating Disorders, Inc. (ANRED)
P. O. Box 5102
Eugene, Oregon 97405
(541) 344-1144

National Eating Disorders Organization (NEDO)
6655 South Yale Avenue
Tulsa, Oklahoma 74136
(918) 481-4044

National Association of Anorexia Nervosa and Associated Disorders (ANAD)
1920 Thornwood Lane
Riverwoods, Illinois 60035
(847) 831-3438

Overeaters Anonymous
6075 Zenith Court, NE
Rio Rancho, New Mexico 87124
(505) 891-2664

These national organizations and services, along with thousands of smaller local ones, offer helpful support for those seeking healthier eating patterns and more fulfilling lives. Overeaters Anonymous and some organizations offering weight-control programs are among those frequently cited for compassionate assistance to individuals and their families in overcoming eating, weight, and codependency problems. Many find this type of group a resource for developing co-independent relationships and a sense of personal worth and identity. In times of distress, they can be a resource for emotional support, direction, companionship, and strength. You can find Overeaters Anonymous, or similar support organizations, listed in most local telephone directories or by phoning your Chamber of Commerce. Local community mental health clinics, college health centers, medical associations, and hospitals are also sources of referrals.

Suggested Reading

Alberti, Robert E., and Michael L. Emmons, *Your Perfect Right,* Sixth Edition (Calif.: Impact, 1990).

Beattie, Melody, *Codependent No More; How to Stop Controlling Others and Start Caring for Yourself* (New York: Harper/Hazelden, 1987).

Beattie, Melody, *Beyond Codependency; and getting better all the time* (New York: Harper/Hazelden, 1989).

Berne, Eric, *Games People Play* (New York: Ballantine, 1978).

Bradshaw, John, *Bradshaw On: The Family; A Revolutionary Way of Self-Discovery* (Deerfield Beach, Fla.: Health Communications, 1988).

Bradshaw, John, *Bradshaw On: Healing the Shame That Binds You* (Deerfield Beach, Fla: Health Communications, 1988).

Chernin, Kim, *The Hungry Self; Women, Eating and Identity* (New York: Harper & Row, 1986).

Dowling, Colette, *The Cinderella Complex: Women's Hidden Fear of Independence* (New York: Summit Books, 1982).

Dyer, Wayne W., *Pulling Your Own Strings* (New York: Avon Books, 1979).

Dyer, Wayne W., *The Sky's the Limit* (New York: Simon and Schuster, 1980).

Eisler, Riane, *The Chalice and the Blade; Our History, Our Future* (New York: Harper & Row, 1988).

Eisler, Riane, and David Loye, *The Partnership Way; New Tools for Living & Loving* (New York: HarperCollins, 1990).

Evatt, Cris and Bruce Feld, *The Givers and the Takers* (New York: Fawcett, 1990).

Forward, Susan, *Toxic Parents; Overcoming Their Hurtful Legacy and Reclaiming Your Life* (New York: Bantam Books, 1990).

Gawain, Shakti, *Creative Visualization* (Mill Valley, Calif.: Whatever Publishing, 1978).

Harris, Thomas A., *I'm OK, You're OK* (New York: Avon Books, 1973).

Hutchinson, Marcia Germaine, *Transforming Body Image; Learning to Love the Body You Have* (Freedom, Calif.: The Crossing Press, 1985).

James, Muriel, and Dorothy Jongeward, *Born to Win; Transactional Analysis with Gestalt Experiments* (Mass.: Addison-Wesley, 1971).

Kinoy, Barbara P., and John A. Atchley, *When Will We Laugh Again? Living and Dealing with Anorexia Nervosa and Bulimia* (New York: Columbia University Press, 1984).

Levenkron, Steven, *Treating and Overcoming Anorexia Nervosa* (New York: Warner Books, 1983).

Middelton-Moz, Jane, *Shame and Guilt: Masters of Disguise* (Deerfield Beach, Fla: Health Communications, 1990).

Orbach, Susie, *Hunger Strike; The Anorectic's Struggle as a Metaphor for Our Age* (New York: Avon Books, 1988).

Rubin, Theodore I., *The Angry Book* (New York: Macmillian, 1970).

Russianoff, Penelope, *Why Do I Think I Am Nothing Without a Man?* (New York: Bantam Books, 1982).

Sanford, Linda T., and Mary Ellen Donovan, *Women and Self-Esteem, Understanding and Improving the Way We Think and Feel About Ourselves* (New York: Penguin, 1985).

Thoele, Sue Patton, *The Courage to Be Yourself; A Woman's Guide to Growing Beyond Emotional Dependence* (Emeryville, Calif.: Conari Press, 1991).

Vincent, L. M., *Competing with the Sylph; Dancers and the Pursuit of the Ideal Body Form* (New York: Berkley Books, 1981).

White, Marlene Boskind, and William C. White, Jr.: *Bulimarexia; The Binge-Purge Cycle* (New York: W.W. Norton, 1987).

Woititz, Janet G., *Struggle for Intimacy* (Deerfield Beach, Fla.; Health Communications, 1985).

Helping the
Compulsive Eater

It's natural that, if someone close to us has bulimia or some other compulsive problem, it affects our relationship with that individual; so we need to decide how we are going to deal with the situation.

Corrosive emotions aroused by a daughter, mother, sister, wife, or other loved one who is damaging her health with problematic eating behavior, and may even be flirting with death, can keep a household in continual turmoil. It's difficult to deal with the bewilderment and anxiety of watching as she starves herself and/or insists on purging, uses excessive amounts of laxatives or diuretics, or in some other way distorts the normal eating process.

Anorexics are often adolescent girls living with their parents, while bulimics are frequently older and live away from home. Many bulimics are married, and some have children of their own. Parents of a dependent daughter still at home have a distinct advantage, as do other relatives living with the individual who has the compulsive-eating problems. Parents of a minor can *intervene* when their daughter is damaging her health and see that she gets proper treatment, as can others who are living with an individual who is in crisis due to aberrant eating-related behavior.

The situation is more difficult, however, for relatives of an eating-disorder adult living on her own. In that case, they may be limited to long-distance phone calls, letters, and periodic visits to share concern and perhaps suggest possible courses of action.

The amount and kind of help provided depends on their relation to the affected person — whether she is married, a minor, or an adult, what stage of illness she is in, financial resources (both theirs and hers), and the time and energy available to provide help. Whatever the circumstances, loved ones and concerned friends generally find themselves assuming a nurturing role based on feelings that can be summarized as "We care, we're affected, we want to assist and become part of the recovery process."

If we are caring for an adult who is gravely ill, we may need to assume a supervising, protective stance at the start. We may have to let her know that "This is what we're going to do to see that you don't kill yourself . . . . " with the intention and resolve to turn control back to her when she is able to more responsibly handle her life. In cases of severe illness, it is indeed our responsibility to intervene. This calls for being loving and firm — able to take charge in a crisis situation — while not being domineering.

It's well to remember, though, that from a long-term point of view, it's inappropriate to continue to insist, "Here, let me help you" or "You ought to . . . ," attitudes that indicate a lack of faith in her ability to act capably.

If the individual is an ill child, she will want to feel she can trust parents to be competent, dependable, helpful, and understanding of the trauma that she's living through. Compassion and comforting are in order. Indulgence and coddling are definitely not.

In these circumstances, it's easy to fall into advising and warning, threatening, nagging, begging, dictating, condemning, lecturing, scolding, and complaining, all of which are counterproductive. Such counsel would quite rightly be interpreted as intrusive and unwarranted. The loved one who is having compulsive-eating problems needs to have adequate and appropriate information, but unless she's a child or is physically or emotionally impaired (with the exception of a crisis in which she would be doing herself irreversible harm), she needs to make her own decisions.

In relating to a compulsive eater, we face the problem of inadvertently sending conflicting messages. Even as we *say*, "I love you; I think you're terrific," we may be *thinking*, "How could you behave so foolishly? I wish you'd get yourself straightened out and act normal again!" We express loving words and think critical ones — and it shows. This message comes down to, "You're messed up, and the rest of us are fine" (a subtle ranking in which the compulsive eater is placed one down from us).

Characteristically, these girls and women already feel inadequate and self-critical. It's better to take the attitude that "Your illness is not okay, but *you* are" and look at the individual's bizarre behavior (including drug and alcohol abuse, shoplifting, even prostitution to obtain money for bingeing) as illness-related.

Striking a Balance

A common complaint of women with eating disorders is that they feel that their environment while growing up was overly restrictive, protective, and authoritarian, with little freedom to express themselves and little room for self-directed growth toward individuation and autonomy. Therefore *self-responsibility* is an important issue for the compulsive eater that others need to respect.

Though it may not be easy, it's necessary to strike a balance between under- and overreacting. The goal must be to take appropriate, well-considered action. Like everyone else, the compulsive eater has a right to her own feelings, to express her own desires and needs, and to choose her own values and goals. We do her a great disservice if we act in controlling ways that deprive her of the freedom to make her own aware choices when she is capable of doing so. Being compassionate, loving, and caring is appropriate. Taking over responsibilities for the anorexic or bulimic of any age, who can — and should — be handling them for herself, is an act of "rescue." This implies that she is incompetent and unable to act responsibly. It deprives her of opportunities to decide and act in her own behalf, to be self-reliant and thereby build a sense of accomplishment, competence, and self-direction.

If we regularly do more for her than is reasonable; if we neglect our own needs, interests, friends, because we're busy sacrificing ourselves on her account; if we help without first having been asked; if we do things for her that we would really prefer not to do; if we take charge of matters that are logically her responsibility — then we're rescuing (or, what I refer to as, giving "hyper-help"). This overly-concerned, excessive helping is characteristic of codependence.

Though it may seem to us that we are being kind, actually we are creating a situation in which we will eventually feel resentful toward the individual with the compulsive-addictive problems because of all the sacrifices we have made on her behalf, and she will become resentful of our controlling ways. This promotes her feeling incompetent and powerless. *We* will feel victimized, and so will *she.*

Whenever we feel martyred because we have been doing things we *didn't really want to do*, the result can be an expectation on our part that she *should* feel obligated to us (again, for her, a one-down position). However we look at it, doing more than is appropriate creates resentment. Such rescuing does not help the individual and can even be an attempt by the caretaker to feel better about her- or himself.[1]

In discussions of *codependence*, "caretaking" is often mentioned. In this context it refers to an attitude and manner of behaving that is self-sacrificial. It has to do with obsessive attempts at trying to force one's will on someone else. Additionally, it refers to being *other*-directed rather than *self*-directed. Caretaking, enabling, rescuing — call it what you will — is unhealthy and unwarranted. This abnormal "hyper-help" entails self-neglect, self-denial, and inappropriate attempts at control. The answer to the temptation to be a so-called caretaker is to concentrate on *real help*.

One of the cultural messages that women need to overcome in order to provide appropriate help (not rescue) is the belief that they should be "caretakers and nurturers,"[2] or that accepting self-sacrifice and giving "hyper-help" is admirable. Women are taught early to believe that they should put the needs of others before their own rather than to establish co-independent relationships.

It's difficult to know how to break through a bulimic's or anorexic's defense or denials; how to intervene in some appropriate and effective manner. However, denials can sometimes be "collapsed" in what John Bradshaw has referred to as "a confrontation process called intervention" in which we become involved in the healing process and are really "there for" the individual in question.[3]

Professional Help

Since these are complex illnesses, and we are most often emotionally involved, it may be helpful to get some professional advice on how to proceed since the decisions are often not easy or clear cut.[4] This can give perspective and direction as well as emotional support in what is a very trying time, when a daughter — wife — sister — mother (or a son, husband, or brother) is eating inadequately while also resisting treatment and possibly risking her, or his, life.

Professional guidance can help a family establish new patterns of interaction that are likely to be conducive to recovery. Various family members may resist this idea since cohealing requires them to question their own attitudes and behavior, plus a willingness by them to change.[5] Most parents, family members, and friends are willing to step in to do whatever is necessary to halt devastating effects of anorexia or bulimia. Yet consulting professionals sometimes provides little reassurance or information about the specific eating disorder or the anticipated course of treatment,[6] so we need to be persistent in getting our questions answered.

It can be distressing to consider putting a young daughter into a treatment program. This carries with it feelings of having failed as a parent, of uncertainty about a program that's not fully understood, of worry over expenses that could wipe out family savings and put the household into debt.[7]

For many, there are bills for long-term hospital care and physician fees along with the costs of psychotherapy, and with bulimia, additional expenses for dental repair. These expenses can have a catastrophic effect on a family's finances, particularly because insurance companies frequently do not cover such costs. Even if a policy includes them, insurance companies have been known to simply disallow coverage.

Some hospitals have reduced or eliminated their eating-disorder clinics because the refusal of insurance companies to cover these problems has made it impossible for many women to avail themselves of these badly needed services. In addition to what can amount to years of continuing medical bills, there is also the cost of the food the bulimic eats, which, at times, can be substantial. In families facing the extended course of these illnesses, the financial burden can be overwhelming. Thus, there is not only the emotional drain, but also the financial drain. For many this becomes a matter of not being able to obtain the therapeutic help that is needed.

It's easy to feel that we ought somehow to be coping better with our own emotions and with helping our loved one who is ill, as well as dealing with doctors, therapists, nurses, other family members, and paying the related expenses. It's agony watching someone close to us starve herself, or purge and do other things that are dangerous and harmful to her health. Yet we need to resist cajoling, arguing, bribing, or punishing; remembering that none of these work, and none are appropriate.

Group Support

Self-help and therapy groups that support those with compulsive-eating disorders as well as their families, have been springing up across the country in recent years in response to the growing need for them. This is a hopeful trend since, in years past, there were no such groups to turn to for assistance, and the way seemed lonely and tenuous indeed.

The group setting can be particularly useful for providing information, mutual cohealing support, and a place where angry, helpless feelings of distress can be shared; a place to be fully accepted with no denials or hidden agendas. Self-help groups often include women who have recovered from eating addictions, whose input can be invaluable to those still having these problems. The lingering physical consequences that sometimes remain after recovery can be discussed with those who have already learned to deal with them.

As with alcoholics, in a group setting, those with eating addictions cannot get away with defenses and denials that they ordinarily use with others. They eventually have to face themselves and their demons and, with the support of the group, can make progress working through them. Since compulsive eating is a means of blocking painful feelings, when the individual begins giving up her former bulimic or anorexic patterns, she may experience heightened anger, frustration, sadness, grief, fear, or whatever other feelings have been deadened by the addictive behavior. Once these core emotions are uncovered, they can be faced and dealt with in a more direct and constructive manner.

Having a bulimic or anorexic in the family can put a heavy strain on a marriage. Some that were already shaky may continue to weaken or even head toward divorce. For others, though, the strain of illness brings the couple closer together, and through the cohealing experience, they draw renewed strength from their relationship.[8]

Family counseling can provide vital assistance by offering insights into present interactions between parent, child, and sibling, between husband and wife, and between them and other family members. It can indicate ways to improve those interactions and provide guidance on how individual members of the family can develop more satisfying lives and support each other in cohealing.

Epilogue

Since the major body of this book was completed, several years have passed. Because eating disorders are addictive, it takes time to know whether healthy patterns will be sustained. Fortunately, both Jacque and Brenda continue on a positive course with abundant health and satisfying lives that are filled with warm friendships, travel, and career commitments. Brenda has also reconciled with her step-father and they now have a cordial, co-independent relationship.

In the months immediately after completing the manuscript, both of my parents died within a few weeks of each other. My mother had stuck with her decision not to communicate with me after I chose to divorce. Interestingly, after her passing, relatives told me that she had saved the cards and letters I'd sent her over the intervening years and had kept them among her treasured possessions. While I was writing COHEALING, my father was strongly supportive of the project and one of the last things he said to me was, "I'm rooting for you" in reference to wanting the book to have a significant impact.

I'd been concerned, however, about the effect the book might have on my mother, if she were to read it, because of the references to her role in our family system, and had held back on its publication, but now that is no longer a consideration.

I am no longer involved in property investing and renovation, and now devote myself to lecturing, consulting, and writing, which bring me great personal satisfaction.

More than ever I sense the oneness, the interconnectedness of all that is. I recognize "the all" as far too complex to understand but, as I mentioned earlier, imagine it as being somewhat like a spider web, in that we can not remove or influence any specific section of it and leave the whole unaffected. Each segment of reality — of time, space, energy — that we consider is as intimately connected to the whole as is any segment of a spider's web. Every move we make, every thought or feeling we have, reverberates through and affects the rest of existence.

As we and others move toward wholeness, we affect and benefit our environment (the all), which in turn benefits not only others but also ourselves as well.

Knowing how uncertain the way seemed when my daughters and I first were working to shed the hurtful, restrictive legacy of the past and overcome addictive problems, and how inadequate were the guidelines for accomplishing this, it's my hope that this book will provide direction as you search for answers. Toward this end, it is suggested that it be circulated among support groups, individuals in therapy, in hospital units, in workshops dedicated to recovery and healing, as well as at work and among friends and family members.

This book is for sharing, for underlining, and for adapting to overcoming whatever limitations — societal, political, religious, familial, or personal — keep you from freely reclaiming your right to a satisfying, fulfilling life.

References

Preface — The Cohealing Response

1. Riane Eisler, *The Chalice and the Blade* (New York: Harper & Row, 1988), p. xvii.

CHAPTER 2: Dieting Becomes Addiction

1. Jean Rubel, Ph.D., Workshop on "Psychology of Eating Disorders" (Monterey, Calif.: Monterey Peninsula College, November 6, 1981).
2. Dennis P. Cantwell, M.D., et al., "Anorexia Nervosa," *Archives of General Psychiatry* (Chicago: September 1977), 34, pp. 1087–1093.
3. Ari Kiev, M.D., *The Courage to Live* (New York: Thomas Crowell, 1979). Excerpted in *Cosmopolitan*, September 1980, pp. 303–307.

CHAPTER 4: Pitfalls in Helping a Compulsive Eater

1. Nancy Young, "Full Stomach & Empty Lives," *Glamour*, September 1979, p. 206.
2. Hilde Bruch, M.D., *The Golden Cage* (Cambridge, Mass.: Harvard University Press, 1978), p. 47.
3. Marlene Boskind-White, Ph.D., and William C. White, Jr., Ph.D., *Bulimarexia, The Binge/Purge Cycle* (New York: W.W. Norton, 1987), p. 33.
4. G. F. M. Russell, "General Management of Anorexia Nervosa and Difficulties in Assessing the Efficacy of Treatment," in *Anorexia Nervosa,* edited by R. A. Vigersky (New York: Raven Press, 1977), p. 282.
5. William A. Nolen, M.D., "Anorexia Nervosa: The Dieting Disease," *McCall's* (June 1977), p. 72.
6. Preston Zucker, M.D., "President's Column," *American Anorexia/Bulimia Association Newsletter*, Vol. IX, No. 5, p. 2.

CHAPTER 5: Dual Personalities

1. Hilde Bruch, M.D., *The Golden Cage* (Cambridge, Mass.: Harvard University Press, 1978), p. 56.
2. Jean Rubel, Ph.D., Workshop on "Psychology of Eating Disorders" (Monterey, Calif: Monterey Peninsula College, November 6, 1981).
3. Ibid.
4. K. R. W. Norton et al., "Why do Some Anorexics Steal? Personal, Social, and Illness Factors," *Journal of Psychiatric Research*, Vol. 19, No. 2/3, p. 388.
5. D. Alun Jones et al., "Anorexia Nervosa, Bulimia, and Alcoholism — Association of Eating Disorders and Alcohol," *Journal of Psychiatric Research*, Vol. 19, No. 2/3, p. 380.
6. Ibid., p. 379.

CHAPTER 6: Body-Image Distortions

1. Marlene Boskind-Lodahl, Ph.D., and Joyce Sirlin, "The Gorging Purging Syndrome," *Psychology Today*, March 1977, p. 50.

2. Hilde Bruch, M.D. *Eating Disorders* (New York: Basic Books, 1973), p. 90.
3. Alison Bass, *Boston Globe*, "Psychology: New research links sexist society and eating disorders," *San Francisco Examiner and Chronicle*, November 4, 1990, p. D–15.
4. Ibid.
5. Ibid.
6. Ibid.

CHAPTER 8: Male Rejections

1. Herb Goldberg, *The New Male* (New York: Signet, 1979), p. 78.

CHAPTER 9: To Get Well or Not Get Well

1. Ron Davis et al, "Mood and Food: An Analysis of Bulimic Episodes," *Journal of Psychiatric Research*, Vol. 19, No. 2/3, pp. 332–333.
2. Ibid., pp. 331, 333.
3. Ibid., p. 334.
4. Ibid., pp. 332, 333.
5. L. K. G. Hsu et al., "Outcome of Anorexia Nervosa," *The Lancet* (London, U.K.), January 13, 1979, p. 61.
6. Kelly M. Bemis, "Current Approaches to the Etiology and Treatment of Anorexia Nervosa," *Psychological Bulletin*, Vol. 85, No. 3, p. 600.

CHAPTER 10: Bulimic Dreams

1. Frances Kennett, *How to Read Your Dreams* (London, (U.K.: Marshall Cavendish, 1975), p. 9.

CHAPTER 11: Food Rules and the Internal Voice

1. Jean Rubel, Ph.D., Workshop on "Psychology of Eating Disorders" (Monterey, Calif.: Monterey Peninsula College, November 6, 1981).
2. Dr. Steven Levenkron, *The Best Little Girl in the World* (Chicago: Contemporary Books, 1978), p. 179.
3. Barbara P. Kinoy in collaboration with Estelle B. Miller, John A. Atchley, and the Book Committee of the American Anorexia/Bulimia Association, *When Will We Laugh Again?* (Guildford, Surrey, N.Y.: Columbia University Press, 1984), p. 122.
4. John Bradshaw, *Bradshaw On: The Family* (Deerfield Beach, Fla.: Health Communications, 1988), p. 100.
5. Ibid., p. 15.
6. William Duffy, *Sugar Blues* (New York: Warner Books, 1975).
7. Stanton Peele, "Addiction: The Analgesic Experience," *Human Nature*, September 1978, p. 67.
8. Catherine Houck, "The Addiction Trap: How to Get Unhooked," *Cosmopolitan*, March 1981, p. 220.
9. Ibid.
10. Ibid., p. 234.
11. Ibid.
12. J. Hubert Lacey and Elizabeth Gibson, "Controlling Weight by Purgation and Vomiting: A Comparative Study of Bulimics," *Journal Psychiatric Research*, Vol. 19, No. 2/3, p. 337.
13. Ibid., p. 340.
14. Ibid., p. 341.
15. Ibid., p. 340.

16. Hilde Bruch, M.D., *The Golden Cage* (Cambridge, Mass.: Harvard University Press, 1978), p. 55.
17. Ibid., p. 56.
18. Ibid., p. 12.
19. Eric Berne, M.D., *Transactional Analysis and Psychotherapy* (New York: Grove Press, 1961).
20. John M. Dusay, M.D., *Egograms* (New York: Bantam Books, in association with Harper & Row; 1980).

CHAPTER 12: Expanding Food Choices

1. Daniel Zwerdling, "The Risks of Eating," *Playgirl Presents: Diet & Exercise*, March 1979, p. 27.
2. Ibid.
3. Michael F. Jacobson, Ph.D., *Nutrition Action Newsletter*, 1982, pp. 1, 4.
4. Ibid.
5. Rose D. Frisch, "Food Intake, Fatness, and Reproductive Ability," in *Anorexia Nervosa*, edited by Robert A. Vigersky, M.D. (New York: Raven Press, 1977), p. 155.
6. Anne Scott Beller, "Pregnancy: Is Motherhood Fattening?" in *A Woman's Conflict*, edited by Jane Rachel Kaplan (Englewood Cliffs, N.J.: Prentice-Hall, 1980) pp. 147–148.
7. Judith Willis, "The Gender Gap at the Table," *FDA Consumer, Department of Health and Human Services*, June 1984, p. 2.

CHAPTER 13: New Awareness — New Choices

1. Maj. Britt T. Rosenbaum, "Gender-Specific Problems in the Treatment of Young Women," *The American Journal of Psychoanalysis*, 37, pp. 215–221.
2. Ibid.
3. A. H. Crisp et al., "The Long-Term Prognosis in Anorexia Nervosa: Some Factors Predictive of Outcome," in *Anorexia Nervosa*, edited by Robert A. Vigersky, M.D. (New York: Raven Press, 1977), p. 56.
4. Mona Charen, "Mirrors in Mind — Women Hate Their Bodies," *San Francisco Chronicle*, January 15, 1989, *This World*, p. 6.
5. Ibid., p. 8.
6. Ibid., p. 7.
7. Ibid.
8. Chris Chase, *The Great American Waistline* (New York: Coward, McCann & Geoghegan, 1981), p. 210.
9. *Weekly World News*, May 27, 1980, p. 19.
10. Newspaper advertising campaign by Jules J. Garfield, of Hollywood, Calif., 1979.
11. Ibid.
12. *National Enquirer*, June 19, 1984, p. 22.
13. *American Home*, February 1978, p. 91.
14. *Family Weekly*, October 3, 1982, p. 13.
15. Richard B. Stuart and Barbara Davis, *Slim Chance in a Fat World* (Champaign, Ill.: Research Press, 1972), p. 139.
16. Pat Patrick, "'How I Stay Slim,' Eight wafer-thin women tell the secrets of their success," *Playgirl Presents: Diet & Exercise*, April 1980, p. 26.
17. "A Grand Tour of Spectacular Desserts," *McCall's*, January 1979 cover.
18. Mallen De Santiss, "Up and Out of the House in 45 Minutes Flat," *Cosmopolitan*: March 1980, pp. 254–257.
19. Newspaper advertising campaign by Jules J. Garfield, of Hollywood, Calif., "The A, B, C (and D's) of Breast Enlargement," 1979.

20. Mark Eden Mark II, "Instant Inches on the Bustline," *Cosmopolitan*, June 1979, p. 351.
21. Slim-Skins, "Monday morning I woke up a *Size 12* — Monday night I went to bed a *Size 9* . . . ," *Cosmopolitan*, June 1979, p. 355.
22. "The Cellulite Dissolver," *Playgirl's Slimmer*, New York: March 1981, p. 72.
23. "Nobody's Perfect — So Start Enjoying Who You Are, Warts and All," *Cosmopolitan*, June 1979, cover.
24. "Wasting Away. Why You *Can* Be Too Thin," *Cosmopolitan*, March 1981, cover.
25. Ibid., "The Most Important Love Affair of Your Life — With Yourself! How Are You Handling It?" *Cosmopolitan*, June 1979, cover.
26. Alice E. Courtney and Thomas Whipple, "Women in TV Commercials," *Journal of Communications*, Spring 1974, p. 116.
27. Bill Moyers, "TV or Not TV?," *Bill Moyers' Journal*, WNET/13, P.B.S. (Air Date: April 23, 1979).
28. Nancy S. Tedesco, "Patterns in Prime Time," *Journal of Communications,* Spring 1974, pp. 120, 122.
29. Op. cit., *Bill Moyers' Journal* (quote by Dr. George Gerbner).
30. John Carman, "Male Disdain In Prime Time, A pungent strain of gender anger comes through," *San Francisco Chronicle*, July 12, 1990, p. E–1.
31. Ibid.
32. Ibid.
33. Joyce Millman, "Prime time: Where the boys are, Strong women have weak presence in fall lineup," *San Francisco Sunday Examiner and Chronicle*, September 9, 1990, p. F–1.
34. Ibid.
35. Ibid.
36. Ibid.
37. "Why You Hate the Way You Look," *Women's Day*, May 15, 1990, p. 6.
38. Arnold Levinsons, "Amenorrhea May Affect Loss of Bone Minerals," UC [University of California, Berkeley] Clip Sheet, Vol. 57, No. 30.
39. Susan Okie, *Washington Post*, "Why You Gain Weight — Blame Your Genes," *San Francisco Chronicle,* May 24, 1991, p. A–1, 20.

CHAPTER 14: Living with Male-Female Stereotypes

1. *Vogue Patterns* (New York: Vogue Pattern Service: August 1979).
2. Ernest Dichter, "Why People Follow the Dictates of Designers," *U.S. News & World Report*, April 9, 1979, p. 53.
3. "thin," *Webster's New Collegiate Dictionary* (Springfield, Mass.: G. & C. Merriam, 1956), p. 796.
4. "female," *Roget's Thesaurus,* edited by Norman Lewis (New York: Washington Square Press, 1966), p. 156.
5. Op. cit., "broad," *Webster's New Collegiate Dictionary,* p. 106.
6. Ibid., "slender," p. 796.
7. Op. cit., "thinness," *Roget's Thesaurus,* p. 433.
8. Op. cit., "lean," *Webster's New Collegiate Dictionary,* p. 478.
9. Ibid., "healthy," p. 380.
10. Morton M. Hunt, "The Direction of Feminine Evolution," in "The Male Revolt," from *The Potential of Women*, edited by Seymour M. Farber and Roger H. L. Wilson (New York: McGraw-Hill, 1963), p. 262.
11. Alan Watts, "The Spectrum of Femininity," in "The Woman in Man," from *The Potential of Women* (ibid), p. 79.
12. Jeanne Parr Lemkau and Carol Landau, "The 'Selfless Syndrome': Assessment and Treatment Considerations," *Psychotherapy*, Vol. 23, No. 2, p. 227.

13. Geneen Roth, *Breaking Free from Compulsive Eating* (New York: Signet, 1986), p. 197.
14. Zane Kotker, "The 'Feminine' Behavior of Powerless People," *Savvy*, March 1980, p. 36.
15. Ibid.
16. Ellen Forman, *Fort Lauderdale News & Sun-Sentinel*, "Careers blocked for women," *San Francisco Sunday Examiner and Chronicle*, July 15, 1990, p. D–3.
17. Theodore Isaac Rubin, *The Angry Book* (New York: Collier Books, 1969), p. 51.
18. Niles Newton, "An Answer for Troubled Women," *San Francisco Sunday Examiner and Chronicle*, April 4, 1971, Women Today Supplement, p. 8.
19. Riane Eisler, *The Chalice and the Blade* (New York: Harper & Row, 1988), p. xvii.

CHAPTER 15: Problems with Low Self-Esteem

1. *New York Times*, "Male College Students Taken More Seriously," *San Francisco Chronicle*, April 12, 1990, p. B–3.
2. Ibid.
3. Ibid.
4. Ibid.
5. Graduate School of Business, Stanford University admissions bulletin (Palo Alto, Calif.: 1982).
6. Op. cit, "potential," *Webster's New World Dictionary*, pp. 1114–1115.
7. Morton M. Hunt, "The Direction of Feminine Evolution," in "The Male Revolt," *The Potential of Woman* (New York: McGraw-Hill, 1983), p. 265.
8. Jan Salisbury et al., "Counseling Victims of Sexual Harassment," *Psychotherapy*, Vol. 23, No. 20, p. 317.
9. Jean Shinoda Bolen, "Point Blank," *Forum* (Monterey, Calif.: June 1980).
10. Op. cit., Jan Salisbury et al., p. 318.
11. Ibid.
12. Joan Ryan, "A different abuse," *San Francisco Examiner and Chronicle*, March 4, 1986, p. F–1.
13. Jonathan Tilove, Newhouse News Service, "Wife battering ends in 6 deaths," *San Francisco Examiner and Chronicle*, January 8, 1989, p. A–5.
14. Harriet Chaing, "Sexism Pervades State's Courts Committee Says," *San Francisco Chronicle*, March 24, 1990, p. A–1.
15. Associated Press, "Working women with secret money," *San Francisco Sunday Examiner and Chronicle*, October 27, 1985, p. A–31.
16. Linda Ellerbee, "Girls and Women and Progress," *San Francisco Sunday Examiner and Chronicle*, March 1989, *This World*, p. 4.
17. Evans Witt, "Report: Women Haven't Made It," *Contra Costa Times*, Walnut Creek, Calif.: July 22, 1987, p. B–1.
18. Combined references:
    Examiner, Staff Report, "Women in top management still scarce," *San Francisco Examiner*, April 1, 1986, C–1.
    United Press International, "Job Gains Still Slight for Women," *San Francisco Chronicle*, July 12, 1989, B–3.
19. Associated Press, "Poverty Soaring Among Women, Study Says," *Monterey[,California] Peninsula Herald*, February 15, 1985.
20. Statistics Abstract of the United States, 1991, U. S. Census Bureau, Table 750, p. 464.
21. Margo Burke, "Don't Get Mad; Get Equal," *Monterey, [California] Peninsula Herald*, September 19, 1985, *Peninsula Life*, p. 28.
22. Ibid. Associated Press, February 15, 1985.

23. Daniel Bar-Tal and Leonard Saxe, "Physical Attractiveness and Its Relationship to Sex-Role Stereotyping," *Sex Roles*, Vol. 2, No. 2, p. 129.

CHAPTER 18: Healing — A Shared Experience

1. Philip J. Webster and Hope Sinclair, *Dreamers, Dreaming, Dreams* (Oakland, Calif.: Regent Books, 1991).
2. David Loye, Ph.D., *The Sphinx and the Rainbow; Brain, Mind, and Future Vision* (New York: Bantam, 1984).
3. Allan Combs, and Mark Holland, *Synchronicity* (New York: Paragon House, 1990).
4. Sheila Murray Bethel, *Making a Difference, 12 Qualities That Make You a Leader* (New York: G.P. Putnam's Sons, 1990), p. 273.
5. Riane Eisler, *The Chalice and the Blade* (New York: Harper & Row, 1988), p. xvii.

CHAPTER 19: Cohealing and Co-Independence

1. Sue Patton Thoele, *The Courage To Be Yourself* (Nevada City, Calif.: Pyramid Press, 1988), p. 232.
2. Melody Beattie, *Beyond Codependency* (New York: Harper & Row, 1989), p. 102.
3. Ibid., p. 103.
4. John Bradshaw, *Bradshaw On: Healing The Shame That Binds You* (Deerfield Beach, Fla.: Health Communications, 1988), p. 39.
5. Ibid., p. 204.
6. Ibid., p. 55.
7. Ibid., p. 89.
8. Ibid.
9. Ibid., p. 40.
10. David Bohm, Ph.D., *Wholeness and the Implicate Order* (New York: Ark, a division of Routledge, Chapman and Hall, 1983), pp. 172–213.
11. Op. cit., John Bradshaw, p. 105.
12. Riane Eisler, *The Chalice and the Blade* (New York: Harper & Row, 1988), p. xvii.
13. Ibid.

NOTES

Reclaiming Our Rights

1. Robert E. Aberti and Michael L. Emmons, *Your Perfect Right: A Guide to Assertive Living* (San Luis Obispo, Calif.: Impact, 1990), Sixth Edition, cover.
2. Sue Patton Thoele, *The Courage To Be Yourself* (Nevada City, Calif.: Pyramid Press, 1988), p. 170.
3. Ibid., p. 199.
4. Ibid., p. 142.

Extent of the Problem

1. Combined references:
   James Mitchell and Elke D. Eckert, "Scope and Significance of Eating Disorders," *Journal of Consulting and Clinical Psychology*, (Washington, D.C.: October 1987), Vol. 55, N5, pp. 628-634.

Walter Vandereycken and Rolf Meermann, "Anorexia Nervosa: Is Prevention Possible?," *International Journal of Psychiatry in Medicine* (Amityville, N.Y.: 1984), Vol. 14(3), pp. 191–205.
2. Combined references:
    James E. Mitchell and Richard L. Pyle, "The Bulimic Syndrome in Normal Weight Individuals: A Review," *International Journal of Eating Disorders* (New York: 1982), Vol. 1(2), pp. 61–73.
    Barbara Schlesier-Stropp, "Bulimia: A Review of the Literature," *Psychological-Bulletin* (Washington, D.C.: March 1984), Vol. 95(2), pp. 247–257.
3. Ibid., James E. Mitchell and Richard L. Pyle.
4. Combined references:
    James J. Gray, Kathryn Ford, and Lily M. Kelly, "The Prevalence of Bulimia in a Black College Population," *International Journal of Eating Disorders* (November 1987), Vol. 6(6), pp. 733–740.
    Mark S. Smith, "Anorexia Nervosa and Bulimia," *Journal of Family Practice* (Norwalk, Conn.: May 1984), Vol. 18(5), pp. 757–766.
5. Preston Zucker, M.D., "President's Column," *American Anorexia/Bulimia Association Newsletter* (Teaneck, N.J.: November 1986–February 1987), Vol. IX, No. 5, p. 3.
6. Kim Chernin, *The Hungry Self* (New York: Harper & Row, 1985), p. 13.
7. Marlene Boskind-White, Ph.D., and William C. White, Jr., Ph.D., *Bulimarexia, The Binge/Purge Cycle* (New York: W.W. Norton, 1987), pp. 35, 22, 43, 5, 28.
8. Ibid., p. 12, 22, 5, 28.
9. Catherine Steiner-Adair, "Developing the voice of the wise woman: college students and bulimia," *Journal of College Student Psychotherapy* (New York: 1988–89), Vol. 3(2/3), pp. 151–165.
10. Victoria Secunda, "Swerve Toward Curves," *Sacramento Bee* (Sacramento, Calif.: January 22, 1987), p. C–1.
11. Barbara P. Kinoy in collaboration with Estelle B. Miller, John A. Atchley, and the Book Committee of the American Anorexia/Bulimia Association, *When Will We Laugh Again?* (Guildford, Surrey, N.Y.: Columbia University Press, 1984), p. 14.
12. Mary Deanna VanThorre, M.A., and Francis X. Vogel, Ph.D., "The Presence of Bulimia in High School Females," *Adolescence* (Roslyn Hts., N.Y.: Spring 1985), Vol. 20, No. 77, p. 48.
13. Susan A. Basow and Renae Schneck, "Eating Disorders Among College Women," paper presented at the Annual Meeting of the Eastern Psychological Association, Philadelphia, Penn.: April 6–9, 1983).
14. Combined references:
    Jo A. Carter and Pamela A. Duncan, "Binge-Eating and Vomiting: A Survey of a High School Population," *Psychology in the Schools* (Brandon, Vt.: April 1984), Vol. 21(2), pp. 198–203.
    Statistics from Gallup polls conducted in 1985.
15. Paula M. Howat and Arnold M. Saxton, "The Incidence of Bulimic Behavior in a Secondary and University School Population," *Journal of Youth and Adolescence* (New York: June 1988), Vol. 17(3), pp. 221–231.
16. Ibid., James J. Gray, Kathryn Ford, and Lily M. Kelly, pp. 733–740.
17. Ibid., Mary-Deanna VanThorre and Francis X. Vogel, pp. 45–51.
18. Lionel W. Rosen, M.D., et al., "Prevalence of Pathogenic Weight-control Behaviors Among Native American Women and Girls," *International Journal of Eating Disorders* (1988) Vol. 7, No. 6, p. 808.
19. Mary B. Harris, "Disordered Eating in Southwestern Pueblo Indians and Hispanics," *Journal of Adolescence* (London, England: September 1989), Vol. 12(3), pp. 329–336.
20. Ibid., Lionel W. Rosen, M.D., et al., p. 807.

21. Ibid.
22. Ibid., p. 808.
23. Ibid., p. 809.
24. Ibid.
25. Ibid., Mary B. Harris.
26. Combined references:
    George I. Szmukler, "The Epidemiology of Anorexia Nervosa and Bulimia," *Journal Psychiatric Research* (Elmsford, N.Y.: 1985), Vol. 19, No. 2/3, pp. 143–145, 151.
    Angela D. Mickalide and Arnold E. Andersen, "Subgroups of Anorexia Nervosa and Bulimia: Validity and Utility," *Journal of Psychiatric Research* (1985), Vol. 19, No. 2/3, pp 112, 127.
27. Preston Zucker, M.D., "President's Column," *American Anorexia / Bulimia Association Newsletter* (February–April 1987), Vol. X, No. 1.

Glossary of Terms

1. "Eating Disorders," *The Harvard Medical School Mental Health Letter*, Vol. 1, No. 2.
2. P. J. V. Beumont, "Bulimia: Is It an Illness Entity?," *International Journal of Eating Disorders*, Vol. 7, No. 2, p. 167.
3. Ibid.
4. George I. Szmukler, "The Epidemiology of Anorexia Nervosa and Bulimia," *Journal of Psychiatric Research*, Vol. 19, No. 2/3, p. 149.
5. Marlene Boskind-White, Ph.D., and William C. White, Jr., Ph.D., *Bulimarexia, The Binge / Purge Cycle* (New York: W.W. Norton, 1987), p. 20.
6. Ibid., p. 174.
7. Gerald F. Russell, "The Changing Nature of Anorexia Nervosa," Introduction to Anorexia Nervosa and Related Disorders Conference, Swansea, Wales, *Journal of Psychiatric Research*, Vol. 19, No. 2/3, pp. 101–109.
8. Craig L. Johnson and Susan Q. Love, "Bulimia: Multivariate Predictors of Life Impairment," *Journal of Psychiatric Research*, Vol. 19, No. 2/3, pp. 346, 347.
9. Combined references:
    I. Eisler and G. I. Szmukler, "Social Class as a Confounding Variable in the Eating Attitudes Test," *Journal Psychiatric Research*, Vol. 19, No. 2/3, p. 173.
    Katherine A. Halmi, "Classification of the Eating Disorders," *Journal of Psychiatric Research*, Vol. 19, No. 2/3, p. 113.
10. Ibid., I. Eisler and G. I. Szmukler, p. 173.
11. Ibid., George I. Szmukler, p. 144.
12. Ibid.
13. Op. cit., Craig L. Johnson and Susan Q. Love, p. 343.
14. Op. cit., P. J. V. Beumont, p. 171.
15. Arthur Reber, "anorexia nervosa," *The Penguin Dictionary of Psychology* (New York, N.Y.: Viking Penguin, 1985), p. 39.
16. Stuart Sutherland, "anorexia nervosa," *MacMillan Dictionary of Psychology* (London, U.K.: MacMillan Press, 1989), p. 26.
17. "What Are the Symptoms?," *American Anorexia Nervosa Association*, brochure, p. 2.
18. Op. cit., Arthur Reber.
19. Barbara P. Kinoy in collaboration with Estelle B. Miller, John A. Atchley, and the Book Committee of the American Anorexia/Bulimia Association, *When Will We Laugh Again?* (Guildford, Surrey, N.Y.: Columbia University Press, 1984), p. 9.

20. Dale L. Coovert, Bill N. Kinder, and Kevin J. Thompson, "The Psycho-sexual Aspects of Anorexia Nervosa and Bulimia Nervosa: A Review of the Literature," *Clinical Psychology Review* (Oxford, U.K.), Vol. 9(2), pp. 169–180.
21. Harold I. Kaplan and Benjamin J. Sadock, editors, "bulimia," *Comprehensive Text Book of Psychiatry*, Fourth Edition, (Baltimore, Md.: William & Wilkins, 1985), p. 1732
22. Op. cit. Marlene Boskind-White, Ph.D., and William C. White, Jr. Ph.D.
23. Op. cit., P. J. V. Beumont, pp. 169–171.
24. Op. cit., Katherine A. Halmi, p. 116.
25. Op. cit., William Wilkins, p. 1732.
26. David M. Garner, Marion P. Olmsted, and Paul E. Garfinkel, "Similarities Among Bulimic Groups Selected by Different Weights and Weight Histories," *Journal of Psychiatric Research*, Vol. 19, No. 2/3, p. 129.
27. Combined references:
    Op. cit., Arthur Reber, "bulimia," p. 103.
    Op. cit., Stuart Sutherland, "bulimia," p. 61.
    Op. cit., Marlene Boskind-White, Ph.D., and William C. White, Jr., Ph.D., p. 44.
28. Pamela S. Grace, Romey S. Jacobson, and Clive J. Fullager, "A Pilot Comparison of Purging and Non-purging Bulimics," *Journal of Clinical Psychology*, Vol. 41(2), pp. 173–180.
29. Combined references:
    Op. cit., *The Harvard Medical School Mental Health Letter.*
    Robert A. Moss, Gerald Jennings, and John H. McFarland, "Binge Eating, Vomiting, and Weight Fear in a Female High School Population," *Journal of Family Practice*, Vol. 18(2), pp. 313–320.
    Shirley A. Segal and Charles R. Figley, "Bulimia: Estimate of Incidence and Relationship to Shyness," *Journal of College Student Personnel*, Vol. 26(3), pp. 240–244.
30. Ronna Saunders, "Bulimia: An Expanded Definition," *American Anorexia/Bulimia Association Newsletter,* Vol. X, No. 1, p. 12.
31. Op. cit., Marlene Boskind-White, Ph.D., and William C. White, Jr., Ph.D., p. 44.
32. "compulsion," American Psychiatric Association: Diagnostic and Statistical Manual of Mental Disorders, Third Edition, Revised (Washington, D.C., American Psychiatric Association, 1987), p. 139.
33. Op. cit., Arthur Reber, "compulsion," p. 139.
34. Combined references:
    Ibid., "addiction," p. 12.
    Op. cit., Stuart Sutherland, "addiction," p. 9.
35. Combined references:
    Ibid., "obsession," p. 287.
    Op. cit., Arthur Reber, "obsession," p. 486.
36. Ibid.
37. Frank M. Webbe and Joanne Clontz, "Differentiation Between Bulimia and Food Addiction in a Community Sample," paper presented at the Annual Meeting of the Southwestern Psychological Association, Houston, Tex.: April 13–15, 1989.
38. John Bradshaw, *Bradshaw On: Healing The Shame That Binds You* (Deerfield Beach, Fla.: Health Communications, 1988), p. 100.
39. Preston Zucker, M.D., "President's Column," *American Anorexia/Bulimia Association Newsletter*, Vol. X, No. 1.
40. Hubert J. Lacey and Ginny Smith, "Bulimia nervosa: The impact of pregnancy on mother and baby," *British Journal of Psychiatry* (London, U.K., Royal College of Psychiatry), Vol. 150, pp. 777–781.

Considerations in Selecting a Therapist

1. Combined references:
    Barbara P. Kinoy in collaboration with Estelle B. Miller, John A. Atchley, and the Book Committee of the American Anorexia/Bulimia Association, *When Will We Laugh Again?* (Guildford, Surrey, N.Y.: Columbia University Press, 1984), p. 117.
    "Eating Disorders," *The Harvard Medical School Mental Health Letter*, Vol. 1, No. 2.
2. Op. cit., Barbara P. Kinoy et al., p. 63.
3. Ibid.
4. Ibid., p. 118.
5. Marlene Boskind-White, Ph.D., and William C. White, Jr., Ph.D., *Bulimarexia, The Binge/Purge Cycle* (New York: W.W. Norton, 1987), p. 19.
6. Ibid., p. 166.
7. Ibid., p. 19.
8. Op. cit., Barbara P. Kinoy et al., p. 117.
9. Op. cit., Marlene Boskind-White Ph.D., and William C. White, Jr., Ph.D., p. 8.
10. Stan Theander, "Outcome and prognosis in anorexia nervosa and bulimia," from Conference on Anorexia Nervosa and Related Disorders in Swansea, Wales in 1984, *Journal of Psychiatric Research*, Vol. 19, No. 2/3, pp. 493–508.
11. Op. cit., Barbara P. Kinoy et al., p. 118.
12. Moshe Talmon, Ph.D., *Single Session Therapy* (San Francisco, Calif.: Jossey-Bass, 1990), p. 59.
13. Ibid., p. 58.
14. Ibid.
15. Ibid., p. 59.

Helping the Compulsive Eater

1. John Bradshaw, *Bradshaw On: Healing The Shame That Binds You* (Deerfield Beach, Fla.: Health Communications, 1988), p. 92.
2. Jody Hayes and Maureen Redl, *"Smart Love"* (Los Angeles, Calif.: J.P. Tarcher, 1989), pp. 8, 9.
3. John Bradshaw, *Bradshaw On: The Family* (Deerfield Beach, Fla., Health Communications, 1988), p. 195.
4. Barbara P. Kinoy in collaboration with Estelle B. Miller, John A. Atchley, and the Book Committee of the American Anorexia/Bulimia Association, *When Will We Laugh Again?* (Guildford, Surrey, N.Y.: Columbia University Press, 1984), p. 54.
5. Ibid., p. 50.
6. Ibid., p. 54.
7. Ibid.
8. Ibid., p. 48.

Index

Abandonment (*see also* Rejection), 74, 222, 223
Abstinence, 13, 15, 101, 252
Abuse, 187
    physical, 132, 143, 154, 155, 157, 159, 183, 185, 188, 202, 221–223
    sexual (*see* Rape [incest])
Acceptance (*see also* Approval), 8, 10, 13, 15, 49, 66, 78, 161, 163, 170, 174, 175, 203, 211, 215, 216, 226, 267
    destruction of, 224
    of the past, 175, 179, 195, 200, 213
    self-acceptance (belief), *xii, xviii, xix,* 61, 108, 151, 162, 163, 165, 179, 209, 216, 229, 233, 235, 236, 257
    struggle for, 18, 55, 76, 117, 153, 224
    unacceptability (*see also* Self-devaluation), *xvii,* 76, 107, 117, 118, 137, 151, 200, 233, 243
Achievement, 137
Actualization (*see also* Affirmation), 9, 49, 153, 196
Adaptive (overly), 134, 224, 235
Addiction (dependence), 6, 9, 11, 98, 99, 221, 222, 250
    alcohol, 55, 108, 221, 222, 226, 251, 264
    behavior, 268
    cross addiction, 226
    drugs, 108, 226, 251, 264
    food, *xvii,* 98, 99, 249–251, 254
    vomiting, 227
"Adult" (*see* Parent, Adult, Child)
Affection, 137
Affirmation(s), *xix,* 61, 84, 90, 145, 163, 196, 233, 234, 236

Agreements, 238
Agressive(ness), 141, 142, 159, 229
Alcohol abuse (*see* Addiction)
Alienation, 156, 241
Allowing, 8, 226, 236
Alternatives (*see also* Options), 22
Amenorrhea, 129, 248
Amphetamines, 237
Anemia, 252
Anger (*see also* Rage), 7, 28, 41, 42, 46, 48, 86, 87, 135, 143–149, 155–157, 172, 178, 183, 185, 186, 189–192, 201, 202, 213, 216, 221, 223, 233, 268
    displacement, 148
    perpetuation, 148
Anorexia nervosa, 8, 43, 133, 135, 136, 144, 172, 243, 246, 248–250
    anorexic(s), 45, 54, 57, 58, 62, 63, 77, 97, 101, 102, 110, 137, 218, 249, 263
    anorexic reasoning, 68
    anorexic "self," 50–54, 67, 71, 110
    anorexic fears (*see also* Fear), 69
    pre-anorexic, 101, 243, 247
    split-screen (*see also* Split selves), 83
Anxiety (*see also* Worry), 7, 8, 9, 27, 82, 84, 86, 87, 150, 156, 158, 220, 235, 251, 263
Apologize, 148
Appetite, 156, 233
Apprehension (*see also* Fear), 150, 198
Approval (*see also* Acceptance), 8, 19, 41, 49, 61, 198, 215, 216, 264
    appreciation (assurance), 216
    lack of, 197–200
Arrhythmia (*see also* Medical consequences), 32, 33

Cohealing and
Co-Independence
Highlights

"COHEALING: The Shared Quest for Optimal Well-Being"
offers guidelines for recovery from restrictive dieting, compulsive eating, purging, self-starvation, and body-image
distortions. It explores *core issues* behind today's alarming
epidemic of eating and weight problems, and addresses
them from a personal as well as a cultural perspective.
Most importantly, it reveals ways to overcome these negative influences and at last *feel good about yourself.*

THIS BOOK demonstrates how to:

- Break the habit of restrictive dieting and self-starvation

- Overcome self-sabotaging binge/diet and/or binge/purge cycles

- Re-establish and maintain healthful eating and weight

- Acquire a realistic body-image and learn to like your body

- Recognize influences detrimental to your self-esteem

- Move from inertia and procrastination to constructive action

- Shift negative self-talk to positive self-talk

- Find freedom from self-doubt and inhibiting perfectionism

- Replace feelings of helplessness with competency and confidence

- Work through repressed anger and express anger effectively

- Release the habits of "reflected" guilt and self-blame

- Move from depression and lethargy to emotional buoyancy

- Make healing a mutually beneficial, shared experience

- Create relationships that promote recovery from dependencies

- Reclaim the personal rights that are basic to your well-being

> Cohealing is the cooperative, shared process for achieving optimal well-being. It is an attitude and approach that fosters personal involvement and growth beyond dependency and addiction.

COHEALING is a shared recovery process in which:

COMPULSIVITY and addiction give way to healing
AUTHORITARIANISM is replaced by partnership
DYSFUNCTIONAL relationships become healthfully co-independent

COHEALERS are essential to recovery because they:

ARE in the process of self-discovery, as we are
VALIDATE our reality
RESPECT our perceptions and feelings
ALLOW us to grieve our losses and release distress
NURTURE and believe in us
ACCEPT us as we are, and do not try to change us
HELP us heal and grow

COHEALING is beneficial and supportive when:

COMPULSIVITY and addiction are part of our lives
OUR RELATIONSHIPS are persistently painful
WE COME FROM dysfunctional, "dominator" family backgrounds
WE ARE overly other-directed rather than self-affirming
WE SUFFER frequent ongoing distress or depression
LIFE seems stressful and unsatisfying
WE LACK the courage to be ourselves

COHEALERS develop a reciprocal relationship in which:

ALL involved benefit
ALL have a personal commitment to recovery and well-being
EACH cohealer accepts the need to share the recovery process
EACH includes supportive, caring people in her or his life

COHEALING NETWORKS are built with:

Family, counselors and other professionals, friends, co-workers, self-help and therapy groups, participants in various organizations, and others who choose to share the cohealing process with us

> **Co-independence combines mutuality and partnership with individuation and autonomy. It is a condition that honors each individual and is grounded in equal power, trust, affirmation, and respect. This approach is essential to justice and the actualization of individual potential.**

CO-INDEPENDENCE is essential to relating since it:

PROVIDES a mind-set that overcomes codependence
PROMOTES authentic, mutual, healthy interactions
FOSTERS individual self-identity and self-determination
COUNTERACTS detrimental hierarchical social systems
ENCOURAGES overall health and well-being

CO-INDEPENDENT RELATIONSHIPS release us from:

BEING VICTIMIZED and controlled by others
STRUGGLING to control and dominate others
EMOTIONAL NEEDINESS that limits our personal choice
    and free will
INABILITY to commit ourselves to intimate relationships
CODEPENDENCY and compulsivity in relating to others

CO-INDEPENDENCE:

OVERCOMES the problems of such words as inter*dependence*
    (which describes dependence between ourselves and others)
    and *partnership* (which emphasizes connection but disre-
    gards the fact we each need to need to maintain our own
    independent identity in relationships)
IS A MUCH NEEDED way to describe, visualize, and create
    healthy relationships
OFFERS us a clearer understanding of our relationships and
    how to improve and enhance them

COHEALING AND CO-INDEPENDENCE lead to:

PERSONAL GROWTH, recovery, and building a good life
A PARTNERSHIP attitude and approach
A BASIS for healing and for hope

Personal Cohealing Journal

I accept my past, pain and all. It is what brought me to the present.

Personal Cohealing Journal

I will choose attitudes that are beneficial to healing.

Personal Cohealing Journal

I need caring relationships in which I am my best self.

Personal Cohealing Journal

I deserve people in my life who encourage and believe in me.

Personal Cohealing Journal

I choose to move beyond past limitations by trying new things!

Personal Cohealing Journal

I can count on myself, believe in myself, trust myself.

Personal Cohealing Journal

I will choose cohealers who accept and respect me.

Personal Cohealing Journal

There are people who can help me. I am not alone.

The Internet

Keep in touch with the *Center for Cohealing* through the Internet. Find out about our activities including "Cohealing for Couples" workshops, speaking engagements, and cohealing groups. Contact us at: http://WWW.cohealing.com/cohealing (or by email at: Hope@Cohealing.com).

About Ordering

Books available by Hope Sinclair:

COHEALING: The Shared Quest for Optimal Well-Being $16.95
(Self-Help, Healing and Recovery, Relationships)

DREAMERS DREAMING DREAMS: A Celebration of the $ 7.95
Human Spirit & the Wisdom That Comes With Age
(Inspirational Poetry and Prose)

Forthcoming book by this author:

THRIVE! You Have a Right to *Thrive* . . . Not Just Survive $12.95
(Relationships, Personal Rights, and Getting the Most Out of Life)
     Orders are now being accepted for this forthcoming
     book which will be shipped as soon as it is available.

Order from your local bookstore or send check or money order to the:

> Center for Cohealing
> 4546 El Camino Real
> B 10 — Suite 150
> Los Altos, CA 94022

WHEN ORDERING: List items *(title and quantity)* and include:

Total amount for items plus $3.00 shipping charge for first book and
$1.50 each additional book (CA residents add applicable sales tax).
Your name and address.

Make checks payable to the *Center for Cohealing.*

> The above books are available in quantity discounts. Cohealing
> Groups, therapists, corporations, schools, and organizations please
> specify whether purchase is for resale, distribution, or fund rais-
> ing. For more information write the Center for Cohealing.

ABOUT THE AUTHOR:

Hope Sinclair, the mother of four children, including two who recovered from life-threatening eating disorders, has been a newspaper feature writer as well as columnist for a large metropolitan daily. She has a degree in economics from the University of California, Berkeley, and studied journalism at Oregon State University, Corvallis. Her ongoing work on social issues began in college when she conducted research studies and reported on economic and educational disparities between the genders. A forthcoming video series, featuring highlights from her pioneering work with *cohealing* and *co-independence*, is being coordinated with her speaking engagements, Cohealing Groups, and "Cohealing for Couples" workshops.

Is Cohealing for You?

Answer the following by putting a check for "Yes" responses:

___ I often feel anxious or worried.
___ I feel trapped in relationships that are frustrating or unrewarding.
___ Compulsive-addictive problems are disrupting my life.
___ I review my past and feel distressed about what happened.
___ I find it difficult to feel relaxed around other people.
___ I feel lonely much of the time.
___ I keep wishing for things that I can't seem to make happen.
___ I am frequently self-critical.
___ Life seems stressful much of the time.
___ I often feel unable to stand up for myself and what I believe.
___ I frequently blame other people for my problems.
___ I often feel hurt, insecure, or vulnerable.
___ I feel like a failure much of the time.
___ I often feel envious, jealous, or resentful.
___ I feel helpless or hopeless much of the time.
___ I do things that I know are harmful to me.
___ My anger "gets the best of me" and I blow up at other people.
___ I use threats or demands to control people and get my way.
___ I have a "hidden self" others would consider unacceptable.
___ I feel sad or depressed much of the time.
___ Inertia saps my energy and I find it difficult to function.
___ I frequently feel guilty or inadequate.
___ I don't take good care of myself.
___ My life often feels painful.
___ I don't assert myself and I let people take advantage of me.

If you answered "Yes" to five or more of the above questions (or "Yes" to just one that is particularly troubling), you can benefit from *cohealing*. Now you can resolve these and other difficulties so that you find greater personal comfort and satisfaction.

You might want to consider finding (or establishing) a Cohealing Group or beginning cohealing with a few trusted people in an personal cohealing network. Why not take advantage of this process? Begin using cohealing to improve and enhance your life — you deserve satisfying relationships and an abundant sense of well-being!